Types of
Ecclesiology

Types of Ecclesiology

FIVE THEOLOGICAL APPROACHES

David Emerton

Baker Academic
a division of Baker Publishing Group
Grand Rapids, Michigan

© 2024 by David Emerton

Published by Baker Academic
a division of Baker Publishing Group
Grand Rapids, Michigan
BakerAcademic.com

Printed in the United States of America

Library of Congress Cataloging-in-Publication Data
Names: Emerton, David, author.
Title: Types of ecclesiology : five theological approaches / David Emerton.
Description: Grand Rapids, Michigan : Baker Academic, a division of Baker Publishing Group,
    [2024] | Includes bibliographical references and indexes.
Identifiers: LCCN 2024019820 | ISBN 9781540964977 (paperback) | ISBN 9781540968289
    (casebound) | ISBN 9781493447473 (ebook) | ISBN 9781493447480 (pdf)
Subjects: LCSH: Church. | Bonhoeffer, Dietrich, 1906–1945.
Classification: LCC BV593 .E44 2024 | DDC 262—dc23/eng/20240606
LC record available at https://lccn.loc.gov/2024019820

Cover design by Paula Gibson

Baker Publishing Group publications use paper produced from sustainable forestry practices and post-consumer waste whenever possible.

24   25   26   27   28   29   30   7   6   5   4   3   2   1

For Naomi,
my wife,
to me
the most precious
and beloved blessing of grace

Contents

Acknowledgments

This book has taken (much) longer to write than anticipated. I am deeply grateful therefore to Anna Moseley Gissing at Baker Academic for her grace and editorial patience, which without doubt I have tested sorely. Anna has been an incredibly thoughtful and supportive sounding board throughout the writing of this book, and her wise observations and constructive critique have made it a much better one than it otherwise would have been.

I also owe a debt of gratitude to Dr. R. David Nelson, formerly of the Baker Academic publishing parish but now director of Baylor University Press. When I was a newly minted doctor of philosophy seeking a publisher for my PhD dissertation, Dave was generous with his time and advice as to what I should do in that regard. Subsequently, Dave was generous with his reputation in commissioning this work. I like to think that he saw (and will see) something significant in it, although I worry that Aberdonian theological ties cover over a multitude of sins. Some of those sins—those of a grammatical, syntactical, and typographical nature at least—have been expunged by the expertise and theological acumen of those who have helped in the editing of this work, making the final manuscript more accessible and far easier to read. I am deeply grateful to project editor Alexander DeMarco and copyeditor Brittany McComb in this regard. I am also grateful to those who have read and provided feedback on either a part or the whole of an earlier draft of this book. My thanks in this regard are due to Rev. Dr. Alex Irving, the Rt. Rev. Dr. Graham Tomlin, and Dr. Anna Westin; their comments were all remarkably kind and supportive, even when disagreeing. Any errors that remain—of whatever nature—are of course my own, and no one but me should be held responsible for the text that follows.

The origins of this text lie in my PhD research at the University of Aberdeen, and in my thinking in that context about how the ecclesiological thought of Dietrich Bonhoeffer might relate to contemporary approaches to ecclesiology.[1] I am forever grateful for the tutelage of Professor Tom Greggs during my time in Aberdeen, and for Tom's continuing friendship and willingness to offer wise counsel to me both personally and professionally. It is in large part because of Tom's theological ingenuity, particularly in matters ecclesial, that I am in a position to be able to submit this book to the academy and the church for consideration.

I do so, however, with a certain degree of fear and trembling. This is not only because of the extent of the ecclesiological terrain that I try to traverse in this book but because of my own fallibility and vocational insecurity. There have been any number of moments during the process of writing this book when I have doubted my ability not only to complete the manuscript but also to compose a coherent sentence, not least in what was a difficult final few months. For enabling me to get over the finish line, I owe thanks to my dean at St. Mellitus College, Rev. Russell Winfield; the staff at St. Mellitus College, East Midlands; Rev. Dr. Hannah Steele; and most especially the Venerable Victoria (Tors) Ramsey and her husband Adrian. I am honoured to be able to count Tors and Adrian as my closest friends. Their faithful companionship through the ups and downs of life has been such a source of personal support, understanding, and grace that it is difficult to imagine life without them, not least because of their unhesitating willingness to share a life lived in faith before God over a bottle of wine (or two), and to do so in a way that is normal, honest, and fun.

My greatest thanks and deepest debt of gratitude are due to my family, however. As I wrestled with this book, my wife has borne the brunt of my doubting, despairing, and anxiety-ridden moments, and she has loved and supported me through them without ceasing. I genuinely do not know where I would be without Naomi, and her compassion, consolation, and constant encouragement, not to mention her remarkable self-giving in bearing the burden of family life so that I might write, have helped bring this book into its existence. Naomi always saw the endpoint even when I could not. It is therefore only right that the book be dedicated to her. (Although, given her inclination to find theological things far from interesting, I imagine I will need to tell her that it is.) And in ways that will be unknown to them, my daughters

---

1. For the revised version of this research, see Emerton, *God's Church-Community*. The text that follows in this book in part represents a reimagination and substantial expansion of (significantly) reworked ideas found in chap. 1 of *God's Church-Community*.

Lois and Sophie-Joan have brought me joyous relief from the self-absorbed solitude of book writing, be it through countless cuddles, the playing of the piano, or their ability by their very presence to pull me back to what really matters in life.

I say my greatest thanks and deepest debt of gratitude are due to my family, but in truth that would be to speak an untruth, for it would be to pass over the One who gifted them to me, the One in whose being we live and move and have our being, and who therefore rightfully has the first place in my life. To the One who is Father, Son, and Holy Spirit, my thanksgiving and praise can only ever be unending. It is my prayer that what is written in this book will therefore serve in some way to honor and glorify God.

Introduction

The primary task of ecclesiology is to account theologically for what the church is. This task is pressing, not least in the context of the twenty-first century West. The Western church is currently bedeviled by its decline and the prospect of its own death. Of course, learning how to die is elemental to Christian faith: it is through death that resurrection life comes in the Spirit. Jesus makes this clear to those who would follow Him in the moments after Peter's confession that Jesus is the Messiah of God: "Whoever wants to be my disciple must deny themselves and take up their cross daily and follow me. For whoever wants to save their life will lose it, but whoever loses their life for me will save it" (Luke 9:23–24). The church stands on perilous theological ground if it does not take seriously the force of Jesus's call to discipleship and embrace the prospect, and even necessity, of its own death. Yet all too often, this is precisely where the church stands. The church today commonly reacts to its decline and the prospect of its own death either with inertia or with what Michael Jinkins has aptly described as "the hyperactivity of panic."[1] This panic, Jinkins observes, "manifests itself in clutching for any and every programmatic solution and structural reorganization in the desperate hope that survival is just another project or organizational chart away."[2]

The church to which I belong and that I seek to love and serve as a priest-theologian, the Church of England, has repeatedly reacted to its own decline and the prospect of its death in this way.[3] In its episcopal leadership,

1. Jinkins, *Church Faces Death*, 9.
2. Jinkins, *Church Faces Death*, 9.
3. Average weekly church attendance in the Church of England has declined by 40 percent in just twelve years (from 2010 to 2022). See Church of England, "Statistics for Mission 2011"

synodical governance, and parochial life, it has manifested both problematic reactions—inertia and "the hyperactivity of panic"—in equal measure.[4] Both reactions work contrary to the paradoxical movement of faithful Christian discipleship that Jesus establishes. Given the limitations of space, I cannot set out my concerns in this regard as fully as I would like, but will content myself with three indicative observations. First, we have recently lived through a global pandemic, yet the Church of England was largely content to accept its prescribed status as "non-essential" throughout the COVID-19 crisis. To many outside the church—indeed to many inside the church—this appeared to be a rather disconcerting "disappearance" of the church from UK national life, at a time when people were confronted by the reality of death in an intensely powerful way. As one political commentator put it at the time: "This could have been a great opportunity for the Church. With everyone in the land forced to reflect on their potentially imminent mortality, I imagine that a fair few were wondering if something other than Netflix might fill the void. Yet the Church was silent."[5] Of course, there were examples of practice that contradicted such a sobering critique,[6] but all too often the Church of England's inertia simply contributes to its becoming ever more irrelevant to contemporary society.

Second, and in the context of the COVID-19 crisis itself, the Church of England set out its vision and strategic priorities for the 2020s: to become a "simpler, humbler, bolder" church that is "Christ centred and Jesus shaped."[7] This is certainly an attractive vision. But whether the specified goals of creating "10,000 new Christian communities"; developing "3,000 churches . . . to be worshipping hubs for children and young people"; and instigating a plethora of working groups to steer the church toward these arbitrary numerical outcomes amount to anything more than yet further initiatives in a long line of similar initiatives—for which no one, seemingly, is ever held to account—is an altogether different matter.[8] And despite the insistence of the Church of England's most senior leadership that it is not "downward sloping graphs, or burning platforms or melting icebergs that motivate us,"[9] that we even

---

and "Statistics for Mission 2022." According to these (2022) statistics, the median Anglican church in the Church of England has an average weekly congregation of twenty-five, of which one and a half is a child.

4. Anglican ecclesial polity is often described as "episcopally led and synodically governed." Synods are decision-making bodies and are composed of elected clergy and laypeople who represent each parish church in a diocese and the Anglican church as such.

5. Murray, "Great Opportunity."

6. See, e.g., Tomlin, "Too Late to Think about Death When You're Dying."

7. See Cottrell, "Church of England in the 2020s."

8. See Cottrell, "Simpler, Humbler, Bolder," 9–11.

9. Cottrell, "Simpler, Humbler, Bolder," 12.

have to deny such perceptions is itself symptomatic of "the hyperactivity of panic" that Jinkins speaks of.

Third, in the name of missional creativity, but in response to the downward-sloping graphs that ostensibly do not motivate us, what might be described as a pernicious pragmatism is currently sweeping the Church of England. The symptoms of this pragmatism are readily observable. For example, at the same time that the Church of England set out its vision and strategic priorities for the 2020s, an Anglican parachurch movement set out its own vision "to support the planting of thousands of new, predominantly lay-led churches throughout the Church of England and church in England in the next ten years."[10] Now, I have no desire to take sides in the trenchant and distasteful culture war that surrounds the implementation of such a vision,[11] but I do think the Church of England's increasing desire to release those who are, theologically speaking, minimally trained, and in some cases even altogether untrained, more quickly, and in ever-increasing number, into positions of lay and ordained church leadership is a further symptom of the hyperactivity of panic. And this is taking place at a time when theological "debate" in contemporary church culture occurs most frequently in the space of 140 characters and training for senior church leadership positions—at least in the Church of England—increasingly emphasizes business management skills while de-emphasizing theological literacy. This marginalization of the slow and costly work of theological education in the Church of England's life is all the more baffling when what is perhaps most needed in the church today is theologically astute followers of Jesus Christ who can out narrate a sin-sick world.[12]

As a theological educator in the Church of England, I find the hyperactivity of panic also manifesting itself in some less obvious but equally problematic ways in much of what is written or taught about the church today. Contemporary speech about the church is concerned predominantly with the question of how to "be" and therefore how to "do" church: material concerning how the church should relate to post-Christian secular culture, address issues of contemporary ethics, practice its worship, engage in mission and evangelism, or raise up its future leaders abounds.[13] The suggestion in one sense being that if the church could only "do" differently in the matter of its form and practice—and therefore "be" different—then it would reverse the downward

10. Gregory Center for Church Multiplication, "Lay-Led Planting."
11. See Wyatt, "Tensions Are Running High."
12. I owe this turn of phrase to Lincoln Harvey.
13. The kind of material I am thinking of here includes Drane, *McDonaldization of the Church*; Gibbs and Bolger, *Emerging Churches*; Ward, *Selling Worship*; Turner, *Christian Ethics and the Church*; Paas, *Pilgrims and Priests*; and Lawrence, *Growing Leaders*.

sloping graphs, be less bedeviled by its decline and the prospect of its own death, and experience more of the resurrection life that comes through the Spirit. But as Karl Barth once warned, "No polity can create renewal or reformation. But this it can and must do. . . . The polity of the Church can and must give a form to the Church which expresses the conviction that Jesus Christ alone is its hope."[14]

Reflection on matters of form and practice are without doubt important to resurrection life coming to the church in the Spirit—charts, projects, programs, structural reorganizations, *and* business management skills included. But are we not in danger of putting the proverbial cart before the horse here, and failing to heed Barth's warning? For the question of *how* we should "be" or "do" church can be addressed only once we have answered the question of *what* the church is. The importance of this order for anyone interested in thinking and speaking theologically about the church cannot be overstated. If we do not first seek to understand *what* the church is, then how can we begin to consider how to "be" or "do" church? Yet so much of today's speech about the church floats free from this task. As someone who shares in the oversight of men and women training for ordained ministry in the Church of England, I carry a nagging fear about the number of ordained clergy—or those involved actively, one way or another, in church leadership—who would struggle to articulate a theological response to the question of what the church is. Do those who are called to serve and lead the church really know what it is they are called to lead and serve?

My hope is that this book will encourage those who seek to lead and serve the church—priests and pastors, teachers and professional theologians, students and lay leaders and practitioners—to consider afresh what the church is, and to engage this question before they engage the question of how to "be" or "do" church. In the pages that follow, I propose a fivefold typology of contemporary approaches to ecclesiology. This typology is conceived in relation to the fundamental and decisive ecclesiological question—*What is the church?*—with the intention of bringing this question sharply into view. My hope, therefore, is that this book may provide a constructive orientation to the field of contemporary ecclesiology, and that in doing so it may also, in some small way, help the church to live and act in ways that are ever more faithful to its true being at this time in which the church faces the prospect of its own death.

14. Barth, *God Here and Now*, 76.

1

Types of Ecclesiology

A PROPOSAL

The concern in this chapter is to outline the fivefold typology of contemporary approaches to ecclesiology that this book proposes. The subsequent chapters will then articulate each type of ecclesiological approach. However, before outlining the typology, it will be instructive to first turn to the pages of Scripture, and in particular to the apostle Paul's description of the church in Corinth. For in Paul's description of the Corinthian church we find a basic theological grammar for talking about what the church is. It is from this basic theological grammar that the framework of my fivefold typology of contemporary approaches to ecclesiology is drawn.

Considering Corinth

Most basically, for Paul, the Corinthian church is a reality that is both divine and human. The church in Corinth is the "church of God [*ekklēsia tou theou*]" (1 Cor. 1:2; 2 Cor. 1:1).[1] Its origin is in God's calling and choosing (1 Cor.

---

1. Contemporary New Testament scholarship considers it anachronistic—but not illegitimate—to translate *ekklēsia* as "church." While the debate concerning the origin and meaning of *ekklēsia* as Paul used it lies beyond the scope of this book, readers should exercise caution against overinterpreting Paul's use of *ekklēsia* on the basis of preconceived ideas and experiences of what church is or is not: the meaning of *ekklēsia* is certainly not exhausted by "church." I am indebted to Chris Tilling for drawing my attention to this concern in contemporary New Testament scholarship. For more on this subject, see the in-depth discussion of Korner, *Origin*

1:2, 24, 26, 27–28). And as the sanctified creature of God's Word (1 Cor. 1:2, 18; 2:1–5; 3:9–11), the church is inconceivable without reference to the gospel of God (2 Cor. 11:7). The church, Paul emphatically insists, is the building that God constructs and the field that God grows (1 Cor. 3:9). It is, as John Chrysostom once observed, the possession, "not 'of this or of that [person],' but of God."[2] The church, in other words, does not belong to its members or its leaders (ordained or otherwise, no matter how gifted they may be); to its boards of elders or **parochial church councils**;[3] to one denomination or church tradition or another; or to any one of its self-styled "movements," in-groups of "spiritual" people who manifest "this gift or that gift," who believe "this but not that," who worship "in this way and not that way," or who even dress "like this and not like that." Indeed, the Corinthian Christians' erroneous belief that the church did, in fact, belong to them, together with the destructive behavior that flowed from that belief, is perhaps the principal problem that Paul seeks to illuminate and address in his letters to them. "The main defect of Corinthian conditions," Barth notes, "consist[s] in the boldness, assurance, and enthusiasm with which they believe, not in God, but in their own belief in God and in particular leaders and heroes." In doing so the Corinthians "confuse belief with specific human experiences, convictions, trends of thought and theories."[4] Hence Paul's emphatic insistence that all that the Corinthian Christians are, all that they have and hope to be—including their existence as the church—"is from God" (2 Cor. 5:18). The Corinthian church belongs to God alone; it is, Paul says, "of God" (1 Cor. 1:2).

However, this church that is "of God" is, at the same time, existing "in Corinth [*ousē en Korinthō*]" (1 Cor. 1:2; 2 Cor. 1:1). And it exists "in Corinth" *as it is*. It exists, that is, contingently, particularly, and fallibly. Indeed, the content of Paul's letters to the Christians in Corinth makes it clear that the Corinthian church is divided (1 Cor. 1:10–12; 3:3–4); suffering (2 Cor. 1:3–7); and engaged in any number of destructive passions and contentious practices (1 Cor. 5:1–2; 6:1–6, 12–16; 8:1–13; 10:14–22; 11:17–34; 12:1–31) that reflect the competitive, entitled, and self-sufficient culture of the day.[5] But the content of Paul's letters also makes clear that the Corinthian church is called to overcome these fallible and sinful realities of their pre-Christian culture by

---

and Meaning of Ekklēsia; or, for a succinct summary of the debate, see Esler, "Adoption and Use of the Word ΕΚΚΛΗΣΙΑ."

2. John Chrysostom, *Homilies on the Epistles of Paul to the Corinthians*, 3. I owe this reference to Anthony Thiselton.

3. Bolded terms are defined in the glossary at the back of the book.

4. Barth, *Resurrection of the Dead*, 15.

5. For a succinct articulation of the culture of Corinth and how it permeated the Corinthian church, see Thiselton, *1 Corinthians*, 1–18.

particular and concrete acts of forgiveness (2 Cor. 2:5–8; 5:16–20); love (1 Cor. 13:4–7); purification (1 Cor. 5:7, 11; 6:18; 10:14, 21; 2 Cor. 6:14); peace (2 Cor. 13:11–12); generosity (2 Cor. 9:6–15); and respect (1 Cor. 8:9–13; 9:19–23; 10:27–28; 12:21–26). Living out in practice such concrete and particular acts is what it means for the church in Corinth to be what God in Christ Jesus has already made them: "sanctified" (1 Cor. 1:2). As Paul puts it to the church in Ephesus, "[God] chose us in [Christ] before the creation of the world to be holy and blameless in his sight" (Eph. 1:4). The Corinthian church is "called to be his holy people" (1 Cor. 1:2) precisely because "in Christ" they are already the sanctified people "of God"—they are people who belong to God and, as such, are called to be God's holy people.

Of course, the logic of this description of the church in Corinth and its peculiar Christian vocation is not novel to the pages of the New Testament, but reflects descriptions of ancient Israel in the Old Testament. Paul himself points the Christians in Corinth in this direction when warning them against attending pagan idol feasts in 2 Corinthians 6:14–18. Amid the catena of Old Testament quotations Paul uses to urge the Corinthian church to be "separate" (2 Cor. 6:17) from such ritual impurity (to be holy, in other words), Paul sets before them God's covenantal promise to ancient Israel: "'I will be their God, and they will be my people'" (2 Cor. 6:16; see also Lev. 26:12; Jer. 32:38; Ezek. 37:27). Why is this the case? Paul wants to remind the church in Corinth of God's commitment to God's people and their corresponding obligation to God. Divine commitment and human obligation are essential to the covenant relationship of divine and human togetherness in which the church has come to participate by virtue of its sharing in God's determination of ancient Israel to be God's people.[6]

Critically, this determination, in which both divine commitment and human obligation are essential, is unilateral in origin: the covenant that God makes with ancient Israel comes into being and is sustained in being by God alone. In an expansive restatement of God's covenant togetherness with Abraham (now reworked to apply to ancient Israel as a whole),[7] notice that it is God and God's gracious acts that determine God's covenant togetherness with God's people: "I will look on you with favor and make you fruitful and increase your

---

6. The way in which the church shares in the identity of God's people in the Old Testament is important: the church does not replace or supersede ancient Israel as the people of God. As Korner shows, Paul envisages ancient Israel and the *ekklēsia tou theou* as "distinct yet covenantly related socio-religious entities." Korner, *Origin and Meaning of Ekklēsia*, 19. Paul indexes this distinction to the gospel of God and more specifically to the new existence "in Christ" (2 Cor. 5:17), which belief in the crucified and resurrected Jesus as Messiah inculcates.

7. On this reworking, see Goldingay, *Old Testament Theology*, 1:370–74.

numbers, and I will keep my covenant with you. . . . I will put my dwelling place among you, and I will not abhor you. I will walk among you and be your God, and you will be my people" (Lev. 26:9–12). And as Moses reminds ancient Israel just before they enter the land of Canaan,

> You are a people holy to the LORD your God. The LORD your God has chosen you out of all the peoples on the face of the earth to be his people, his treasured possession. The LORD did not set his affection on you and choose you because you were more numerous than other peoples, for you were the fewest of all peoples. But it was because the LORD loved you and kept the oath he swore to your ancestors that he brought you out with a mighty hand and redeemed you from the land of slavery, from the power of Pharaoh king of Egypt. (Deut. 7:6–8)

God's determination of ancient Israel to be the people of God is not conditioned, then, by ancient Israel itself—that is, by something inherent in Israel's own being that would somehow qualify Israel to be chosen as God's people, distinct from all those nations of the earth not chosen. Nor is it conditioned by Israel's response to God's choosing. It is instead conditioned by God alone. Indeed, the scandal of God choosing ancient Israel as God's people out of all the nations of the earth is not that God chooses one and not others (Abel, not Cain; Abraham, not another; Isaac, not Ishmael; Jacob, not Esau; Ephraim, not Manasseh, and so forth[8]) but that God chooses anyone at all. And that God does is only, as Deuteronomy 7:7–8 makes clear, because of God's love and faithful commitment to keep God's own covenantal promise. Put otherwise, God's choosing is, as Barth forcefully argues, grounded wholly in God's gracious act: "God elects. It is this that precedes absolutely all other being and happening."[9]

Nevertheless, God's determination of ancient Israel to be God's people requires—as an indivisible aspect of it—a particular and contingent human response. As God makes clear to Moses on Mount Sinai, Israel, having seen that God carried them out of Egypt "on eagles' wings" and brought them to Godself (Exod. 19:4), must obey God fully and keep God's covenant (Exod. 19:5). In other words, as the people *of God*, ancient Israel is to follow God's decrees and keep God's commands (Lev. 26:3). As God's "treasured possession" (Exod. 19:5), Israel is to be—both for God's sake and for the sake of the world—"a kingdom of priests and a holy nation" (Exod. 19:6).[10] As John

8. See Gen. 4:4–5; 12:1–3; 21:12; 25:21–34; 48:8–20.
9. Barth, *Church Dogmatics* II/2, 99.
10. As Gerhard von Rad maintains, "There can be no doubt that it is the proclamation of the Decalogue over her which puts Israel's election into effect." See von Rad, *Old Testament Theology*, 1:192. This is why ancient Israel's observance of the Mosaic Torah is indivisible

Goldingay writes, "There is nothing behind 'I lifted you on eagles' wings' that somehow qualifies Israel to be beneficiaries of Yhwh's activity in Egypt (Ex. 19:4). Here as elsewhere Scripture declares that everything depends on Yhwh, but that a responsive reciprocal commitment to Yhwh on Israel's part is an absolute necessity (Ex. 19:5)."[11] As the contingent and particular sociohistorical reality that they are, ancient Israel must be God's people, therefore—a people who respond by identifying with their minds the covenant God, Yahweh, as their God, and orient themselves with their wills toward this God by following God's decrees and faithfully keeping and observing God's commandments, so that salvation can reach out from them to the ends of the earth (Isa. 49:6).

It is this divine determination, and necessary human vocation, of ancient Israel to be God's people that the church has come to share in. This is what Paul wants to remind the church in Corinth of. This is why Paul sets before them God's covenantal promise in 2 Corinthians 6:14–18. He reminds the Corinthian Christians of God's commitment to them, but he also reminds them of their obligation to God as an indivisible aspect of the covenant togetherness in which they exist and are to exist as God's people. And as with ancient Israel, there is nothing about the Corinthian church that somehow qualifies the church to be beneficiaries of God's calling and choosing—far from it, in fact. Paul has reminded them already that in their origin and continued existence they are the people "of God" (1 Cor. 1:2). That is, they are determined by God in Jesus Christ as God's holy people.

According to Paul, the church is so determined before the creation of the world (Eph. 1:4). As he writes to the Ephesians, the church is "the mystery of Christ," (Eph. 3:4) "which for ages past was kept hidden in God" (Eph. 3:9). For Paul, the church exists, then, prior to Christian believers. The church is not produced or made by believers. Rather, the church, chosen and called by God, makes or produces them: the church is truly the mother of those who have been "born of God" through belief in Jesus Christ by the power of the Holy Spirit (1 John 5:1; Rom. 8:14–16), being raised to life through death **proleptically** in baptism (Rom. 6:3–6), and thus being adopted into the preexisting reality of the church as God's children.[12] Yet notwithstanding what God has already made the Christians in Corinth by virtue of this divine determination, as with

---

from their determination by God to be God's people. Israel's observance of the Torah is both an instrument and a sign of this determination.

11. Goldingay, *Old Testament Theology*, 1:372.

12. Speaking of the church as "mother" is largely absent from contemporary (Protestant) ecclesiology, but it was a favorite theme of the early church fathers. The sentiment is repeated, for example, by Origen of Alexandria, Cyprian of Carthage, and Augustine of Hippo. See de Lubac, *Motherhood of the Church*, 47–58. See also Braaten, *Mother Church*.

ancient Israel, a reciprocal commitment to God on the part of the Corinthian Christians is an absolute necessity. By their particular and contingent human response to the God now revealed in Christ by the Spirit, the Corinthian Christians must identify this God as their God and orient themselves toward this God by following Christ in loving God and neighbor (Matt. 22:37–40; Luke 9:23). In their sociohistorical existence, the Corinthian church indeed is called to be God's holy people—to live out in practice (as Paul urges them throughout his letters) concrete and particular acts that will overcome the fallible and sinful realities of their pre-Christian culture, as they encounter that culture in both the church in Corinth and in Corinth itself.

Accordingly, the church in Corinth is God's *people* ("they will be my people"), but these people are not just any people. Rather, they are a people who, in their human response to God, are determined by God as *God's* people ("I will be their God"). Paul's point here is also made by Peter in what might be seen as Peter's own summary statement of what the church is: "But you are a chosen people, a royal priesthood, a holy nation, God's special possession, that you may declare the praises of him who called you out of darkness into his wonderful light" (1 Pet. 2:9).[13] For Peter, as for Paul, the church is the people of God because the gentiles who "once . . . were not a people" have now been made God's people (1 Pet. 2:10) together with ancient Israel. They have been "chosen according to the foreknowledge of God" (1 Pet. 1:2) and have received God's mercy (1 Pet. 2:10). But having been made by God to be God's people, the church is to declare God's praises and thereby witness to what Douglas Harink describes as the "people-making mercy" of God.[14] Indeed, as Peter indicates, that the church may declare the praises of God is the very purpose of God's choosing and making them God's people. The church, then, is both the people that praises God and the people that God mercifully chooses. This covenantal relationship is a unilateral work of God in its origin and continued existence, but human response is also essential to it.

Church and Covenant

By describing what the church is in this covenantal way, it could be said that Paul's speech about the Corinthian church functions in a twofold manner.

---

13. In contemporary New Testament scholarship, it is a matter of debate whether 1 and 2 Peter were in fact written by Peter himself or whether they were written by someone else using Peter's name (a common practice at the time)—that is, whether these letters are apostolic in authorship or pseudepigraphical. In referring to the author of 1 Peter as "Peter," I am simply following the canonical text: the letter begins, "Peter, an apostle of Jesus Christ" (1 Pet. 1:1).

14. See Harink, *1 & 2 Peter*, 74.

First, it establishes the truth that the church is at once a divine and human reality. And second, it delineates a specific and given order to the relationship of divine and human togetherness within this reality. That "I will be their God" precedes, in God's covenantal promise, "they will be my people" makes a crucial theological point that must never be lost in ecclesiological description. The point is that the relationship of divine and human togetherness in the church's being is asymmetrical. In other words, the church's sociohistorical existence is derivative of, and dependent upon, God and God's gracious acts. It is God alone who brings the church into being as the church's originating and sustaining cause.[15]

This is to highlight the ecclesiological importance of the fundamental distinction—but also relation—between God and creation that is foundational to Christian theology, and which the **doctrine** of *creatio ex nihilo* ("creation out of nothing") affirms. The affirmation of "creation out of nothing" means that the most basic categories of creation—time and space— and all that exists in time and space, including the church, are brought into being by God and are entirely dependent on God for their continued existence.[16] As Paul puts it to the church in Corinth, "There is but one God, the Father, from whom all things came and for whom we live" (1 Cor. 8:6). Or, in the words of the book of Revelation, "You are worthy, our Lord and God, to receive glory and honor and power, for you created all things, and by your will they were created and have their being" (Rev. 4:11). And as the letter to the Colossians delineates it, "In [Jesus Christ] all things were created: things in heaven and on earth, visible and invisible . . . ; all things have been created through him and for him. He is before all things, and in him all things hold together" (Col. 1:16–17). This is what Robert Jenson describes as "a drastically revisionary metaphysics." "We exist," he says, "and exist as we do because God determines that we shall."[17] Existence itself *is* only because of God's graciousness in creating out of nothing and sustaining creation continually. This moment—the moment that I write these words and the moment that you read them—is held in existence only by the sustaining power of God. As Rowan Williams puts it (quoting Hildegard of Bingen), "Reality rests 'like a feather on the breath of God.' It *is* because God speaks, because God loves and it *is* for no other reason."[18] As with the rest of creation, the church exists as a sociohistorical human

---

15. On the need to affirm the asymmetrical but related agency of divine and human action in Christian theology, see Schwöbel, "Creature of the Word," 110–55, esp. 116–21.

16. For a helpful overview of "creation out of nothing," see McFarland, *From Nothing*.

17. Jenson, *Canon and Creed*, 91. See the glossary for a definition of **metaphysics**.

18. Williams, "Thomas Merton and Karl Barth" (emphasis original).

community only because of the love of God, only because of God's choosing and willing.

Thus, the church is a creature of God and God's gracious acts.[19] If we want to account theologically for what the church is, therefore, we must speak about it as that which God graciously, and without necessity, creates and sustains in its sociohistorical existence. And we must speak about it in this way—that is, with reference to divine agency—before we speak about it in any other way. In this way, speech about the church is ordered in accordance with Scripture and the Christian tradition, and so ordered in a genuinely theological fashion.

At once, however, the order that God's covenantal promise gives to the relationship of divine and human togetherness in the church's being makes a further crucial point that also must never be lost in ecclesiological description. Aside from establishing that the church is graciously created and sustained in its sociohistorical existence by God, that "they will be my people" follows "I will be their God" in God's covenantal promise indicates that any reference to divine agency in speech about the church must necessarily be indexed to the church as a sociohistorical reality that God graciously creates and sustains. To affirm that God creates out of nothing and sustains creation continually is indeed to recognize that God is distinct to creation and that God is free from creation in God's own life. But it is also to recognize that God's freedom is such that God freely chooses to unite creation to Godself as creator, reconciler, and redeemer. As Dietrich Bonhoeffer writes, "Even in creating, God remains wholly free over against what is created. God is not bound to creation; instead God binds creation to Godself."[20] Or, as he puts it elsewhere,

It is not so much a question of the freedom of God—eternally remaining within the divine self, aseity—on the other side of revelation, as it is of God's coming out of God's own self in revelation. It is a matter of God's *given* word, the covenant in which God is bound by God's own action. It is a question of the

---

19. We profess this point in the Nicene Creed through the creedal preposition *in*: "We believe in one God, the Father Almighty . . . And in one Lord Jesus Christ . . . And in the Holy Spirit." The Latin reads, "Credo in unum Deum, Patrem omnipotentem . . . Et in unum Dominum Iesum Christum . . . Et in Spiritum Sanctum." By this creedal preposition, we affirm the triune God as creator in distinction from creation and thus as the One *in* whom we believe and place our faith. The Latin rendering of the creed emphasizes the theological significance of this affirmation by the omission of the preposition before the word "church" (*Ecclesiam*): "Et unam, sanctam, catholicam et apostolicam Ecclesiam" (And one, holy, catholic and apostolic Church). As Yves Congar comments, "It is . . . possible to believe *in* God, to accept him as the end of one's life, but it is not possible to believe in the same way *in* the Church." Congar, *I Believe in the Holy Spirit*, 2:5 (emphasis original). Thus, we profess to "believe the church." As John Calvin contends, "There is no good reason why many insert the preposition 'in.'" Calvin, *Institutes*, 4.1.2.

20. Bonhoeffer, *Schöpfung und Fall*, 38 (my trans.).

freedom of God, which finds its strongest evidence precisely in that God freely chose to be bound to historical human beings and to be placed at the disposal of human beings. God is free not from human beings but for them.[21]

This is to say that the being of God always involves God's relationship to creation and creatures. For Bonhoeffer, God's being (from the perspective of humankind, at least) exists in God's act of becoming "for us." As such, the being of God is, as Barth maintained, "God's being in act," and God is "the event of His action."[22]

In the story of Scripture, this point is perhaps most vividly illustrated in the context of God revealing Godself to Moses in the burning bush. In response to Moses's request for God to reveal God's name (Exod. 3:13), God says, "I AM WHO I AM ['ehyeh 'asher 'ehyeh]" (3:14)—a name that is equally well translated, "I am being that I am being" or "I am the One who always is." John Durham describes this as the "Is-ness"[23] of God: God has neither a beginning nor an end; God simply "is." This is why we read in the scriptural story that "the bush does not burn up" (3:3). Ordinarily, fire is dependent on fuel, but this fire does not consume the bush. Rather, this fire has its own source of being and power. This is an important part of what God is revealing about Godself to Moses in the name "I AM." God, you might say, does not need any fuel; God is "Is-ness"—existence in-and-of Godself. In other words, absolutely no power or being has caused God "to be" because God is the cause of all being and power. This is what we recognize when we speak (as Bonhoeffer does in the quote above) of the **aseity** of God—that God is entirely self-sufficient and independent, and all that is not God is entirely dependent on God. In this sense, God is free from creation in God's own life. Yet the God who reveals Godself to Moses as "I AM WHO I AM" also makes it clear to Moses that the One being revealed to him is one and the same as the God of his fathers, "the God of Abraham, the God of Isaac and the God of Jacob" (3:15). This God is "the Lord," the God who has "heard" the Israelites' groaning and "remembered his covenant" with them (2:24); the God who says, "I have indeed seen the misery of my people in Egypt" and "come down to rescue them" (3:7–8). This rescuing, further, is to "a good and spacious land, a land flowing with milk and honey" (3:8). As Moses leads God's people to this place of plenty, God promises to be with them and with Moses especially

---

21. Bonhoeffer, *Act and Being*, 90–91 (emphasis original). See the glossary for a definition of **aseity**.

22. Barth, *Church Dogmatics* II/1, 262. For more about this aspect of Barth's theological ontology, see Nimmo, *Being in Action*.

23. Durham, *Exodus*, 39.

(3:12), helping him to speak and teaching him what to say (4:12). In other words, the God who is existence in-and-of Godself, and is free from creation in the life of God, is at the same time the God of Israel who is actively present with God's people concretely and particularly. As Durham notes, God's "Is-ness means Presence."[24] And that "I Am" has chosen to be present with the people of God means that God is in this relationship irrevocably, is "for" them, and through them is in relationship to creation and creatures.

This is how Bonhoeffer describes the covenant in the quote above. God chose to bind creation to Godself and determine Israel to be God's people; thus, God is irrevocably bound both to creation and to humankind as a consequence of God's own free action. Put otherwise, and to follow Bonhoeffer, God does not have God's being "alone."[25] Rather, God "is" only in relationship. In Barth's words, God enters "a relationship outside of which God no longer wills to be and no longer is God, and within which alone He can be truly honoured and worshipped as God."[26] And the basis of this relationship (at least for humankind) is God's own act of becoming "for us" creator, reconciler, and redeemer, paradigmatically in Jesus Christ.[27] Thus, in the same way that God's people are not just any people, but a people determined by God as God's people, so God then is not just any God. Rather, in and through Jesus Christ, God is God in relationship to creation and creatures, and God is God in this way with and for a particular and concrete people: the people of ancient Israel and now—because it shares in God's determination of Israel to be God's people in and through Jesus Christ—the church. This is the way in which "I will be their God" is followed in God's covenantal promise by "they will be my people." Thus, not only must God's being and action always be described simultaneously, but any description of God and God's gracious action must necessarily be indexed to this concrete and particular people as the people of God. Reference to divine agency in ecclesiological description must, therefore, be mindful of this indexing, and a genuinely theological account

24. Durham, *Exodus*, 39.
25. Bonhoeffer, *Schöpfung und Fall*, 60 (my trans.).
26. Barth, *Church Dogmatics* II/1, 7. This is true of God's own immanent life as Father, Son, and Holy Spirit as well. The doctrine of the Trinity affirms that the being of God in Godself exists in three persons in relation. See the glossary for a definition of **immanent Trinity**. For a helpful introduction to trinitarian doctrine, see Sanders and Crisp, *Advancing Trinitarian Theology*.
27. Jesus Christ is "the climax of the covenant." See Wright, *Climax of the Covenant*. Not only does Jesus take the name "I Am" upon himself (John 8:58; see also John 6:35; 8:12; 10:7; 10:11; 11:25; 14:6; and 15:5), but as the incarnate and crucified risen One, Jesus is God *for us*; as we confess in the Nicene Creed, it is "for us and for our salvation" that "he came down from heaven." What is more, Jesus is God *for us* as the faithful Israelite. Unlike ancient Israel, Jesus is true to the covenant purposes of Israel's God: Jesus is truly "the light of the world" (John 8:12), and the efficacy of His redemptive history means that God's salvation truly does reach "to the ends of the earth" (Isa. 49:6).

of the church will account fully for the being and form of the sociohistorical human community that God graciously creates and sustains as the church.

If we want to account theologically for what the church is, then, we must, on the basis of Paul's description of the church in Corinth, speak about the church as a creature of God and God's gracious acts. But having spoken about the church with reference to divine agency, we must subsequently speak about the church as the sociohistorical reality that God and God's gracious acts create and sustain the church as—that is, with reference to *human* agency. For the church is at once a divine and human reality. Given the asymmetrical relationship of divine and human togetherness in this reality, however, there is a need for divine agency to be spoken about in such a way that it relativizes but does not minimize human agency. Such is the force of Paul's appropriation of God's covenantal promise to the church in Corinth. First, it functions to establish that the church is at once a divine and human reality; second, it delineates a specific and given order to the relationship of divine and human togetherness in this reality. It is by virtue of this twofold function that Paul's description of the Corinthian church offers a basic theological grammar to account for what the church is. Paul's speech establishes the need to hold together in ecclesiological description both divine and human agency, but to do so in a way that reflects the asymmetrical relationship of divine and human togetherness in the church's being.

Most significant for what follows in this book, Paul's speech about the church in Corinth could therefore be said to function in a third way, for his description raises the question of how theologians can give due attention in their speech about the church to both the sociohistorical human community that the church is and the gracious divine acts of God that create and sustain the church as that community. And how might theologians hold together in their accounts of the church both divine and human agency in an ordered and proportionate way, so as to ensure that the former relativizes but does not minimize the latter? In other words, how do theologians give voice in their speech about the church to the asymmetrical relationship of divine and human togetherness in the church's being?

The Church as a Topic of Systematic Theology

To put these questions in a more formal register, the issue at stake here is one that falls within the purview of systematic theology particularly.[28] Systematic

---

28. This is a matter I have discussed elsewhere. See Emerton, "Jesus Christ: The Centre of the Church," 236–55, esp. 237–40. This paragraph and the next one include language adapted and borrowed from this publication.

theology is concerned with the material content and ordering of Christian doctrine and with how doctrines are understood in relation to one another, especially with respect to the proportionality of the doctrines represented and which doctrine (if any) is considered foundational.[29] As A. N. Williams points out, Christian theology can be understood to be systematic in two different ways.[30] On the one hand, Williams identifies what she describes as "explicit" systematic theologies. What she means by an explicit systematic theology is a comprehensive and coherent single account of Christian theology ordered doctrine by doctrine. While the exact scope and ordering of doctrines varies in these accounts considerably, examples of this form of systematic theology include Aquinas's *Summa Theologica*; Calvin's *Institutes*; Barth's *Church Dogmatics*; the systematic theologies of Wolfhart Pannenberg and Robert Jenson; and more recently, the first two volumes of the *Systematic Theology* of Katherine Sonderegger.[31] On the other hand, Williams identifies what she describes as "implicit" systematic theologies. What she means by an implicit systematic theology is an account that treats any one Christian doctrine as a single subject of theological inquiry but is concerned to demonstrate in that inquiry how the one doctrine is informed by or determines the shape of other doctrines, an account that thereby exhibits "an impetus towards coherence and comprehensiveness."[32] For Williams, this impetus likens theology that is systematic in this sense to a jigsaw puzzle: "Even if one does not have all the pieces, the shape of any one of them reflects its orientation towards others as parts of a larger pattern. When there are enough such pieces to hand, a complete picture forms, but even in the absence of a whole, unified image, a solitary piece displays by its very shape its trajectory towards linkage."[33] Whether implicitly or explicitly, therefore, the systematic theologian is alive to the way in which any one Christian doctrine is shaped or misshaped by another doctrine; and, further, to the way the expansion or contraction—or, indeed, prioritization—of one doctrine in relation to another doctrine can distort the coherence of Christian doctrine as a whole. Accordingly, a major task for the systematic theologian is to register and repair any such distortions.[34]

29. See Webster, introduction to the *Oxford Handbook of Systematic Theology*, 1–15, esp. 12–13; and Greggs, *Dogmatic Ecclesiology*, 1:xxx–xxxvi.

30. See Williams, *Architecture of Theology*, 1–22.

31. Pannenberg, *Systematic Theology*; Jenson, *Systematic Theology*; Sonderegger, *Systematic Theology*.

32. Williams, *Architecture of Theology*, 1.

33. Williams, *Architecture of Theology*, 1.

34. See Webster, introduction to the *Oxford Handbook of Systematic Theology*, 13.

The importance of this task—and the alertness that it requires of the systematic theologian—cannot be overstated: no Christian doctrine is treatable in isolation from other doctrines, and each doctrine must be treated always with reference to the way it interconnects coherently with Christian doctrine as a whole. However, it is also the case that the doctrine that is considered foundational to that whole, or prioritized particularly within it, will tend to shape (or misshape) the doctrines treated subsequently.[35] As Sarah Coakley says, "*Wherever one chooses to start* [one's systematic theology] *has implications for the whole, and the parts must fit together.*"[36] So, for example (and to apply this to the subject matter of this book), theologians who teach **theological anthropology** as foundational to the whole of Christian doctrine, and subsequently relate their ecclesiological description to a doctrine of humanity, will produce radically different accounts of the church than theologians who prioritize teaching about God's aseity and thus relate their accounts of the church subsequent to a doctrine of God's own immanent life as Father, Son, and Holy Spirit. Alternatively, theologians who treat ecclesiology subsequent to **soteriology** will produce different accounts of the church than theologians who treat ecclesiology subsequent to **pneumatology**.

All of this is to say that, in ecclesiology, "dogmatic topography"[37] matters. It matters where theologians choose to start their ecclesiological descriptions because different doctrinal foundations for ecclesiological speech give rise to different theological accounts of the church. And those accounts—because of those different doctrinal foundations—may be misshaped and thus theologically deficient to one extent or another. Indeed, the threefold force of Paul's appropriation of God's covenantal promise to the church in Corinth is such that theologians must ensure that their accounts of the church are founded on a doctrine of God's own life and work ("I will be their God") and, because of that foundation, always include duly proportionate speech about the sociohistorical human community that God creates the church as ("they will be my people"). Further, the material content and formal presentation of this speech will always be concerned to speak of both a doctrine of God and a doctrine of humanity together, but only as these two doctrines relate, one to another, in accordance with the logic of God's covenantal promise.

It is not too great an exaggeration to say, then, that in Paul's appropriation of God's covenantal promise to the church in Corinth we are given, not only a basic theological grammar to account for what the church is, but also

---

35. For more about this aspect of systematic theology, see John Webster, *God without Measure*, 1:3–10; and Greggs, "Proportion and Topography in Ecclesiology," 89–106.

36. Coakley, *God, Sexuality, and the Self*, 41 (emphasis original).

37. Greggs, *Dogmatic Ecclesiology*, 1:xxx.

the most basic ecclesiological task—the task, that is, of holding together in speech about the church, in an ordered and proportionate way, an account of both divine and human agency, thereby ensuring that the church is spoken of as both creature of God and sociohistorical human community, with due concern for the asymmetrical relationship of divine and human togetherness in the church's being. To the extent that theologians successfully perform this task, their speech about the church will be genuinely theological. Additionally, the resulting account of the church and the basic theological grammar with which it operates will work to repair what I see to be a fundamental problem in contemporary approaches to ecclesiology: the tendency to attend either to the church's human empirical form (to "they will be my people") or to the life and work of God (to "I will be their God"). This either/or tendency generates speech about the church that pries apart what most properly should be held together in ecclesiological description, and which, accordingly, is theologically deficient in light of this most basic task. The typology of contemporary approaches to ecclesiology that I propose in this book works, therefore, both to demonstrate this fundamental either/or problem and also, in the course of its analysis, to point out the concomitant theological deficiencies. The first, second, third, and fourth types of ecclesiological approach, in particular, will demonstrate this fundamental problem, in chapters 2, 3, 4, and 5, respectively.

Five Types of Ecclesiology

To put the matter quite provisionally for now, in the first type of contemporary approach to ecclesiology theologians prioritize description of the church's human empirical form. As an expression of the "ethnographic turn" in contemporary approaches to ecclesiology, and the prior and related convergence on culture in theological inquiry,[38] what I will call *empirical ecclesiology* seeks to account fully for the church as a lived sociohistorical reality, treating the church's human empirical form as the proper object of ecclesiological speech. However, I suggest empirical ecclesiology does so at the expense of speech about the life and work of God: in empirical ecclesiology, the church essentially is what humans do, and an account of human agency is paramount. Empirical ecclesiology is therefore theologically deficient because it risks collapsing speech about divine action into language about ecclesial human reality without remainder. In other words, empirical ecclesiology ultimately "forgets

---

38. I explore this "ethnographic turn" and convergence on culture in the articulation of type 1, empirical ecclesiology, in chap. 2.

God" (to borrow a phrase from Barth[39]), and the charge of methodological agnosticism—if not atheism—is a clear and present threat.

In type 2 ecclesiology, and perhaps arising as a symptom of the legacy bequeathed to ecclesiological description by the **Magisterial Reformation**,[40] the theological deficiency is speech about the church that, proportionately speaking, is inadequately attentive to God's life and work. In this type, which I call *performative ecclesiology*, notwithstanding its support of ecclesiological description with an account of divine agency (in contrast to empirical ecclesiology), the account of human agency proffered in relation to lived ecclesial life and performed church practice treats the doctrine of the church too independently from a doctrine of God. More specifically, performative ecclesiology gives inadequate attention to the unique nature of the church that God and God's gracious acts create *as* a sociohistorical reality. Performative ecclesiology fails to account adequately for the church's uniqueness, for the fact that the church is not just one creaturely reality among others.

In type 3 ecclesiology, in direct contrast to the first and second types, the theological deficiency is instead ecclesiological description that, proportionately speaking, marginalizes the lived sociohistorical reality of the church by its account of the life and work of God. In this type, which I call *communion ecclesiology*, the church's human empirical form is almost swallowed up by an account of God's own triune life and activity indexed to the work of the Holy Spirit and, more specifically, to the site of the Eucharist. In seeking to account for the unique nature of the church as a creature of God's grace, communion ecclesiology overidentifies the church's being with the being of God as triune, and in doing so associates the doctrine of the church too closely with the doctrine of God.

The fourth type of contemporary approach to ecclesiology, like the third, but in direct contrast to the first, prioritizes in its account of the church a description of the life and work of God. In this type, which I call *ideal ecclesiology*, the church essentially is what God does. To be sure, an account of divine agency, indexed to a theology of God's aseity, is paramount. However, in its desire to account fully for the church as a creature of God's grace and treat God and God's gracious acts as the proper object of ecclesiological speech, the density and force of the account of divine agency that ideal ecclesiology proffers not only marginalizes the church's human empirical form but risks dissolving it. Ideal ecclesiology is theologically deficient because it presents,

---

39. See Barth, *Church Dogmatics* I/2, 794.

40. I explore this suggestion in the articulation of type 2, performative ecclesiology, in chap. 3.

in somewhat theoretical or abstract terms, an overly idealized account of the church that neglects the church's sociohistorical existence, introducing too great a distinction between that existence and the life and work of God in creating and sustaining it. In ideal ecclesiology, the clear and present threat is not methodological agnosticism but methodological **docetism**, so to speak. In other words, ideal ecclesiology ultimately "forgets human existence" (to borrow another of Barth's phrases).[41]

In the typology of contemporary approaches to ecclesiology that I propose, therefore, one can place type 1, empirical ecclesiology, and type 4, ideal ecclesiology, at opposite poles; and type 2, performative ecclesiology, and type 3, communion ecclesiology, can then be placed between these opposing poles. (See fig. 1.)

Another way to put this is to say that performative ecclesiology is a soft form of empirical ecclesiology, and communion ecclesiology is a soft form of ideal ecclesiology. By using the adjective *soft*, I mean to distinguish theologians who make the problematic either/or tendency an *explicit* methodological claim, and thereby a normative and necessary foundation of their ecclesiological description, and theologians who do not make the either/or tendency a normative and necessary foundation of their ecclesiological description but nevertheless display it therein, making it an *implicit* logical consequence of that description. In other words, while the individual theologians whom I read as illustrating empirical and ideal ecclesiology state the problematic either/or tendency explicitly, the theologians I read as illustrating performative and communion ecclesiology show it implicitly.

A note of caution should be registered here, however. Like all typological analysis, the typology of contemporary approaches to ecclesiology that I propose is a heuristic device and, as such, is (often) a simplification of the complexities of individual theologians' ecclesiological descriptions. The

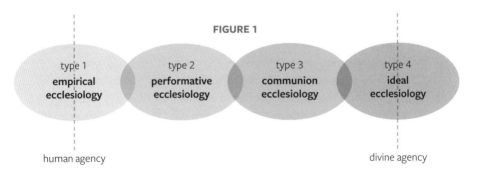

FIGURE 1

type 1
empirical
ecclesiology

type 2
performative
ecclesiology

type 3
communion
ecclesiology

type 4
ideal
ecclesiology

human agency   divine agency

41. Barth, *Church Dogmatics* I/2, 794.

designations *empirical*, *performative*, *communion*, and *ideal* are adopted for the purpose of typological analysis of the field of contemporary ecclesiology only; they are not, in any sense, exhaustive descriptions of the ecclesiological thought of individual theologians. Not everything that is said in relation to a type can be said, therefore, to apply with equal precision to the individual theologians whose works are read as illustrative of that type. To reify a type as a predicate of the work of any individual theologian is thus to tend toward dysfunction. This is simply to register what has long been recognized: the inevitable limitations of typological analysis.

Indeed, space does not allow as thorough-going an analysis of the work of individual theologians as I would like; my purpose here is to make principal points through exemplification. As I noted in the introduction, the typology of contemporary approaches to ecclesiology that I propose is offered principally to provide a constructive orientation to the field of contemporary ecclesiological thought in relation to the question of what the church is. My intent is to bring this question sharply into view. As I have noted in this chapter, however, the typology is also offered in order to suggest how each of the first four types of ecclesiological approach fails to perform successfully ecclesiology's most basic task, and this notwithstanding the ways in which they might seem to correct the problematic either/or tendencies of one another.

In presenting the first four types of approach to contemporary ecclesiology in this mutually corrective and dialogical way, I hope a pathway will necessarily open up to present, in chapter 6, a fifth type—what I call *ecclesiological ecclesiology*. As it is presented, ecclesiological ecclesiology aims to correct the tendency in empirical, performative, communion, and ideal ecclesiology to pry apart in speech about the church the relationship of divine and human togetherness in the church's being; thus, derivatively, it offers an account of divine and human agency. In ecclesiological ecclesiology, there is thus a desire to ameliorate the problematic either/or tendency in contemporary approaches to ecclesiology by holding together in speech about the church, in an ordered and proportionate way, both the life and work of God and the church's human empirical form, with due concern for the asymmetrical relationship of divine and human togetherness in the church's being. Ecclesiological ecclesiology seeks to do this by attending to the person and work of God the Holy Spirit:[42] the Holy Spirit who creates and sustains the church as the church—that is, as both creature of God and sociohistorical human community. Here, then, the

---

42. The suggestion that ecclesiology as a doctrine is most properly derivative of pneumatology is introduced in the articulation of type 3, communion ecclesiology, in chap. 4, and considered more fully in the articulation of type 5, ecclesiological ecclesiology, in chap. 6. For a helpful introduction to pneumatology itself, see Kärkkäinen, *Pneumatology*.

"how" of this unity is not, as Claude Welch once maintained, "the paradox, the inconceivability, the miracle, beyond which we cannot and must not try to go"[43] but is, rather, the effective and gracious act of God the Holy Spirit. And in speech about the church, it must be understood as such.

Toward a Reparative Ecclesiological Grammar

In light of the above, it is hopefully clear that this book is conceived primarily—in the fashion of Hans Frei's typology of modern Christian theology—as a work *about* rather than *of* ecclesiology.[44] However, as Frei himself notes, "In practice the distinction will not always be clear."[45] That said, this book does not seek to offer a specific theology or doctrine of the church. There are multiple books that offer such a thing and do so with a precision and sophistication that I could never hope to match.[46] What this book seeks to do instead is to press at fundamental ecclesiological questions in order to elucidate ecclesiology's primary task of accounting theologically for what the church is. Further, by describing a fundamental problem in contemporary approaches to ecclesiology and seeking to articulate a reparative theological grammar for ecclesiological description, the book is also set apart from other introductory works to ecclesiology, of which there are many.[47] On the whole, such works tend to offer overviews of specific ecclesiological traditions; the ecclesiology of individual theological thinkers; church identity indexed to particular biblical motifs, historical periods, or models of what the church is like; or, indeed, a combination of all of these things. These overviews are not offered, however, from the perspective of ecclesiological method, nor are they intended to describe a fundamental problem in contemporary approaches to ecclesiology and to articulate a possible reparative theological grammar. That is what this book aims to provide.

In a sense, therefore, the only directly comparable book to this one is the book that has been the go-to for the majority of students of ecclesiology over the past forty-five years: Avery Dulles's *Models of the Church*. While Dulles works from a careful study of a number of theological thinkers to construct

43. Welch, *Reality of the Church*, 38.
44. See Frei, *Types of Christian Theology*, 1.
45. Frei, *Types of Christian Theology*, 1.
46. See, e.g., Schillebeeckx, *Church*; Volf, *After Our Likeness*; Badcock, *House Where God Lives*; Cross, *People of God's Presence*; and Greggs, *Dogmatic Ecclesiology*.
47. See, e.g., Newbigin, *Household of God*; Harper and Metzger, *Exploring Ecclesiology*; Jenson and Wilhite, *Church*; Pickard, *Seeking the Church*; Avis, *Oxford Handbook of Ecclesiology*; and Kärkkäinen, *Introduction to Ecclesiology*.

and evaluate five—and, in the expanded edition, six—models by which the church can be understood, the overview of ecclesiology he presents has a particular (Roman Catholic) slant and, more importantly, is now limited due to the passing of time.[48] Indeed, in the forty-five years since Dulles's work was first published—and despite the revisions his work has gone through in this time—discourse about the church has changed. The landscape of ecclesiological description now includes methodological approaches and theological assumptions that Dulles could not have imagined. There is thus a need to address these differences and to do so in a way that is attentive to how these differences both shape and misshape ecclesiological description. My hope is that this book will meet this need and thereby be of service to contemporary ecclesiological discourse. With all of this in mind, let us now proceed to the articulation of each of the five types of contemporary approach to ecclesiology, beginning with type 1, empirical ecclesiology.

48. See Dulles, *Models of the Church*.

2

Empirical Ecclesiology

In the first type of contemporary approach to ecclesiology, description of the church's human empirical form is the normative and necessary foundation of all ecclesiological speech. In empirical ecclesiology, theologians speak properly of what the church is only if they attend first to the church's human empirical form and thereby make accounts of human agency paramount in their ecclesiological descriptions. There is thus a desire in empirical ecclesiology to account fully for the church as a lived sociohistorical reality, and so to treat this reality as the proper object of ecclesiological discourse.

This desire arises, primarily, out of a concern to establish what has been described as "plausibility" in ecclesiological description—that is, to offer an account of the church in which what is said theologically about the church's being corresponds to, or at least shares a commonality with, the experience of the church's lived sociohistorical reality.[1] In other words, the concern in empirical ecclesiology is to address the often apparent disconnect between one's experience of lived ecclesial life and what is affirmed theologically about the church in ecclesiological discourse. As Nicholas Healy puts it, "Ecclesiology in our period has become highly systematic and theoretical, focused more upon discerning the right things to think about the church rather than oriented to the living, rather messy, confused and confusing body that the church actually is."[2] For the sake of ecclesiology's credibility and to ensure ultimately that ecclesiology is most helpful to the life and mission

1. See Ward, *Perspectives*, 4–6.
2. Healy, *Church, World and the Christian Life*, 3.

of the church, there is thus a need for theologians to establish "plausibility" in ecclesiological description, and to do so by starting their accounts of the church not from abstract theological first principles but from the lived experience of the church as a concrete and particular sociohistorical reality that is both fallible and sinful.

It is from this foundation that theologians will best understand the church's being and have proper concern for accounting theologically for what the church is, in an ordered and proportionate way. This is because the church *is* a sociohistorical human community. In Roger Haight's words, "The principal object of ecclesiology consists in the empirical organization or collectivity or communion called church," and "this empirical, human church is the starting point for the study of the church and the basic referent for the word 'church.'"[3]

Ecclesiology and the Ethnographic Turn

If this is so, then theologians are necessarily required to describe the human empirical form of the church—to describe, that is, the concrete coming together of the particular group of people called "the church" and the practices and beliefs that distinguish and define them as such.[4] This necessity, in turn, means that in empirical ecclesiology ethnography has particular, and perhaps determinative, explanatory power in accounting theologically for what the church is.

While a singular definition of ethnography is elusive in contemporary fields of study, the word derives from the Greek *ethnos*, meaning "people," and *graphia*, meaning "writing." Minimally, therefore, ethnography is writing about the lived experience of people; or, as Christian B. Scharen puts it, the concern of ethnography is with "writing culture"[5]—writing being both descriptive and interpretative, and based on direct qualitative research usually undertaken in the form of participant observation and interviewing in the context of a particular site of study. For Scharen, the "judicious narratives" that such description and interpretation are able to fund are precisely what is needed in ecclesiology if the disjunction that Healy identifies in the quote above is to be addressed.[6] More fundamentally, however, ethnography

3. Haight, *Christian Community in History*, 1:5, 37.

4. See Komonchak, "Ecclesiology and Social Theory," 262–83, esp. 262.

5. Scharen, "'Judicious Narratives,'" 125–42, esp. 125. For a helpful introduction to ethnography, see Jones and Watt, *Ethnography*.

6. See Scharen, "'Judicious Narratives,'" 125. Scharen's argument itself is a response to the ecclesiological thought of John Milbank. I explore Milbank's ecclesiology in the articulation of type 4, ideal ecclesiology, in chap. 5.

itself, Scharen contends, "ought to be a means of doing theology."[7] This is because Scharen sees theology—following the programmatic suggestion of Nicholas Adams and Charles Elliot—as best practiced through the work of detailed practical description of God's world.[8] In such description, theological presuppositions "are *already* at work," and hence "description is the medium in which dogmatics and ethnography include each other."[9] Specific clarification of theological presuppositions adds little or even nothing, then, to what Adams and Elliot see as the inherently theological work of ethnographic description. They therefore propose an approach to theology in which "theologians take ethnographic description at least as seriously as dogmatics: indeed, the latter is, and should be," they argue, "the slave of the former."[10]

It is this approach that Scharen subsequently connects to ecclesiology explicitly, and that, to a certain extent, Healy himself prefigures in his own identification of ecclesiology's need to "find ways to make theological use of those forms of discourse that critically examine the complexities and confusions of human activity, such as sociology, cultural analysis, and history."[11] In this way, empirical ecclesiology considers speech about the church to be a matter of practical, rather than theoretical, wisdom.[12] At the heart of empirical ecclesiology is the methodological conviction that "the real" in ecclesiological discourse is the church's sociohistorical and cultural reality, and that to make ecclesiology "more recognisably real,"[13] theologians must work toward their accounts of the church inductively, "from below"—that is, from the church's human empirical form.

7. Scharen, "'Judicious Narratives,'" 125.
8. See Adams and Elliot, "Ethnography Is Dogmatics," 339–64.
9. Adams and Elliot, "Ethnography Is Dogmatics," 346 (emphasis original), 362.
10. Adams and Elliot, "Ethnography Is Dogmatics," 363. To redescribe theological work in this way is contentious, not least in light of Barth's assertion that "dogmatics is the self-examination of the Christian church in respect of the content of its distinctive talk about God" (Barth, *Church Dogmatics* I/1, 11). The reader might worry whether Adams and Elliot therefore occlude in their redescription of theology a constitutive element of the discipline: its critical and corrective function in inquiring into the content of that which is described, and thus assessing the agreement or lack thereof of the *fides quae creditur* (the "faith that is believed") with the scriptural witness—a witness that stands external to any such description.
11. Healy, *Church, World and the Christian Life*, 5. I have added the qualification "to a certain extent" because Healy ultimately makes ethnographic description the slave of a doctrine of God in his ecclesiological description. It is for this reason that I explore Healy's ecclesiology in the articulation of type 2, performative ecclesiology, in chap. 3.
12. The distinction between theoretical wisdom (*sophia*) and practical wisdom (*phronēsis*) is Aristotle's, and it is found in book 4 of his *Nicomachean Ethics*. See Aristotle, *Nicomachean Ethics*, 102–17. Such a distinction is, of course, heuristic, as hard-and-fast lines between theory and practice are often difficult to demarcate.
13. Scharen, "'Judicious Narratives,'" 125.

What is more, to work in this way theologians must take seriously in ecclesiology the explanatory power of **phenomenology**. As John Swinton summarizes aptly, "Phenomenology asks us to put aside our presuppositions,
plausibility structures, standard explanatory frameworks, expectations, and
assumptions and return to look at the thing itself, the experience as it is lived
rather than as it is theorized."[14] To apply this to ecclesiology, phenomenology asks theologians to turn to the church as it is—as the church is lived
and experienced, and not as the church is theorized from theological first
principles. And for theologians to do this effectively, they will necessarily
have to draw on ethnography, and on the disciplines of the social sciences
more widely, to describe the church's concrete and particular sociohistorical
existence—its phenomenal surface, in other words—in *all* of its concrete
particularity. Indeed, ethnography is understood to be "the right-sized tool"
for this work precisely because it is able to fund a complex understanding
of the cultural and communal identity within the life of any one particular
Christian community.[15]

Central to the methodological conviction of empirical ecclesiology, then,
is not just the explanatory power of phenomenology worked out through
a turn to ethnography, but ethnography's own defining feature: the idea of
thick description. In his essay "Thick Description: Toward an Interpretative
Theory of Culture,"[16] Clifford Geertz defines ethnography as a venture in such
description—description, that is, that moves beyond recorded observation of
mere fact and surface-level appearance to exegete the meaning that people
inscribe those appearances and facts with. Thick description therefore requires
the ethnographer to observe, record, analyze, and—critically—interpret social
discourse, and to do so in such a way that "the 'said' of such discourse" is
"fixed" so that others outside of that discourse can understand its complexity
in all of its concrete particularity.[17] In the words of Norman Denzin, a thick
description "presents detail, context, emotion, and the webs of social rela-
tionships that join persons to one another. It enacts what it describes. Thick
description evokes emotionality and self-feelings. It inserts history into experience. It establishes the significance of an experience, or the sequence of events,
for the person or persons in question. In thick description, the voices, feelings,
actions, and meanings of interacting individuals are heard, made visible."[18]

---

14. Swinton, *Finding Jesus*, 42. For a helpful overview of phenomenology, see Moran, *Introduction to Phenomenology*.
15. See Scharen, "'Judicious Narratives,'" 142.
16. See Geertz, *Interpretation of Culture*, 3–30.
17. Geertz, *Interpretation of Culture*, 20.
18. Denzin, *Interpretive Interactionism*, 100.

Put otherwise, thick description requires the ethnographer to exegete the complexity of the culture of a particular sociohistorical phenomenon by interpreting the socially established structures of meaning that make up that culture.[19] And if the particular group of people called "the church" is the basic referent for what the church is, then thick description of this group and of the socially established structures of meaning that compose its culture is what theologians must engage first and foremost in order to account theologically for the church's being. In this sense, all theologians who want to speak about the human empirical form of the church must, then, become ethnographers;[20] and ecclesiology itself must be seen as the ethnography of Christian belief and practice as that belief and practice is enacted corporately in the cultural context of the church.[21]

Theology and the Convergence on Culture

This ethnographic turn in contemporary approaches to ecclesiology is dependent on a prior convergence on culture in theological inquiry. This convergence is traced, most frequently, to George Lindbeck's decisive and influential work *The Nature of Doctrine*, and in particular to his proposal therein for a "cultural-linguistic" approach to theology over against a "cognitively propositional" or an "experiential-expressive" one.[22] For Lindbeck, a "cognitively propositional" approach to theology understands Christianity as an informational or cognitive enterprise in which Christian doctrines function in the manner of first-order truth claims about objective reality: "For a propositionalist, if a doctrine is once true, it is always true, and if it is once false, it is always false."[23] In contrast, in an "experiential-expressive" approach, Christianity is understood as an aesthetic enterprise and Christian doctrines function as "noninformative" symbols of subjective feelings, beliefs, and practices.[24] For such a symbolist, doctrine is "polyvalent in import and therefore subject to changes of meaning or even to a total loss of meaningfulness."[25]

As an alternative to both types of approach, Lindbeck seeks to understand Christianity as neither a cognitive enterprise nor an experiential-expressive

19. See Geertz, *Interpretation of Culture*, 12.
20. See Scharen, "'Judicious Narratives,'" 142.
21. For more about the relationship between ethnography and ecclesiology, see the collection of essays in Ward, *Perspectives*, together with its partner volume, Scharen, *Explorations*.
22. Lindbeck, *Nature of Doctrine*, 16–19.
23. Lindbeck, *Nature of Doctrine*, 16.
24. Lindbeck, *Nature of Doctrine*, 17.
25. Lindbeck, *Nature of Doctrine*, 17.

one, but rather as a language or culture.[26] In this "cultural-linguistic" approach, Christian doctrines function neither as first-order truth claims with objective import nor as subjective, expressive symbols whose meanings are subject to change, but as "communally authoritative rules" that govern or regulate the behavior, beliefs, and practices of the church and the institutional forms it takes.[27] In this way, Christianity is understood by Lindbeck as "grammatical" and "can be viewed as a kind of cultural and/or linguistic framework or medium that shapes the entirety of life and thought."[28]

Lindbeck's proposal for a "cultural-linguistic" approach to Christian theology and the paradigmatic shift toward culture as a controlling **hermeneutic** for theological inquiry it signals, has, more recently, been taken up prominently by Kathryn Tanner.[29] For Tanner, a postmodern, anthropological notion of culture serves to thicken theological discourse precisely because theology itself is a form of culture: "Theology is something that human beings produce. Like all human activities, it is historically and socially conditioned; it cannot be understood in isolation from the rest of human sociocultural practices. In short, to say that theology is a part of culture is just to say in a contemporary idiom that it is a human activity."[30] And, further, it is a human activity that takes place in, or is at least shaped by, a specifically Christian cultural context and the practices and beliefs that it comprises.[31] Theology, then, is thought of by Tanner as a human-social activity that is specific to the culture of a Christian way of life.[32] As such, theology has to do with everyday Christian practices and beliefs and with the exploration of their "meaning dimension."[33]

These practices and beliefs, additionally, are themselves forms of culture. For Tanner, Christian beliefs and practices are *lived* beliefs and practices. They are, therefore, conditioned in ever-changing ways by a variety of everyday social, economic, and political forces to which the Christian who holds them is necessarily subject.[34] As Tanner maintains, it is not that one is a Christian and then a social, economic, or political agent, or that one is such an agent

---

26. See Lindbeck, *Nature of Doctrine*, 17–18.

27. See Lindbeck, *Nature of Doctrine*, 18.

28. Lindbeck, *Nature of Doctrine*, 33; see also 79–84. Lindbeck's proposal is thus reminiscent of what Ludwig Wittgenstein called a "language game," the distinctive grammar of which "tells what kind of object anything is." Wittgenstein, *Philosophical Investigations*, 123e.

29. See Tanner, *Theories of Culture*. The concern is also prominent in the work of Graham Ward. See Ward, *Cultural Transformation*.

30. Tanner, *Theories of Culture*, 63.

31. See Tanner, *Theories of Culture*, 63–69.

32. Tanner, *Theories of Culture*, 69.

33. Tanner, *Theories of Culture*, 70.

34. See Tanner, *Theories of Culture*, 74–75.

and then a Christian; rather, the Christian is the agent *and* the agent is the Christian.[35] Indeed, it is only in the concrete and particular contexts in which Christian beliefs and practices are lived that their meaning becomes clear, and it becomes clear only as those practices and beliefs are themselves understood in a mutually interpreting way. In Tanner's own words, "In the concrete circumstances of life, actions and interests do not exist per se isolated from the beliefs one holds; nor do beliefs exist per se isolated from one's actions and interests with reference to others."[36]

From this perspective, the nature of Christian belief and practice as culturally situated becomes the proper subject matter of theology. For Tanner, theological inquiry does not exist in some sort of "derealized sphere"[37] and must never be content to operate in such a sphere. To think that theology is a purely informational or cognitive activity that is concerned with abstract first-order truth claims is to make a basic category mistake. This is not only because theology is a context- and culture-specific human activity, but because its subject matter necessarily resists any type of first-order classification. Indeed, the meaning of mutually interpreting Christian beliefs and practices that are inextricably implicated in the vicissitudes of everyday life because they are lived, can only ever be contextual and thus marked by change, conflict, and contradiction.[38] There is, then, no truth claim that carries objective import. As Tanner writes, "The meaning of a Christian belief may have a fairly definite sense in an established context of uses to which it is put, but that meaning presents no absolute standard that predetermines future uses. No given context can control the meaning of a particular belief or value; that belief or value can always be inserted in some other context, the given context itself being perhaps revised or rearranged. The context of usages that establishes meaning is itself ultimately unanchored, in other words."[39]

The implication of this for theologians is that theological inquiry most properly proceeds not by "theoretical logic" but by the "cultural logic of everyday practice."[40] Theology, then, arises organically out of Christian beliefs and practices, and theological ideas are "found" on an everyday level.[41] As

35. See Tanner, *Politics of God*, 9.
36. Tanner, *Politics of God*, 9.
37. Tanner, *Theories of Culture*, 73.
38. See Tanner, *Theories of Culture*, 77.
39. Tanner, *Theories of Culture*, 78.
40. Tanner, *Theories of Culture*, 82.
41. Tanner, *Theories of Culture*, 71 and 85. On the relationship between theology and that which is "found" empirically, see also Quash, *Found Theology*. I explore this relationship further in the articulation of type 2, performative ecclesiology, in chap. 3.

such, theological creativity amounts to what Tanner describes as "the creativity of a postmodern 'bricoleur.'"[42] This creativity, she contends, is expressed "through the modification and extension of materials already on the ground."[43] Thus, theologians are called to construct their theologies internal to, and out of, what they find empirically in the world. In this sense, theological inquiry is to be "worldly" and thereby dependent on, in Sheila Greeve Davaney's words, a "move away from the study of ideas abstracted from their concrete histories and contexts."[44]

The Legacy of Liberation Theology

This concern to construct a more worldly theology out of the cultural situatedness of Christian belief and practice partly echoes what liberation theology—Latin American, Black, and feminist—has long maintained.[45] Indeed, to seek to establish the primacy of situation in theological inquiry is necessary for the liberationist because theology itself is a reflective act from within praxis and on praxis. As Gustavo Gutiérrez writes, "Theology is reflection, a critical attitude. Theology *follows*; it is a second step. . . . The pastoral activity of the Church does not flow as a conclusion from theological premises. Theology does not produce pastoral activity; rather it reflects upon it."[46] In other words, the point of departure for theology is not abstract and objective first-order truth claims about God, but rather the cultural and socio-religious experience of God had by a particular people in the midst of oppression. For the liberationist, truth itself is subjective. It is found, as James H. Cone notes, "in the stories, songs, dances, sermons, paintings, and sayings of . . . peoples"[47] who are struggling to overcome oppression. For the liberationist, there is no truth independent of such human experience, and theology must therefore have this experience as its point of departure. As Cone puts it, summarizing

42. Tanner, *Theories of Culture*, 166.
43. Tanner, *Theories of Culture*, 166.
44. Davaney, "Theology and the Turn to Cultural Analysis," 9.
45. Liberation theology understands the gospel of God as liberation for the poor and oppressed from economic, patriarchal, political, racial, social, or spiritual oppression. It is committed—by cultural affirmation and political concern—to solidarity with the poor and oppressed; to aiding the victims of oppression in practical ways in their struggle against oppressive structures; and, ultimately, to liberating these victims. For the paradigmatic description of liberation theology as it arose in Latin America, see Gutiérrez, *Theology of Liberation*. For the archetypal account of Black theology as liberation theology, see Cone, *Black Theology of Liberation*. And for that of feminist liberation theology, see Schüssler Fiorenza, *In Memory of Her*.
46. Gutiérrez, *Theology of Liberation*, 11 (emphasis original).
47. Cone, *For My People*, 153.

this methodological commitment from the perspective of Black theology, "We do not begin our theology with a reflection on divine revelation as if the God of our faith is separate from the suffering of our people. We do not believe that revelation is a deposit of fixed doctrines or an objective word of God that is then applied to the human situation. On the contrary, we contend there is no truth outside or beyond the concrete historical events in which persons are engaged as agents. Truth is found in the histories, cultures, and religions of our peoples."[48]

Theology, then, is necessarily culturally situated. It arises out of personal experience of God in the context of human degradation—or at least in solidarity with such an experience—and proceeds as a reflection on that experience with a conscious this-worldly emphasis on concrete, oppressed humanity. As a reflective act, the goal of liberation theology, further, is the actual liberation of humankind from its oppression as a faithful witness to God's gospel. What is more, for the liberationist, theology is not *Christian* theology unless it is concerned directly and unreservedly with the human situation that gives rise to it, and thereby participates actively in emancipating humankind from that situation.[49] In this sense, Cone concludes, "Theology is anthropology."[50] Therefore, if theology is to be true to what it, in fact, is and avoid being what Cone describes as "idle talk," at best, and "blasphemy," at worst,[51] theologians must steadfastly refuse to engage in theoretical analysis of abstract theological first principles with a view to applying those principles subsequently to cultural and socioreligious life. As Rosemary Radford Ruether avers, "The prophetic-liberating tradition is not and cannot be made into a static set of 'ideas.' Rather it is a plumb line of truth and untruth, justice and injustice that has to be constantly adapted to changing social contexts and circumstances."[52] Theologians must always reflect, then, from within and on these social contexts and circumstances in all their particularity and concreteness.

Theologians are able to do this, however, only as they draw on the resources of cultural anthropology and the critical tools of social-scientific analysis.[53] Indeed, these particular resources and tools enable theologians to investigate cultural and socioreligious life from an anthropocentric point of departure.

48. Cone, *For My People*, 148.
49. See Cone, *Black Theology of Liberation*, 60.
50. Cone, *Black Theology of Liberation*, 82. Cone's assertion restates the fundamental commitment of Ludwig Feuerbach. See Feuerbach, *Essence of Christianity*, x.
51. Cone, *God of the Oppressed*, 47.
52. Ruether, *Sexism and God-Talk*, 23.
53. See, for example, Gutiérrez, *Theology of Liberation*, 5, 81–82, 86–87, 139, 273; and Cone, *For My People*, 151–52.

This is because the resources of cultural anthropology and the social-scientific tools of analysis are best suited to fund description of, and thereby theological reflection on, the Christian beliefs and practices that life comprises as it is lived concretely and particularly. The critical importance of recourse to such tools and resources in theological inquiry is heightened further for the liberationist by the fact that Christian belief itself is evidenced not by what people say they believe (i.e., not *theoretically*) but by what people do (i.e., *practically*). In liberation theology, Christian practice is considered to be the proof of Christian belief: "Doing and saying are therefore bound together so that the meaning of what one says can be validated only by what one does."[54] Hence the need for theologians to make everyday Christian practice—in relation to which Christian belief is established—the primary locus of theological inquiry and, in that inquiry, to draw on the analytical and critical gaze of the social-scientific fields to enable them to reflect fully on those culturally situated beliefs and practices.

This primacy of the cultural situation and the attendant concern for praxis over theory that liberation theology calls for is perhaps seen most clearly in the liberationist's speech about the church. For Leonardo Boff, the disconnect between the positing of "theological hypotheses" about the church and "ecclesial practices" at work within the church means that "true ecclesiology" can only ever arise as a reflective consequence from within and upon such practices.[55] Only to the extent that theologians start their ecclesiologies with critical reflection on concrete historical practice—and, in particular, on the socioeconomic, political, patriarchal, and racialized realities that inevitably condition that practice—will their ecclesiologies be true. In other words, true ecclesiology ("true ecclesiogenesis," as Boff puts it) arises only as theologians conceive the church from the ground up—that is, from "the 'base,'" from "basic ecclesial communities" comprising the poor who seek liberation from economic, social, spiritual, and political oppression.[56] As Ruether observes, from the perspective of a liberation theology for women, "Women-church—and indeed all base Christian communities—are engaged in a revolutionary act of reappropriating to the people what has been falsely expropriated from us."[57] What is more, for the liberationist (whether feminist, Black, or Latin American), this is precisely what the church is. The church is not an institution or a building, and it is not defined

54. Cone, *For My People*, 148. I explore the relationship between Christian belief and practice further in the articulation of type 2, performative ecclesiology, in chap. 3.

55. See Boff, *Church: Charism and Power*, 1, 32–46.

56. Boff, *Church: Charism and Power*, 44; Boff, *Ecclesiogenesis*, 15.

57. Ruether, *Women-Church*, 25.

by its elders, administrators, or leaders, by its bishops or priests, or even by those who faithfully come week by week to worship. Rather, the church is defined by the desires and struggles—and therefore the faith—of the poor and oppressed.[58]

Indeed, in liberation theology, the church is, definitively, the suffering people of God.[59] It is, as Cone argues, that group of people who take seriously the words of Jesus in Matthew 5:11: "Blessed are you when people insult you, persecute you and falsely say all kinds of evil against you because of me."[60] Further, it is that group of people who, in faithful witness to God's gospel, participate in Christ's own liberating work to identify with the suffering of the poor and oppressed and thereby liberate them. "The Church is, first of all," writes Ruether, "the poor and oppressed,"[61] but "to *be* Church means an exodus from patriarchy."[62] To argue thus is not just to contend for an understanding of the church as a church with a preference for the oppressed and poor, but more acutely for an understanding of the church as a church *of* and *with* the oppressed and poor—or, as Boff puts it, a church *from* the oppressed and poor.[63] In liberation theology, the experience and faithful practice of the oppressed and poor is the genesis of what the church actually is.

Given this, it follows that theologians' ecclesiological descriptions must begin and end in the lived sociohistorical reality of God's suffering people. For Boff—as for Cone and Gutiérrez—theologians do this by "deciphering" the various ecclesial practices in effect in their church contexts through the use of social-scientific tools of analysis.[64] From there, and to ensure that their ecclesiologies go beyond mere phenomenological analysis, theologians must subsequently arrive at "the theoretical premises and formulations behind these practices."[65] Theologians do this by reading ecclesial practices and the sociohistorical contexts that condition them with "the eyes of faith and theology, discerning the paths of sin and the avenues of grace."[66] The final step for theologians in their ecclesiological description is then, for Boff, an articulation of the praxis that aids the suffering people of God concretely in the process of their complete liberation.[67] Accordingly, if ecclesiological

58. See Boff, *Church: Charism and Power*, 10.
59. See Cone, *Black Theology and Black Power*, 74.
60. See Cone, *Black Theology and Black Power*, 74.
61. Ruether, *Sexism and God-Talk*, 132.
62. Ruether, *Women-Church*, 64 (emphasis original).
63. See Boff, *Church: Charism and Power*, 8–10.
64. Boff, *Church: Charism and Power*, 20.
65. Boff, *Church: Charism and Power*, 1.
66. Boff, *Church: Charism and Power*, 20.
67. See Boff, *Church: Charism and Power*, 20.

description is to be true to what the church is, it can never be speech that is abstract or static, and thus indifferent to how the traumas of history are experienced by the oppressed and poor in their struggle against oppression.[68] Rather, true ecclesiology will only ever involve speech about the church that is wholly conditioned by that struggle and experience, and in this way it will always be passionate—that is, it will always be speech that has the concrete wounds of the oppressed and poor as its point of departure. And in its desire to be at one with the depths of those wounds, it will be speech that reflects on ecclesial practice in the context of them and works always in practical ways to bind up and liberate the wounded.[69]

A Worldly Theology for a Wounded Church

The convergence on culture in theology and the turn to ethnography in contemporary approaches to ecclesiology can be seen to echo, albeit in redrawn terms, the call of liberation theology for an ecclesiology (and a theology more broadly) that is passionate. Indeed, in all of these movements, the concern is one and the same: to construct a more worldly theology out of the cultural situatedness of Christian practice and belief by recourse to social-scientific fields of inquiry, and thus, ultimately, a more plausible ecclesiology. This concern is expressed perhaps most clearly and recently in contemporary approaches to ecclesiology by Mary McClintock Fulkerson.

McClintock Fulkerson's ecclesiological speech—like that of the liberationist—proceeds as a reflective act from within and on ecclesial practice.[70] For McClintock Fulkerson, this point of departure for ecclesiology is necessitated by the call to make "full theological sense" of the "worldly" nature of what the church is, together with the "situational character" of lived ecclesial life.[71] The church that McClintock Fulkerson has in view—as the site of her study and participant observer—is a particular United Methodist

---

68. Boff, *Church: Charism and Power*, 2.

69. See Cone, *Black Theology of Liberation*, 17.

70. See McClintock Fulkerson, *Changing the Subject*; McClintock Fulkerson, *Places of Redemption*; and McClintock Fulkerson, "Interpreting a Situation," 124–44. The reader should note that while I read McClintock Fulkerson's ecclesiology as standing in relation to feminist liberation theology, McClintock Fulkerson herself is critical of aspects of this theology—in particular, of what she sees as its generic and normalizing appeal to "women's experience," which fails to take seriously the simple fact that the meaning and identity of the subject "women" is not fixed or universally the same. See McClintock Fulkerson, *Changing the Subject*, esp. 3–8, 50–53.

71. McClintock Fulkerson, *Places of Redemption*, 6–7; and McClintock Fulkerson, "Interpreting a Situation," 125.

Church (UMC) congregation, along with its "worldliness," the way in which this church is "racialized, gendered, [and] marked by valuations of ability."[72] Accounting for "the density of lived faith" in this particular and concrete situation, and understanding the sociohistorical and cultural context that conditions it is what it means, for McClintock Fulkerson, to make "full theological sense" of it.[73]

To do so, however, necessitates that the discipline of theology be shaped not by "historically normative texts," or by "any kind of Christian orthodoxy," but by "empirical study."[74] Accordingly, McClintock Fulkerson appropriates the tools of ethnography—and, in particular, the resources of cultural anthropology and the tools of social-scientific analysis—to fund a thick description of the "situational character" of Good Samaritan UMC and its lived ecclesial life. Indeed, only in this way, she argues, do theologians avoid neglecting "the worldly way" in which the church lives out the Christian faith and the way in which God is "God-with-us."[75] Hence, only by writing about the lived faith of particular and concrete people—by "writing their culture" (to recall Scharen's phrase)—do theologians avoid bypassing or obscuring in their ecclesiological descriptions "the primary 'analytic object' for theological reflection."[76] As McClintock Fulkerson puts it with regard to Good Samaritan UMC, "To do theological justice to this community will be to write about its people, about its habits and idiosyncrasies, its mistakes and its blindness, as well as its moments of honesty and grace."[77] There is thus a need for theologians to recognize that ecclesiology most properly is the task of practical—not systematic—theological inquiry.[78]

For McClintock Fulkerson, any theology conceived in "purely ideational"[79] or overly cognitive-propositional terms and concerned with "doctrine, rightly understood,"[80] is ill-equipped to account fully for the density of the situational character of lived ecclesial life. This is because the "ideational" framework of systematic theology simply bypasses or obscures "the complex

72. McClintock Fulkerson, *Places of Redemption*, 251n48.
73. McClintock Fulkerson, "Interpreting a Situation," 125.
74. See McClintock Fulkerson, "Interpreting a Situation," 129, 125.
75. McClintock Fulkerson, *Places of Redemption*, 6.
76. McClintock Fulkerson, "Interpreting a Situation," 129.
77. McClintock Fulkerson, *Places of Redemption*, 6.
78. See McClintock Fulkerson, "Interpreting a Situation," 126. David Tracy defines practical theology as "the mutually critical correlation of the interpreted theory and praxis of the Christian fact and the interpreted theory and praxis of the contemporary situation." Tracy, "Foundations of Practical Theology," 76. I owe this reference to McClintock Fulkerson.
79. McClintock Fulkerson, *Places of Redemption*, 233.
80. McClintock Fulkerson, *Places of Redemption*, 232.

configuration of the lived situation."[81] Further, according to McClintock Fulkerson, this conceptual framework problematically seeks to apply or impose "correct" Christian doctrine on that situation and does so without regard for the way in which "lived or everyday theologizing" arises organically out of Christian practice.[82] She writes, "'Belief and value commitments' are usually left underdeveloped and 'ambiguous' in the ordinary practice of faith" because of "the contradictory way [such] commitments occur."[83] This contradiction has to do with the way in which beliefs and value commitments are implicated necessarily in "the banal and opaque realities of ordinary existence," and in the fact that existence itself is shaped necessarily by its own sociohistorical, cultural, and autobiographical aspects.[84] It is not only that systematic theology cannot address the density and complexity of these aspects of ordinary existence, which condition Christian practice and belief; for McClintock Fulkerson, systematic theology actually suppresses these realities. In her words, "It is simply not helpful to ask only whether Good Samaritan UMC is 'biblical' or to interrogate the systematic relations of its doctrinal loci. Instead, the complexity of Good Samaritan must be taken seriously as a 'situation of faith' before even thinking about what a faithful mode of being biblical or doctrinal would look like."[85] Put otherwise, what it means to be "biblical" or "properly creedal" in the context of lived ecclesial life cannot be deduced from "orthodox definitions of Christian faithfulness" but can only ever be conceived from the phenomena of Christian faith in its worldly, situational character.[86] In this "materialist" conceptual framework, "all of the [Christian] tradition is finite and open to scrutiny."[87]

What is most important in ecclesiological description is not, then, doctrinal statements or first-order truth claims about God, or even about the church, but rather the fruit of empirical study. The fruit of empirical study alone is capable of displaying the ambiguity and implication of the church in its particular and concrete sociohistorical existence. Furthermore, for McClintock Fulkerson, systematic theology's conceptual framework not only bypasses and suppresses the worldly situation of lived ecclesial life but is also ignorant of how theological inquiry is initiated.[88] She writes, "Theologies that matter arise out of dilemmas—out of situations that matter. The generative

81. McClintock Fulkerson, *Places of Redemption*, 8.
82. McClintock Fulkerson, *Places of Redemption*, 233–34.
83. McClintock Fulkerson, *Places of Redemption*, 8.
84. McClintock Fulkerson, *Places of Redemption*, 7.
85. McClintock Fulkerson, "Interpreting a Situation," 126.
86. McClintock Fulkerson, *Places of Redemption*, 6–8.
87. McClintock Fulkerson, *Changing the Subject*, 40.
88. See McClintock Fulkerson, *Places of Redemption*, 13.

process of theological understanding is a process provoked, not confined to preconceived, fixed categories."[89] Indeed, for McClintock Fulkerson, only as theologians appropriate "categories foreign to a traditional theological repertoire" is the generative process of theological inquiry provoked at all—for only then do theologians allow descriptions of the situational character of lived ecclesial life to evoke what it means to be faithfully Christian in their particular situations at their particular times.[90] What is more, this generative process that is situationally provoked is provoked, more specifically, by a "wound."[91]

By "wound" McClintock Fulkerson means a particular and concrete situation of harm or suffering that compels theological inquiry in response to a sense that "something *must* be addressed"—that the wound, in fact, must be *redressed*.[92] In the context of Good Samaritan UMC, the wounds that compel McClintock Fulkerson to articulate her ecclesiology are the wounds of racism, ableism, and genderism, together with the associated obliviousness and visceral responses of fear and disgust that all too often characterize the human reaction to the difference of another.[93] McClintock Fulkerson locates the redress of such wounds in the everyday Christian practices of Good Samaritan UMC that create places "*to appear*"—places, that is, "to be seen, to be recognized and to recognize the other,"[94] and that work therefore to transform the situation of harm and suffering, or at least enable the articulation of an emerging impulse for change within it.[95] On this basis, McClintock Fulkerson defines theological inquiry by "an a priori logic of transformation."[96] She describes this logic, further, as the "theo-logic" of theological inquiry.[97] Significantly, this logic is *theo*-logical because a wound and the situations of harm and suffering that give rise to it, while not read by McClintock Fulkerson explicitly as sin, are theo-*logically* suggestive of sin, and the notion of redress is theo-*logically* suggestive of redemption of that sin.[98] Not only, then, does McClintock Fulkerson turn theological inquiry and ecclesiological description decisively to the worldly wounds that inevitably

---

89. McClintock Fulkerson, *Places of Redemption*, 13.
90. McClintock Fulkerson, *Places of Redemption*, 234.
91. McClintock Fulkerson, *Places of Redemption*, 13.
92. McClintock Fulkerson, *Places of Redemption*, 14 (emphasis original), 17.
93. See McClintock Fulkerson, *Places of Redemption*, 12–18.
94. McClintock Fulkerson, *Places of Redemption*, 21 (emphasis original).
95. See McClintock Fulkerson, *Places of Redemption*, 18–23.
96. McClintock Fulkerson, *Places of Redemption*, 14. See the glossary for a definition of a priori.
97. McClintock Fulkerson, *Places of Redemption*, 238.
98. See McClintock Fulkerson, *Places of Redemption*, 236.

mark the situational character of lived ecclesial life, but in doing so—and in consequence of her transformational "theo-logic"—she understands her speech about the church to be theological.[99]

Empirically Located and Theologically Committed Ecclesiological Speech

McClintock Fulkerson's point here should not be lost. For in the move against accounts of the church that trade on theoretical analysis and subsequent application of abstract theological first principles—on "doctrinal reductionism," as James Gustafson describes it—empirical ecclesiology does seek to guard against an overcorrection or collapse into "social reductionism."[100] Put otherwise, in its desire to attend first to the church's human empirical form and to account fully for the worldliness of the church as a lived sociohistorical reality, empirical ecclesiology does not deny that the church is a theological reality.

Indeed, theologians committed to empirical ecclesiology—whether in the liberationist's call for passionate ecclesiological speech, in the turn to ethnography, or in the prior convergence on culture in theological inquiry—do not intend to reduce the theological to the empirical, the doctrinal to the cultural, or for that matter to de-theologize ecclesiology per se.[101] While there is in empirical ecclesiology a deep and full engagement with the church as a lived sociohistorical reality, there is at once—as Pete Ward, one of the leading proponents of the contemporary Ecclesiology and Ethnography network,[102] comments—"no intention of reducing the Church to the human, the historical, or the social."[103] Rather, empirical ecclesiology seeks a "theological interpretation of the social character of the Church," or else an account of the church that is at once located empirically and committed theologically.[104] In this sense, empirical ecclesiology might be seen to echo Edward Schillebeeckx's conviction that the church as one sociohistorical reality must be understood in two irreducibly different languages: on the one hand, the

---

99. See McClintock Fulkerson, *Places of Redemption*, 13.

100. Gustafson, *Treasure in Earthen Vessels*, 105.

101. See Ward, *Participation and Mediation*, 43; Ward, *Liquid Ecclesiology*, 24, 72; and Hegstad, "Ecclesiology and Empirical Research," 41.

102. See Ward, *Perspectives*, together with Scharen, *Explorations*. For a brief history of the network, see Ward, *Liquid Ecclesiology*, 2–5.

103. Ward, *Liquid Ecclesiology*, 68.

104. Gustafson, *Treasure in Earthen Vessels*, 111n9; and see Ward, *Participation and Mediation*, 18.

language of the social-scientific or historic, which analyzes the church as a sociohistorical community in its continuity with all other sociohistorical communities; and on the other hand, the language of the theological or doctrinal, which analyzes the church as a sociohistorical reality in its relation to God.[105] Schillebeeckx's point is recapitulated by Ward himself when he writes, "To talk in solely theological ways or in solely cultural and historical terms, runs the risk of not really seeing the Church. The task of seeing requires that these elements be in some way combined."[106] This combination thus has in view an ecclesiology that accounts for both the human culture and the divine being of the church,[107] and that trades on what Ward describes, further, as a "cultural theology" or "theological ethnography."[108] What is more, according to Ward, this cultural theology or theological ethnography can be expressed christologically.

On the basis of the christological hymn in Colossians 1:15–20, Ward declares: "We want to speak simultaneously about the theological and the social/cultural reality of the church because of Christ who is at once the one in whom 'all things' hold together and 'head of the church.'"[109] On this christological basis, Ward proceeds to note the methodological fallacy of a correlational distinction between empirical and theological description, such that the empirical (often viewed as profane) and the theological (often viewed as sacred) can be regarded as two distinct and subsequently correlatable entities.[110] Rather, "if all things are 'in Christ,'" Ward contends, "then this must relate to social and cultural expressions, and this is also true of the means that might be used to research it."[111] Consequently, theology is said to have no innate disciplinary superiority over—or distinction from—the social sciences; and interdisciplinary conversation in ecclesiology arises precisely because of "the possibility of analogy and dialogue from social and cultural realities that are in Christ."[112]

---

105. See Schillebeeckx, *Church*, 210–13. Schillebeeckx's conception, in turn, might be seen to echo Friedrich Schleiermacher's concern to interpret the church neither in terms of its "variable" nor "invariable" aspects. See Schleiermacher, *Christian Faith*, §§126–56.

106. Ward, *Liquid Ecclesiology*, 78.

107. See Ward, *Liquid Ecclesiology*, 34.

108. Ward, *Liquid Ecclesiology*, 11, 59.

109. Ward, *Perspectives*, 2–3.

110. See Ward, *Perspectives*, 3. For a classic expression of correlation method in theology, see Niebuhr, *Christ and Culture*.

111. Ward, *Perspectives*, 3.

112. Ward, *Perspectives*, 3. A similar point is made by Johannes A. van der Ven in his development of what he describes as a "practical-theological" ecclesiology from a sociological and theological perspective, which in part is funded on the basis of the principles of noncompetition and complementarity between the disciplines of theology and sociology. See van der Ven, *Ecclesiology in Context*, ix–xv.

As Ward puts it elsewhere, "In the incarnation, humanity is transformed, and through the resurrection it is taken into the life of God. . . . Humanity, and by extension human culture, are recapitulated in death and resurrection."[113] This recapitulation is such that, for Ward, there is no difference in the way that Christ is present in the church or in the world: Christ is present wherever and whenever people mourn and lament, are moved by music or art, or gather together in family or community.[114] And this recapitulation with its attendant location of social and cultural realities in Christ serves to establish what Ward sees as the necessarily dynamic interplay—or "liquid" nature—of the empirical and the theological in ecclesiology.[115] "What is required," he writes, "is a way of working theologically which recognizes theology's own cultural contingency and deals with the theological as culture and culture as theological."[116] However, whether or not Ward's christological argument holds good, or empirical ecclesiology is found to be doing here precisely what it intends not to do—that is, reducing the theological to the empirical or denying, effectively, that the church is a theological reality—may depend, in part, on the extent to which the reader is convinced by Ward's reading of Colossians 1:16–17.

Empirical Ecclesiology: An Assessment

The reader might worry that the efficacy of Ward's reading in fact rests on a false exegetical move. What Colossians 1:16–17 says is that "all things have been created through [Christ] and for [Christ]. He is before all things, and in him all things hold together." What it does not say is that all things are in Christ. And to say the former is not to say the latter, though that is what Ward appears to suppose in order to locate social and cultural realities in Christ, and thus to identify the empirical or the cultural with the theological. Put otherwise—and to draw on the associated distinction that is characteristic of the apostle Paul's own thought—what is "in Adam" is not yet "in Christ."[117] Consequently, the reader may wish to consider the extent to which Ward's reading of Colossians 1:16–17 occludes not only this distinction but also the more fundamental distinction between God as creator and that which God creates, which is foundational to Christian theology:

113. Ward, *Liquid Ecclesiology*, 48–49.
114. See Ward, *Liquid Ecclesiology*, 44.
115. See Ward, *Liquid Ecclesiology*; see also Ward, *Liquid Church*.
116. Ward, *Participation and Mediation*, 67.
117. For a helpful summary of these two dominions as they operate in Paul's thought, see Fatehi, *Spirit's Relation to the Risen Lord in Paul*, 263–74.

God is not part of creation, nor is creation part of God. Christian theology is resolutely both anti-pantheistic and anti-panentheistic.[118] But Christian theology also affirms that creation does not exist independently of God. To state, as Colossians 1:16–17 does, that all things were created through and for Christ and that all things are held together (or are sustained continually) in, or by, Christ is to express Christ's agency in God's gracious divine work of creating, sustaining, and redeeming the world. And it is to assert, further, that as the agent of God's work, Christ is supreme over that which is created.[119] What is more, this supremacy is ontological in nature; Christ is "the firstborn over all creation" (Col. 1:15) and "is before all things" (Col. 1:17).

To be clear, I am not suggesting that Ward in any way denies the supremacy of Christ's agency in God's work of creation, reconciliation, and redemption—or that Ward's reading of the christological hymn equates necessarily to either methodological **pantheism** or **panentheism**. What I am suggesting is that Ward's reading unhelpfully lets slip the ontological distinction between God and that which is not God, a distinction that must be maintained in Christian theology. That said, it should be noted that Ward himself does actually allude to this distinction, and also to the distinction that Paul draws between that which is "in Adam" and that which is "in Christ." For Ward, the recapitulation of social and cultural realities that he sees effected in Christ means that they are, indeed, reworked and reincorporated "*into* God" such that they can be said to be *in* Christ.[120] However, Ward continues, "This reworking and reincorporation into God mean that while human society and cultural expression continue to be sinful and imperfect, they are also *capable* of being taken up in revelation."[121] At this point, the worry I want to register—if I understand Ward's argument correctly—is about the affirmation that all social and cultural realities are, on the one hand, already located in Christ and yet are, on the other hand, simply capable of being taken up into Christ. It is surely not the case that the capacity for social and cultural realities to be in Christ equates to them having already been taken up tout court—that is, to them being *in fact* in Christ, and thus to the empirical *being* the theological.

The worry here, then, is that empirical ecclesiology may well be open to the charge that it has done precisely what it intends not to do—that it has effected in its speech about the church a reduction of the theological to the

118. See the glossary for definitions of **pantheism** and **panentheism**.
119. See Thompson, *Colossians and Philemon*, 27–32.
120. Ward, *Liquid Ecclesiology*, 49 (emphasis added).
121. Ward, *Liquid Ecclesiology*, 49 (emphasis added).

empirical, of the doctrinal to the cultural, and thus detheologized ecclesiology per se. In other words, empirical ecclesiology may be presenting an account of the church that prioritizes descriptions of the church's human empirical form at the expense of speech about the life and work of God. The potential consequence of this is not only that empirical ecclesiology might conflate the church as a creature of God and God's gracious acts with the church as a sociohistorical human community, but also that it might risk collapsing speech about divine agency into speech about human subjectivity, and speech about divine action into language about ecclesial human reality. This risk is demonstrated not least, perhaps, by the theo-logic of McClintock Fulkerson's *theo*logical ecclesiology, and its theo*logical* suggestiveness.

Indeed, this theo-logic proposes that speech about divine agency in ecclesiology cannot be proffered as direct speech about God and God's gracious acts, but only as indirect *"testimony to transformations* that are attributable to God."[122] In determining what is *theological* in theological inquiry and ecclesiological description, McClintock Fulkerson affords primacy to the sociohistorical, cultural, and autobiographical experience of redemptive transformation,[123] or to what she describes, alternatively, as "an ecclesial redemptive sociality as mediator or as *appresentor* of transcendence."[124] She continues, "God is never 'present' as a referent or cause of redemption in the way in which other realities are present to consciousness; the theological task is not study of God (nor is it the study of the experience of God)."[125] In other words, the proper object of ecclesiological description and theological inquiry is not God and God's gracious acts but the human experience of transformation, and more specifically, the experience of transformation toward "an ultimate good: redemption."[126] What is more, redemption is an ultimate good that itself is mediated, McClintock Fulkerson contends, through intersubjective and sociohistorical cultural realities.[127] In the words of Harald Hegstad, "Theological statements about the church," ultimately, "are statements about the empirical church."[128] Hegstad's proposition embodies a more radical collapse of speech about divine agency into human subjectivity in ecclesiological description. Such an explicit collapse is not necessarily replicated by others in empirical ecclesiology. What is replicated, however,

---

122. McClintock Fulkerson, *Places of Redemption*, 237 (emphasis original).
123. See McClintock Fulkerson, *Places of Redemption*, 236–37.
124. McClintock Fulkerson, "Interpreting a Situation," 140 (emphasis original).
125. McClintock Fulkerson, "Interpreting a Situation," 140.
126. McClintock Fulkerson, "Interpreting a Situation," 140.
127. See McClintock Fulkerson, "Interpreting a Situation," 140–41.
128. Hegstad, "Ecclesiology and Empirical Research," 41; see also Hegstad, *Real Church*.

is the risk of the collapse of speech about divine action into language about ecclesial human reality.

Haight, for example, argues that the church as a sociohistorical human community has "a certain specific relationship to God, indeed, a constitutive relationship to God."[129] This relationship works to render ecclesiology a *theological* discipline and, by implication, irreducible to the conclusions of cultural anthropology or social-scientific tools of analysis. Indeed, the empirical, human church is "more" than the sum of its sociohistorical and cultural parts, so to speak: "This church is experienced religiously or theologically, because in it and through it people recognize the presence and activity of God."[130] However, that the church is *experienced* religiously or theologically, and in it and through it *people* become conscious of God, might lead the reader to worry that the ultimate emphasis in ecclesiological description is still on human agency rather than divine agency, and in such a way that speech about the latter is at risk of being collapsed into language about the former. The worry is perhaps energized, further, when Haight writes that "specifically Christian faith in response to specifically Christian revelation caused the church to come into being."[131] The ecclesiological "more" that Haight speaks of still seemingly terminates in the church's sociohistorical existence—specifically, in the human experience of God and Christian faith in and through that experience.

Similarly, Joseph Komonchak's intention when he says that the church is a human empirical reality is not to reduce the church to simply one sociohistorical reality in the world among others. "The Church remains the creation of the mysterious God's self-gift in Word and in Spirit."[132] With that said, Komonchak continues, "It is not God but Christian men and women who constitute the Church. . . . The Church is constructed when divine favor transforms and promotes conscious acts of human intentionality and intersubjectivity."[133] This transformation and promotion takes place in such a way that "the Church is not the divine initiative itself, but the human social response to God's grace and word."[134] Ultimately, the church comes to be not because of God and God's gracious acts but through what Komonchak describes as "a process of self-constitution."[135] In the words of Johannes

---

129. Haight, *Christian Community in History*, 1:36.
130. Haight, *Christian Community in History*, 1:5.
131. Haight, *Christian Community in History*, 3:76.
132. Komonchak, *Foundations in Ecclesiology*, 56.
133. Komonchak, *Foundations in Ecclesiology*, 56.
134. Komonchak, *Foundations in Ecclesiology*, 151.
135. Komonchak, *Foundations in Ecclesiology*, 56.

A. van der Ven, "God brings people together by the fact that *people come together themselves*. God inspires them to togetherness by the fact that *they inspire themselves* to togetherness. God motivates them to a community through the fact that *they motivate themselves* to a community."[136] Or, as Gustafson suggests, while the church cannot be understood satisfactorily unless it is seen in relation to divine action as God's gift and work, God in that work "chooses to use that which can be interpreted without reference to him"—that is, the empirical realm and its processes—as the agency by which the human empirical form of the church comes to be.[137] The reader might worry not only that the suggestion that the empirical realm can be interpreted "without reference" to God is at risk of denying the doctrine of creation out of nothing, which is of foundational significance for Christian theology; they might also worry that Gustafson (like van der Ven and Komon-chak) ultimately collapses in ecclesiological description speech about divine agency into language about human subjectivity (albeit human subjectivity understood as expressing a common Christian faith and coming together around this faith).

Such an emphasis on human subjectivity in speech about the church's being might also be seen to be replicated in the liberationist's call for an anthropocentric point of departure in ecclesiological description, indexed to the experience of the oppressed and poor. Indeed, for the liberationist, the experience of oppression itself is such that Christian doctrine is to be analyzed and interpreted only in the context of the emancipation of people living under oppressive degradation.[138] Cone writes, "This does not mean that [Black theology] denies the absolute revelation of God in Christ" or "that [it] makes experience of Christ secondary to the experience of black oppression."[139] But it does mean that "God's revelation in Christ can be made supreme only by affirming Christ as he is alive in black people"[140] and as that aliveness is manifested in the experience of Black oppression. As they might worry about Haight, therefore, readers might worry that, for the liberation-ist, the human experience of oppression conditions the supremacy of God in Christ. Here, too, there is a risk of collapsing speech about divine action into language about human agency.

Similar to Cone, Gutiérrez argues that the truth of theological inquiry and ecclesiological description is dependent on learning to live and think

---

136. Van der Ven, *Ecclesiology in Context*, 40 (emphasis added).
137. Gustafson, *Treasure in Earthen Vessels*, 104, 108.
138. See Cone, *Black Theology and Black Power*, 136.
139. Cone, *Black Theology and Black Power*, 133, 136.
140. Cone, *Black Theology and Black Power*, 133.

according to "what is definitive in what is historical."[141] For Gutiérrez, the church is "that part of [human]kind—gathered into ecclesia—which openly confesses Christ" by being part of the sociohistorical process of liberation.[142] Here, again, liberationists are at risk of ultimately collapsing speech about divine action into language about ecclesial human reality, in this case an ecclesial human reality that opts for the oppressed and poor through solidarity and protest.[143] Like Komonchak, Gutiérrez does not intend to deny that the church is a theological reality. Far from it! That the church is said to be gathered into ecclesia illustrates Gutiérrez's prior point that outside of the work of Christ and the Holy Spirit "the Church is nothing."[144] However, that Gutiérrez locates what is definitive in ecclesiological description in what is historical, and contends that the sociohistorical praxis of the church is what permits theologians to understand what the church is more precisely and to "adjust it more successfully to our times,"[145] does indeed suggest that the being of the church terminates in its own sociohistorical existence, or at least in what Welch once described as "the humanly subjective pole" of the relationship between God and a particular group of Christian people[146]—in this instance, those who act to liberate the oppressed and poor.

What is more, as Boff suggests, what the church is thus arises from the "essential themes" of particular groups of Christian people, whether those themes are social change, human rights and the creation of a more just society, or the sociohistorical liberation of the disinherited and marginalized through concrete service.[147] Consequently, the church emerges, indeed "is born, and is continually reshaped whenever individuals meet to hear the word of God, believe in it, and vow together to follow Jesus Christ"—that is, to live out Christ's own discipleship in the form of these essential ecclesial themes inspired by the Holy Spirit.[148] It is precisely in this sense that Ruether understands the church to be "a community of liberation from patriarchy"—a community that embodies a culture of critique of patriarchy as "the Christian theological expression . . . of feminist collectivization of women's experience."[149] This is to say, again, that what the church is arises from the human experience of a particular group of Christian people. While, as Boff himself puts it, "the

141. Gutiérrez, *Theology of Liberation*, 137.
142. Gutiérrez, *Theology of Liberation*, 15.
143. See Gutiérrez, *Theology of Liberation*, 287–302.
144. Gutiérrez, *Theology of Liberation*, 260.
145. Gutiérrez, *Theology of Liberation*, 79.
146. See Welch, *Reality of the Church*, 48.
147. See Boff, *Church: Charism and Power*, 10.
148. See Boff, *Church: Charism and Power*, 127.
149. Ruether, *Women-Church*, 5, 61.

church community is constituted as a response to Christian faith,"[150] I would point out that this response is a *human* response to Christian faith—that is, the church is born or emerges only when individuals meet to live out what they deem to be "essential themes" of that faith (whether critique of patriarchy or otherwise). This understanding of the church, again, might be seen to fall prey to the tendency of empirical ecclesiology to collapse speech about divine agency into human subjectivity and language about divine action into speech about ecclesial human reality.

To describe the church in this way might also risk conflating the church's being with the being of other forms of sociohistorical human community, notwithstanding "the crucial importance," as Boff notes, "of explicit Christian motivation" through an "ecclesial consciousness" of Christ's own discipleship compelling the church to live out its "essential themes."[151] The risk is made explicit when Boff writes that "all individuals, institutions, and activities directed toward those ideals favoured by the historical Jesus are bearers of [God's] kingdom. The Church is an official and distinctive bearer, but not an exclusive one."[152] In light of this ecclesial nonexclusivity when it comes to bearing the kingdom of God, the reader might ask whether Boff, and indeed the other theologians I have noted in this chapter as exemplifying empirical ecclesiology, therefore occlude in their ecclesiological descriptions the unique nature of the church as both creature of God and sociohistorical human community, a dual nature that God and God's gracious acts have given to the church. We should ask, Is the church just one creaturely reality in creation among others, as Boff seems to suggest? And should all human communities that inculcate "a genuine communion of persons, the conquest of selfishness, [and] the mutual gift of self" be considered *churches*, as Boff seems to suggest?[153]

Ultimately, the question is whether empirical ecclesiology collapses language about divine action into speech about ecclesial human reality to such an extent that the church's originating and sustaining causes, God and God's gracious acts, are essentially evacuated from its ecclesiological description. Put otherwise, does empirical ecclesiology describe the phenomenon that is the church as one that, while standing in a certain (responsive) relationship to God, is nevertheless constituted and sustained in its sociohistorical

---

150. Boff, *Ecclesiogenesis*, 10.
151. Boff, *Ecclesiogenesis*, 11.
152. Boff, *Church: Charism and Power*, 10.
153. Boff, *Ecclesiogenesis*, 11. I further explore inadequate attentiveness in ecclesiological description to the unique nature of the church that God and God's gracious acts create as a sociohistorical reality in the articulation of type 2, performative ecclesiology, in chap. 3.

existence by human agency—that is, by the concrete sociohistorical actions of particular groups of Christian believers who come together to constitute the church in response to their common Christian faith? If the church is at once both creature of God and sociohistorical human community, and if the basic ecclesiological task is that of holding together in ecclesiological description both divine and human agency in an ordered and proportionate way, why must theologians attend first to the church's human empirical form and treat the church most of all as a sociohistorical reality that is wholly accessible to the resources of cultural anthropology and social-scientific tools of analysis? Indeed, if the church is a sociohistorical human community created and sustained by God and God's gracious acts, perhaps the being of the church is not, in fact, wholly accessible to such tools and resources. Why then must theologians work toward their accounts of the church inductively, from the church's human empirical forms, in terms drawn largely from nontheological fields of inquiry?

To be sure, given ecclesiology's basic task, the call of empirical ecclesiology to account fully for the church as a lived sociohistorical reality must be heard by theologians who want to speak about the church in a genuinely theological fashion. In light of this task, it is axiomatic that theologians must offer accounts of the church in which what is said theologically about the church's being does indeed correspond to, or at least share a commonality with, the lived experience of the church as a sociohistorical human community. Indeed, as Christopher Brittain notes, the contradictions and conflicts that arise in the context of lived ecclesial life are themselves "too complicated and painful for the church to be transparent to itself, or to the theologian."[154] The reality of ecclesial sin should itself ensure that speech about the church, "if it is to help the church discern its true nature and calling, cannot remain at the level of ideal and abstract theorizing."[155] The reorientation of ecclesiological description away from theological first principles and toward ecclesial human reality by recourse to empirical study is, indeed, significant for contemporary approaches to ecclesiology because it helps theologians attend more adequately to the reality of ecclesial sin and prevents them from limiting their material treatment of it to an empirical distortion of the church's true theological identity.[156] Such thick description of the church's phenomenal surface—of actual ecclesial life—serves to

154. Brittain, "Ethnography as Ecclesial Attentiveness," 137.
155. Brittain, "Ethnography as Ecclesial Attentiveness," 137.
156. See Brittain, "Why Ecclesiology Cannot Live by Doctrine Alone," 5–30. The tendency in ecclesiological description to either ignore the reality of ecclesial sin or limit material treatment of it to an empirical distortion of the church's true theological identity is explored further in the

enhance the "self-reflexivity" of ecclesiology per se as well as a theologian's own capacity to attend to the church's particular and contingent sociohistorical reality as both fallible and sinful.[157] As Brittain puts it, "By enhancing the church's capacity to confess its sins and to discern God's activity in its midst, ethnography has the capacity to deepen rather than dilute the theological task of ecclesiology."[158]

Notwithstanding this capacity and the desire of empirical ecclesiology to account fully for the church as a lived sociohistorical reality, the reader may still wonder, when confronted by the actual content of speech about the church in this type of ecclesiological approach, whether empirical ecclesiology, in attempting to sound an appropriately proportionate "yes" to the church's lived sociohistorical existence, has in fact forgotten God in the process[159]—or whether it has at least presented theologically disordered and disproportionate ecclesiological speech, considering the basic ecclesiological task of holding together both divine and human agency, with the former relativizing but not minimizing the latter. Beginning and ending with the church's human empirical form, I take it that empirical ecclesiology treats ecclesiology too independently of an account of God's own life and work, such that the nature of the church is permitted to be understood on the basis of human agency alone.

In this way, empirical ecclesiology stands liable to undergirding its account of the church with a capitulation to methodological agnosticism (if not atheism), at worst, or with making the ultimate ground of ecclesiology not God and God's gracious acts, but the sociohistorical and anthropological, at best. There is, then, a further risk in empirical ecclesiology, given its emphasis on human agency in constituting and sustaining the church as a sociohistorical reality—the risk of methodological **Pelagianism**. As the consideration of Paul's appropriation of God's covenantal promise to the church in Corinth established in chapter 1, the church is a creature of God's grace: it is God and God's gracious acts that are the originating and sustaining cause of the church. And this divine grace, which creates the church as a sociohistorical reality, is not only prior to the concrete coming together of a particular group of Christian believers to be the church in response to God's gracious action and their common Christian faith, but is the agency that itself effects that faith and that coming together. The church's human empirical form is not

---

articulation of type 4, ideal ecclesiology, in chap. 5. It is precisely this type of ecclesiology that Brittain has in mind (at least as exemplified by the ecclesiological thought of John Webster).

157. See Brittain, "Ethnography as Ecclesial Attentiveness," 132–35.

158. Brittain, "Why Ecclesiology Cannot Live by Doctrine Alone," 8.

159. See Barth, *Church Dogmatics* I/2, 794.

constituted or sustained by Christian believers. The church, as a creature of God's grace, is prior to those believers, and in its sociohistorical existence is determined by God and God's gracious acts alone.[160] Having articulated and offered an indicative assessment of the first type of contemporary approach to ecclesiology, I will now turn to an articulation and assessment of type 2, performative ecclesiology.

160. In chaps. 4, 5, and 6, respectively, I explore these points further in the articulation of type 3, communion ecclesiology; type 4, ideal ecclesiology; and type 5, ecclesiological ecclesiology.

3

Performative Ecclesiology

In the previous chapter it was suggested that type 1, empirical ecclesiology, in its desire to account fully for the church as a lived sociohistorical reality, and in consequence of its disproportionately thick description of the church's phenomenal surface, risks evacuating from speech about the church God and God's gracious acts as the church's originating and sustaining cause, thereby presenting in an account of the church disordered and disproportionate ecclesiological speech that is treated too independently from a doctrine of God. At the same time, it was suggested that, given the most basic ecclesiological task, theologians who want to speak about the church in a genuinely theological fashion must indeed hear the call of empirical ecclesiology to account fully for the church's human empirical form. It is precisely this call, but also the prior risk, that is the concern of the second type of contemporary approach to ecclesiology that I am proposing.

As in empirical ecclesiology, in performative ecclesiology the proper object of ecclesiological speech is the church as a lived sociohistorical reality, and theologians speak properly of what the church is only if they account fully for the church's human empirical form. However, in contrast to empirical ecclesiology, this does not mean that theologians must attend *first* to that form and thereby make accounts of human agency paramount in their ecclesiological descriptions. In performative ecclesiology, description of the church's human empirical form is not, in other words, a normative and necessary foundation of ecclesiology. The tendency in contemporary approaches to ecclesiology to attend either to the church's human empirical form or to the life and work of God is not stated as an explicit method-ological claim. This tendency is instead an implicit logical consequence of the account of the church that is proffered. In other words, while it is not built on the problematic either/or tendency seen in contemporary ap-proaches to ecclesiology, performative ecclesiology nevertheless displays it. It is for this reason that performative ecclesiology might be seen—as noted in the introduction—as a soft form of empirical ecclesiology. Performative ecclesiology seeks to provide warrant for its account of the church's human empirical form by means of an account of the life and work of God.

There is thus a desire in performative ecclesiology to account for the church as a creature of God's grace. However, performative ecclesiology does this with a heavy emphasis on what the church is in its sociohistorical existence, and, in particular, on the human social form of that existence as it is con-stituted by the agency of Christian believers and embodied in lived ecclesial life and performed church practice. The question that the reader may want to register immediately is whether this heavy emphasis on what the church is as a social body, notwithstanding the attentiveness to the life and work of God, in fact results in an account of the church that is still at risk of treat-ing ecclesiology too independently from a doctrine of God—or, at least, of presenting in ecclesiological description an account of the church that obscures the agency of God's action as the originating and sustaining cause of the unique nature of the church as a sociohistorical reality. Before turn-ing to consider these questions in relation to the specific theologians that I read as illustrating performative ecclesiology in contemporary ecclesiological thought, it will be instructive to first outline what might be seen as something of an insufficient theological inheritance in the discipline of ecclesiology per se, and to which performative ecclesiology as a type of ecclesiological ap-proach might be related.

A Reformation Legacy?

As Wolfhart Pannenberg observes, it is not until the fifteenth century that ecclesiology emerges as a distinct and separate doctrine in systematic presen-tations of Christian theology.[1] This is not to say that theologians before this time had nothing constructive to say about the church.[2] It is instead to say that in **patristic** and **medieval theology** there was no doctrine of the church

---

1. See Pannenberg, *Systematic Theology*, 3:21.
2. See Greggs, *Dogmatic Ecclesiology*, 1:xxxiin21.

per se.[3] It is, at least, to agree with (and extend) the judgment of J. N. D. Kelly that before the fifteenth century there was a lack of "deliberate statements of ecclesiological theory,"[4] which ensured that ecclesiology as a discipline remained nascent and systematically undeveloped. This, of course, changed with the onset of the Magisterial Reformation and the Reformers' efforts to account theologically for what the church of the protest movement was. In Pannenberg's words, "The Reformers were certainly the first to introduce the doctrine of the church into dogmatics."[5] The Reformers did so, however, polemically over against the theology and practice of medieval Catholicism and, in particular, over against the clericalization and essential hierarchy of the Church of Rome. This led the Reformers to place a heavy theological accent on both the inward disposition of Christian faith and the freedom of Christian believers to gather themselves together around Word and sacrament. For the Reformers, this gathering was the church. As Luther puts it, the church is that "crowd or assembly of people who are Christians and holy," who, in consequence of the Holy Spirit giving them faith in Christ and sanctifying them, "believe in Christ" and express their "inward faith" as "a community united in one faith according to the soul."[6] The particular holiness of this assembly of Christian people is then recognized, according to Luther, by their possession of seven "holy possessions," the holiest of which is the Word of God "preached, believed, professed, and lived," after which comes the right administration and reception of the sacraments of baptism and the Eucharist.[7] For Luther, the church exists, therefore, "where the sacraments are purely administered, where there are hearers, teachers, and confessors of the Word,"

---

3. As Henri de Lubac observes, "The writings of the Fathers do not have special chapters on the Church because, quite simply, for them the Church was everywhere. She was, as they saw it, the condition, the milieu, and the end of Christian life." See de Lubac, *Church*, 33. For a helpful introduction to patristic theology, see Pelikan, *Christian Tradition*. For a helpful overview of medieval theology, see van Nieuwenhove, *Introduction to Medieval Theology*.

4. Kelly, *Early Christian Doctrines*, 401.

5. Pannenberg, *Systematic Theology*, 3:22.

6. Luther, *Luther's Works*, 41:143; see also 39:65, 66, 70. To describe Christian faith as "inward" does not mean a Christian lives *in and of themselves*. For Luther, what it means instead is that through the faith that *each* Christian has in Christ they are "caught up" in Christ by the Holy Spirit and therefore "beyond" themselves in love of God and neighbor (Luther, *Luther's Works*, 31:371; see 343–77). To live *in and of oneself*, or *incurvatus in se* ("turned inward upon oneself") is Luther's definition of sin. *Luther's Works*, 25:291–92, 345.

7. Luther, *Luther's Works*, 41:149, 150; and 148–67. The four other "holy possessions" identified here by Luther are: (1) the power to forgive and retain sins; (2) the calling or consecration of ministers to ecclesiastical office; (3) prayer and public praise of God; and (4) the endurance of temptation and suffering after the pattern of Christ's sacred cross.

and this is so irrespective of the number of the assembly or crowd gathered together around Word and sacrament.[8]

Following Luther, the church in Calvin's thought is recognized and constituted similarly: "Wherever we see the Word of God purely preached and heard, and the sacraments administered according to Christ's institution, there, it is not to be doubted, a church of God exists."[9] For Calvin, the church exists as the place in which God's Word is heard and preached and the sacraments are administered and received in order that the faith of Christian believers might be fostered and strengthened.[10] In this sense, the church is seen by Calvin as the way prescribed by God for Christian believers to come to maturity in faith; it is participation in the church as "the society of Christ," he says, that keeps Christian believers "in the society of God."[11] It is therefore logical that in Calvin's *Institutes* discussion of what the church is in book 4 follows a discussion of the individual appropriation of Christ's grace by the Spirit, with the benefits and effects of faith that flow from it, in book 3. For both Calvin and Luther, ecclesiology as a doctrine is considered a consequence of **functional Christology**, and thus subsequent to a doctrine of God's saving work in Jesus Christ.

As Pannenberg again observes, this doctrinal ordering became by and large normative for Reformed dogmatics in the seventeenth century, such that "right up to the 19th and 20th century the account of individual appropriation of salvation usually preceded discussion of the concept of the church."[12] What is more, what then did follow in those discussions, especially in the context of the Reformers' polemical discourse with Rome, were accounts of the church that were oriented more toward pragmatic ecclesial concerns than toward theological considerations of the church's being per se. To be clear, I am not suggesting that Reformation accounts of the church are in any way reducible to matters of ecclesial form, function, or polity: clearly, the Reformers' concern for such things were derivative of their efforts to account theologically for what the church of the protest movement was in distinction to the Church of Rome. What I am suggesting is that in Reformation accounts of the church there is proportionately little discussion of the church's **ontology** compared to that of the church's form, function, and polity. This is perhaps most evident in book 4 of Calvin's *Institutes*, where discussion of the former is the concern of chapter 1, and discussion of the latter is the concern of chapters 2 through 20.

---

8. Luther, *Luther's Works*, 6:149.
9. Calvin, *Institutes*, 4.1.9.
10. Calvin, *Institutes*, 4.1.1.
11. Calvin, *Institutes*, bk. 4, title; 4.1.3.
12. Pannenberg, *Systematic Theology*, 3:24.

The disproportionate emphasis on matters of ecclesial form, function, and polity in ecclesiological description evident in Calvin's work is evident also in the work of other Reformers. For example, the sixteenth-century English Reformer Richard Hooker, while noting in passing the "supernaturall societie"[13] that the church as "the mysticall body of Christ"[14] is, proceeds to unfold his ecclesiological description almost exclusively in reference to the "bodie politique"[15] of the church visible. Hooker's concern, primarily, is with the church's governance and public ordering, and the autonomous exercise or voluntary consent of individual human will to be a member of this particular "politique *Societie*."[16] For Hooker, the church in fact is like any other political society: the church is "alwaies a visible society of men," which has as its foundation the "naturall inclination which all men have unto sociable life" and "some certaine bond of association, which bond is the lawe that appointeth what kinde of order they shall be associated in."[17] At once, however, the church is unlike any other political society. This is because of that part of the "bond of association" that "God himselfe hath revealed concerning the kinde of worship which his people shall doe unto him."[18] What makes the political society that the church is particular, then, according to Hooker, is what Christian believers *do* in worship of God— that is, in performed church practice, in "the publike exercise of such dueties as those mentioned in the Apostles actes, *Instruction*, *Breaking of bread*, and *Prayers*."[19] Thus, as Hooker writes, "The name of a *Church* importeth only a *Societie* of men first united into some publique form of regiment and secondly distinguished from other Societies by the exercise of *Christian* religion."[20]

In a fashion similar to Hooker, the seventeenth-century Puritan theologian John Owen develops his ecclesiology with an almost exclusive focus on "particular congregations" of the "visible and organized" church, and this notwithstanding the "catholic and mystical" nature of the church as Christ's body.[21] For Owen, the essential nature of the church "visible and organized" consists in what he describes further as its "matter and form."[22] While the

13. Hooker, *Lawes*, 1:131.
14. Hooker, *Lawes*, 1:261.
15. Hooker, *Lawes*, 1:195.
16. Hooker, *Lawes*, 3:319 (emphasis original).
17. Hooker, *Lawes*, 1:205, 1:131.
18. Hooker, *Lawes*, 1:131.
19. Hooker, *Lawes*, 1:206 (emphasis original).
20. Hooker, *Lawes*, 3:319 (emphasis original).
21. See Owen, *The Church and the Bible*, 3.
22. Owen, *The Church and the Bible*, 16:11.

former is "the persons whereof the church doth consist, with their qualifi-
cations," the latter is "the reason, cause, and way of that kind of relation
among them which gives them the being of a church."[23] The "formal cause"
of a church, Owen argues (irrespective of the fact that Jesus Christ is the
"supreme efficient cause" of human willing) is thus the "mutual confederation or solemn agreement" of individual human wills, which, "by their own
actual, express, voluntary consent," obediently perform the duties prescribed
by Christ to His disciples.[24] Indeed, the "qualification" of Christian believers who constitute the church is the visible holiness of character that befits
a **regenerate** state expressed in baptism.[25] By voluntary and faithful acts of
obedience to Christ, then, Christian believers join themselves together as the
church.[26] And for Owen, this joining together by individual choice and voluntary consent "completes the confederation intended, which is the formal cause
of the church, and without which, either expressly or virtually performed,
there can be no church-state."[27]

Both Owen and Hooker proffer, therefore, what might be described as
highly individualized theological accounts of what the church is. Further,
there is in these accounts, in a fashion similar to the accounts offered by
Calvin and Luther, proportionately little material theological discussion of
the church's being, compared to that of church form, function, and polity.
And again, speech about the church is treated subsequent to an account of
individual appropriation of God's saving work in Christ and the agency of
Christian believers to form and constitute the church by what they do in the
context of lived ecclesial life and performed church practice.

In the account of the church developed in the nineteenth century by Friedrich Schleiermacher there is further evidence that this doctrinal ordering,
with its disproportionate emphasis on the agency of Christian believers
to form and constitute what the church is, is a legacy of the Reformation.
Schleiermacher's turn to individual subjectivity, and specifically to the interior "feeling" or "immediate self-consciousness" of redemption in Jesus
Christ, is the point from which he develops his theology in *The Christian
Faith*.[28] For Schleiermacher, the inner experience of being assumed, on the
one hand, into the power of Christ's perfect "God-consciousness" (by which

23. Owen, *The Church and the Bible*, 16:11.
24. Owen, *The Church and the Bible*, 16:25–26 (emphasis original).
25. Owen, *The Church and the Bible*, 16:12, 15–17. See the glossary for a definition of
regeneration.
26. See Owen, *The Church and the Bible*, 16:27.
27. Owen, *The Church and the Bible*, 16:28.
28. Schleiermacher, *Christian Faith*, §3; §11. For a succinct summary of Schleiermacher's
understanding of redemption, and in particular of how it relates to his conception of the

the God-consciousness of Christ is simultaneously "implanted" into the individual "as a new vital principle"), and, on the other hand, into the fellowship of Christ's "unclouded blessedness," is the content of **regeneration** in its two elements: conversion and justification.[29] The life of the redeemed individual after regeneration is therefore marked, Schleiermacher argues, by "a living fellowship with Christ."[30] This fellowship is understood in terms of both the individual's "changed relation" to God, which is her justification, and the "creative production" in the individual of "the will to assume Christ" into her own life, which is her conversion.[31] Further, in this living fellowship with Christ, Christ's own life and activity becomes progressively ever more the redeemed individual's life and activity through the work of the Holy Spirit in sanctification.[32] It is the work of the Holy Spirit to ascribe "the right apprehension of Christ,"[33] argues Schleiermacher, such that in the process of being sanctified, the life of the redeemed "ever approximates more to pure harmony with the impulse issuing from Christ, and therefore to indistinguishability from Christ Himself."[34] For Schleiermacher, the goal of redemption is thus the animation of Christ's own God-consciousness in the individual, and the perfect fulfillment of the divine will.[35]

This interior turn in Schleiermacher's theology to a self-consciousness of divine grace and the changed form of life it effects nevertheless proceeds to an exterior turn. As Schleiermacher puts it, "The supernatural in Christ is to become natural," and in the absence of the man Jesus of Nazareth, the natural mechanism for the ongoing communication of the supernatural redemption accomplished by Christ is the church.[36] In Schleiermacher's thought, the church is therefore necessary because, as Eugene Schlesinger notes, "it is only through a shared cultural framework that the inner feelings

---

Reformation antithesis between Protestantism and Catholicism (in §24 of his *Christian Faith*), see Nimmo, "Mediation of Redemption."

29. See Schleiermacher, *Christian Faith*, §100, 425, 427; §101, 431.

30. Schleiermacher, *Christian Faith*, §107.1, 478.

31. Schleiermacher, *Christian Faith*, §107, 478; §100.2, 426; §107.1, 478. The reader should note that the extent to which Schleiermacher's understanding of justification is continuous (or not) with the theology of the Reformation is disputed. For a helpful and constructive overview of the debate, see Nimmo, "Schleiermacher on Justification," 50–73.

32. See Schleiermacher, *Christian Faith*, §110; §118.1, 541. For a discussion of Schleiermacher's understanding of the work of the Holy Spirit, see Hector, "Mediation of Christ's Normative Spirit," 1–22.

33. Schleiermacher, *Christian Faith*, §122.1, 566.

34. Schleiermacher, *Christian Faith*, §110.1, 506.

35. See Schleiermacher, *Christian Faith*, §104.3, 456.

36. Schleiermacher, *Christian Faith*, §117.2, 537; see also §116.3, 535.

of piety [animated in redemption] . . . can be cultivated and sustained."[37] For Schleiermacher, the church is this shared cultural framework; or put otherwise, the church is the corporate fellowship of Christian believers who share a commonality of conviction, activity, and spirit with respect to Christ-formed piety.[38] In Schleiermacher's own words, "The Christian Church takes shape through the coming together of regenerate individuals to form a system of mutual interaction and co-operation."[39] Earlier in *Christian Faith* he writes, "It is only out of this new corporate life that the communication of the divine grace comes to each individual."[40] In other words, through the corporate life of the church and its ecclesial practices the God-consciousness of Christ is communicated both to those inside and to those outside the church.[41] As Kevin Hector puts it in relation to this aspect of Schleiermacher's ecclesiological thought,

> Through their susceptibility to Christ's instruction, the disciples internalize Christ's influence and are recognized by Christ as competent to judge whether others are "going on in the same way." . . . We thus have a picture of how Christ's activity is mediated to us in the present: we accept the judgments of those who know how to "go on in the same way" as Jesus in order to learn what it means to follow him; once we are recognized as competent in making such judgments our judgments provide the basis for others to learn the practice, and so on.[42]

Schleiermacher's account of the church is, in this way, marked by a heavy insistence on human subjectivity and the agency of Christian believers to create and sustain the church. To be sure, what the church is, for Schleiermacher, "springs from no other individual life than that of the Redeemer,"[43] and "the Holy Spirit is the inmost vital power of the Christian Church as a whole."[44] Like the accounts of the church developed by Owen and Hooker, and indeed by Luther and Calvin, Schleiermacher's is not an account that risks collapsing in ecclesiological description speech about divine action into language about ecclesial human reality without remainder, as type 1, empirical ecclesiology, does. For Schleiermacher, the church owes its origin

---

37. Schlesinger, "Schleiermacher," 238.
38. See Schleiermacher, *Christian Faith*, §115.1, 532; §116.3, 535–36.
39. Schleiermacher, *Christian Faith*, §115, 532.
40. Schleiermacher, *Christian Faith*, §90.1, 369.
41. See Schleiermacher, *Christian Faith*, §113.1, 525.
42. Hector, "Mediation of Christ's Normative Spirit," 9.
43. Schleiermacher, *Christian Faith*, §113.1, 525.
44. Schleiermacher, *Christian Faith*, §122.1, 565.

and ongoing existence to the divine causality of Christ and the Spirit.[45] But Schleiermacher, following the example of the Reformers and of Hooker and Owen, nevertheless treats the doctrine of the church only after a prior discussion of individual appropriation of salvation—in his case, as expressed by a self-consciousness of redemption in Christ. What is more, the church as a sociohistorical human community then arises in consequence of regenerate individuals coming together corporately to communicate their common consciousness of Christ-formed piety and the beliefs and practices that constitute it.

The accounts of the church that emerge in the thought of Schleiermacher, Owen, and Hooker, therefore—perhaps as a symptom of the legacy bequeathed to them by the Reformers—are ones that, while certainly cognizant of the church as a creature of God's grace, place a disproportionate emphasis on the church's human empirical form, as that form is constituted by the agency of Christian believers and performed church practice. This highly performative emphasis in ecclesiological description is expressed perhaps most clearly in contemporary approaches to ecclesiology in the work of Stanley Hauerwas.

The Church as Social Ethic

Central to Hauerwas's speech about the church is the conviction that theology, inherently, is a practical discipline. To think of theology in this way, for Hauerwas, is to make the point that "the truthfulness of our theological convictions is inseparable from questions of how we are to live."[46] Indeed, "any consideration of the truth of [those] convictions cannot be divorced from the kind of community the church is and should be."[47] Or, as he puts it elsewhere, "the 'what' of what we believe" as Christians "cannot be separated from the 'how'" we, as Christians, are to live.[48] This echoes the driving conviction of Cone and the liberationists more generally that "doing" and "saying" are inseparably linked in Christian theology such that the former conditions the meaning of the latter,[49] but it also conflates what David Kelsey describes as "the logic of Christian beliefs" with the "logic of the life of Christian believing."[50] The

45. See Schleiermacher, *Christian Faith*, §87.3, 360; §116.3, 535.
46. Hauerwas, *With the Grain of the Universe*, 22.
47. Hauerwas, *Community of Character*, 1.
48. Hauerwas, *Work of Theology*, 269.
49. See chap. 2 on empirical ecclesiology.
50. Kelsey, *Eccentric Existence*, 1:80; see also 1:27–45. Kelsey is drawing here on the thought of Hans Frei. See Frei, *Identity of Jesus Christ*, xi–xiii.

first logic has to do with the meaning and mutual coherence of doctrinal statements about the church's belief in God, and with God's relation to that which God creates. The second logic is concerned with the way in which that belief is lived out in practice, or with how, in Frei's words, "the resurrection of Christ shapes a new life."[51] In conflating positively and intentionally in theological inquiry the first and second logics, Hauerwas affirms that theology must be done "in a way that does not abstract doctrine from ways of life in which doctrine does work."[52]

Indeed, Hauerwas fears that theology, and systematic theology in particular, all too often present Christianity "as a system of beliefs" abstracted from how the church is to live in a distinctly Christian way given Christ's resurrection.[53] He argues that the very grammar of belief upon which systematic theology trades "invites a far too rationalistic account of what it means to be a Christian."[54] In this account, it is assumed that if Christians could only get their "'beliefs' right," then they would know how "to act right."[55] This assumption, contends Hauerwaus, is itself false, however. It wrongly assumes that the logic of belief "implies propositions about which you get to make up your mind before you know the work they are meant to do."[56] For Hauerwas, and precisely in consequence of his positive and intentional conflation of the two logics of belief, "Christianity is not beliefs about God *plus* behaviour."[57] He writes elsewhere, "If you think Christians have 'beliefs' that need to be applied, I assume that something has gone wrong in your understanding of the grammar of theology."[58] This is not to say that the grammar of belief is redundant for Hauerwas, or that doctrinal statements about God are irrelevant for displaying the truthfulness of the church's theological convictions.[59] Nor is it to say that the "what" of what we believe as Christians is unimportant.[60] It is instead to say that the grammar of Christian belief must have purchase on how ecclesial life is lived if theological inquiry

51. Frei, *Identity of Jesus Christ*, xiii. The reader should note that what I identify here as the second logic is in Kelsey's presentation actually a third logic. The second logic in his presentation is what he describes as "the logic of coming to belief." Kelsey, *Eccentric Existence*, 1:27.

52. Hauerwas, *Work of Theology*, 271; see also 267–69.

53. Hauerwas, *Sanctify Them in the Truth*, 157.

54. Hauerwas, *Hannah's Child*, x.

55. Hauerwas, *Sanctify Them in the Truth*, 157.

56. Hauerwas, *Hannah's Child*, x.

57. Hauerwas, *After Christendom?*, 107 (emphasis added).

58. Hauerwas, *Work of Theology*, 23.

59. See Hauerwas, *With the Grain of the Universe*, 22.

60. See Hauerwas, *Sanctify Them in the Truth*, 158: "This does not mean, for example, that questions about God's Trinitarian nature are unimportant. Yet something has gone wrong

is to avoid presenting itself as a set of abstract theological first principles, offering answers to doctrinal questions that no one is really asking.[61] In fact, for Hauerwas, theological inquiry is "a performative discipline"[62] and "must, if it is to be truthful, be embedded in the practices of actual lived communities."[63] When we separate the truth (or falsity) of the church's doctrinal convictions from Christian practice we lose what Hauerwas describes as "our intelligibility as Christians."[64]

Thus Hauerwas sees a need to recover in theological inquiry what he describes, provocatively, as "peasant Catholicism."[65] What he means by this is a particular characterization of Christianity that draws positively on what it means (or did mean) to be a peasant. As Hauerwas defines the term, a peasant is someone who works continually at a craft necessary to sustain life in community, and who therefore has knowledge of that craft habituated in their body.[66] To learn this type of embodied knowing is, in other words, to acquire the virtues of a craft in order to become a skilled practitioner.[67] The characterization of Christianity that follows is that "Christianity is not a set of beliefs or doctrines you believe in order to be a Christian, but rather Christianity is to have one's body shaped, one's habits determined, in a manner that the worship of God is unavoidable."[68] Another way to put this is to say that we cannot think our way to holiness. Holiness instead—salvation, even—has to do with becoming a certain type of person, a skilled practitioner of the craft of Christianity such that Christianity is so inscribed in our bodies that it becomes impossible for us not to worship God with those bodies.[69] And this process of formation or virtue acquisition takes place only as we participate in "that set of cultural habits called church."[70] The church, as Hauerwas understands it, is thus "a school of virtue,"[71] or, as he puts it elsewhere, "a culture which . . . forms bodies to

---

when questions about the Trinity have no purchase on how we make as well as what we do with our money."

61. See Hauerwas, *Work of Theology*, 271; and Hauerwas, *Sanctify Them in the Truth*, 2.
62. Hauerwas, *Work of Theology*, 271.
63. Hauerwas, *Sanctify Them in the Truth*, 157.
64. Hauerwas, *After Christendom?*, 24; cf. 16.
65. Hauerwas, *Sanctify Them in the Truth*, 79.
66. See Hauerwas, *Sanctify Them in the Truth*, 78.
67. See Hauerwas, *After Christendom?*, 103.
68. Hauerwas, *Sanctify Them in the Truth*, 79.
69. See Hauerwas, *In Good Company*, 8: "Christian salvation means, finally, becoming a certain kind of person, one who can enjoy the end of life that the Christian community commends."
70. Hauerwas, *Sanctify Them in the Truth*, 159.
71. Hauerwas, *Community of Character*, 83.

inhabit the world in a distinctive fashion."[72] And the church is this culture because the church embodies a particular set of human practices configured in response to the story of God's gospel. This then leads Hauerwas to his emphatic and abiding ecclesiological claim that "the church is a social ethic."[73]

To describe the church as a social ethic is to affirm that "the church is the place where the story of God is enacted, told, and heard."[74] Critically, however, this story is not something that the church *has* but something that the church *is*: in other words, the story of God's gospel is not just a story. It is instead what Hauerwas describes as "a reality-making claim."[75] This claim not only "tells us the truth about the world and ourselves"—for example, "that we are sinners, yet saved"[76]—but requires a corresponding community of people to be formed in God's likeness to learn to live in a way that makes it possible for the story of God to be heard, told, and enacted in the first place.[77] The church, accordingly, "is not our but God's creation" and lived ecclesial life—as an aspect of creation—is only possible because God makes it so.[78] In this way, the church, says Hauerwas, is "a graced community."[79] That the church is such a community reflects the fact that "'church,' after all, is not a descriptive term but a theological claim about God's creation of a new people."[80]

The theological force of Hauerwas's point here should not be lost. That the church is a graced community ultimately means that it is intelligible only as a creature of God's grace, and therefore only from the perspective of theological inquiry. While Hauerwas does not want to deny the value of social-scientific fields of study for accounting for what the church is, he certainly is concerned about "the uncritical use of social-scientific paradigms which often, if applied rigorously and consistently, methodologically preclude the theological claims necessary for the church's intelligibility."[81] But that the church is a graced community does not mean that it is anything less than a natural community that is sustained in its sociohistorical existence by the

72. Hauerwas, *Sanctify Them in the Truth*, 165.
73. Hauerwas, *Peaceable Kingdom*, 99.
74. Hauerwas, *Christian Existence Today*, 101.
75. Hauerwas, *Christian Existence Today*, 102.
76. Hauerwas, *Christian Existence Today*, 102–3.
77. See Hauerwas, *Christian Existence Today*, 101.
78. See Hauerwas, *Christian Existence Today*, 54.
79. Hauerwas, *Peaceable Kingdom*, 103.
80. Hauerwas, *Christian Existence Today*, 112.
81. Hauerwas, *Christian Existence Today*, 130n15.

agency of human action.[82] The church, as Hauerwas writes, "is a polity like any other, but it is also unlike any other in so far as it is formed by a people who have no reason to fear the truth"of God's story.[83] As a social ethic, the church "in its profoundest expression" is indeed the gathering of Christian believers who have been formed by God's story to be a community of theological virtue, and who thus give witness in habit and speech to the truth of that story.[84] The church in this way is "an attempt to show what the world is meant to be as God's good creation."[85] And so "Christians must attempt to be nothing less than a people whose ethic shines as a beacon to others illumining how life should be lived well."[86] For Hauerwas, it is performed church practice, then, configured in response to the story of God's gospel, that defines what the church is as a social ethic and that constitutes the content of ecclesiological description. And these ecclesial practices—what the church *does*, in other words—form the church as a community of people whose life is shaped distinctively by the resurrection of Christ. As Hauerwas writes, "What is crucial . . . is not whether the Church is primarily understood as 'the body of Christ' or 'the people of God,' but whether the practices exist through which we learn that our bodies are not 'ours.'"[87] Put otherwise, the proper object of ecclesiological discourse must always be the logic of how the church's theological convictions are lived out in practice by Christian believers.

This forcefully performative concept of what the church is and the practical characterization of both Christianity and theological inquiry on which it trades is echoed in the work of Nicholas M. Healy. Despite his own (very) critical analysis of Hauerwas's ecclesiological thought and account of Christian doctrine more generally, Healy identifies with Hauerwas's central conviction that to treat Christianity, and thereby theology, as a system of belief inevitably distorts both Christianity and the discipline of Christian theology per se.[88] Healy sees this distortion most obviously at work in what he describes as "blueprint ecclesiologies."[89]

82. See Hauerwas, *Peaceable Kingdom*, 103.
83. Hauerwas, *Peaceable Kingdom*, 102. For more about the church as a polity, see Rasmusson, *Church as Polis*.
84. Hauerwas, *Community of Character*, 108; see also 109; and Hauerwas, *Peaceable Kingdom*, 102–6.
85. Hauerwas, *Peaceable Kingdom*, 100.
86. Hauerwas, *Peaceable Kingdom*, 34.
87. Hauerwas, *In Good Company*, 24.
88. See Healy, *Hauerwas*.
89. Healy, *Church, World and the Christian Life*, 25; see also 32–49.

The Church as Anti-blueprint?

As Healy describes them, "blueprint ecclesiologies" generally share five
key methodological characteristics. First, the attempt to capture in a single
concept or image—in a "model" (to recall Avery Dulles's phrase)—the essence or true nature of what the church is. Second, the construal of the
church as having "a twofold ontological structure,"[90] in which the church's
human empirical form is described as the sociohistorical expression of its
own true nature. Third, the move to combine these two characteristics to
develop a normative account of what the church is (or should be). Summarizing this move, Healy writes, "If the fundamental reality of the church
is some particular thing, namely model x, then x must be realized in the
visible forms of the church, which can then be described systematically and
normatively in its light."[91] Fourth, and consequently, a "blueprint ecclesiology" has the tendency to account for what the church is in abstraction from
its sociohistorical existence, not least in relation to the reality of ecclesial
sin as "an ever-present aspect of the church's concrete identity."[92] And fifth,
a "blueprint ecclesiology" thereby tends to speak about the church in idealized terms. In sum, "Blueprint ecclesiologies thus foster a disjunction
not only between normative theory and normative accounts of ecclesial
practice, but between ideal ecclesiology and the realities of the concrete
church, too. They undervalue thereby the theological significance of the
genuine struggles of the church's membership to live as disciples within
the less-than-perfect church and within societies that are often unwilling
to overlook the church's flaws. As a consequence, blueprint ecclesiologies
frequently display a curious inability to acknowledge the complexities of
ecclesial life in its pilgrim state."[93]

To acknowledge this state, and to illuminate the sinful nature of its complexities in particular, Healy thinks that ecclesiological description needs to
be oriented away from speech about the church that is theoretically abstract
and universally applicable and toward the particular and concrete realities
of lived ecclesial life. For Healy, in a fashion similar to both Hauerwas and
type 1, empirical ecclesiology, speech about the church is a matter of practical rather than theoretical reasoning.[94] As Paul Avis puts it, in language that
directly echoes Healy's overriding concern, "It will not do to start with a

90. Healy, *Church, World and the Christian Life*, 28.
91. Healy, *Church, World and the Christian Life*, 30–31.
92. Healy, *Church, World and the Christian Life*, 37.
93. Healy, *Church, World and the Christian Life*, 37.
94. See Healy, *Church, World and the Christian Life*, 46.

paper blueprint of the Church and then measure churches against it. . . . The Church is known in ecclesial praxis," in "the practical experience of being the Church."[95] In Healy's own words, it is known in "the church's performance of its tasks."[96] For Healy, the need, then, is not just to orient ecclesiological description toward the concreteness and particularities of lived ecclesial life, but to ensure that ecclesiology as a discipline "arises out of ecclesial practices, and is ordered directly towards them."[97] As Healy goes on to say, echoing the concern of the liberationist, "Contextual ecclesial praxis informs ecclesiology, and ecclesiology informs contextual ecclesial praxis, in a practical hermeneutical circle."[98]

The reordering of ecclesiological description that Healy calls for not only determines, then, that theologians must resist any definitive closure, so to speak, of the material content of the doctrine of the church, but that ecclesiology as a discipline must include "*explicit* analysis of the ecclesiological context as an integral part of properly *theological* reflection upon the church."[99] This is not to suggest, however, that the ecclesiological context can be described independently of the church, such that the latter can be correlated to an empirical account of the former. The point is, rather, that the ecclesiological context is *integral* to understanding what the church is. As Healy writes, "The concrete church lives within and is formed by its context."[100] In other words, what the church is cannot be known **a priori**, in abstraction from the context in which the church is embedded as a sociohistorical human community. Indeed, theologians must see the church's being as constituted, according to Healy, by a matrix of what might be described as theological, nontheological, and even anti-theological elements—"by the actions of the Holy Spirit; by the beliefs, valuations, feeling and experiences of its members; by the relations between its members and both the church collective and the non- or anti-Christian societies around them; by social practices, rituals and institutions the church has developed in the course of its history; by the power structures, the financial considerations, the external constraints and opportunities that the church faces in diverse times and places; and so on."[101]

For Healy, it follows that if theologians are to account theologically for what the church is, then they must make use of disciplines of study that are

95. Avis, *Reshaping Ecumenical Theology*, 63.
96. Healy, *Church, World and the Christian Life*, 11.
97. Healy, *Church, World and the Christian Life*, 46.
98. Healy, *Church, World and the Christian Life*, 46.
99. Healy, *Church, World and the Christian Life*, 39.
100. Healy, *Church, World and the Christian Life*, 39.
101. Healy, *Church, World and the Christian Life*, 167.

able to critically analyze the complexities of the human ecclesiological matrix.[102]
Only by drawing on disciplines such as sociology, cultural analysis, and history will theologians attend appropriately, argues Healy, to what the church
is as a sociohistorical human community, and in doing so present "careful
and critical descriptions of its activity within the confusions and complexities of a particular ecclesiological context."[103] Healy thereby conceives the
discipline of ecclesiology as an "active engagement" between theological and
nontheological fields of study.[104]

Notwithstanding this conception of ecclesiology and the emphasis it places
on the context of lived ecclesial life and performed church practice, Healy
subsequently insists that ecclesiological description must still be authorized
by a robust doctrine of God.[105] The robustness of this doctrine is such that
speech about the church must have as its starting point an account of the immanent life and economic work of the Holy Trinity.[106] Further, this account of
God's own life and work must be offered "initially independent" of the speech
about the church that follows it, so that the former determines the meaning
and force of what is said in the latter.[107] While the position that Healy takes
here thus works to a significant extent against his earlier argument critiquing
the method of "blueprint ecclesiologies," it is necessary because the identity
of the church, he notes (somewhat ironically in the context of that earlier
argument), is "thoroughly theological, for it is constituted by the activity of
the Holy Spirit, without which it cannot exist."[108]

What is more, this activity of the Holy Spirit in first constituting the
church necessitates the prior and initially independent account of the
agency of divine action that warrants speech about lived ecclesial life and
performed church practice. This is because the activity of the Holy Spirit
in constituting the church must be accounted for, says Healy, in a way that
maintains the freedom of the Spirit to act independently or apart from—
and at times prophetically over against—the church and its practices.[109] For
Healy, because the practices of the church are performed by human agents in
ecclesiological contexts that are constituted by theological, nontheological,
and anti-theological elements, they are inevitably subject to distortion and

102. See Healy, *Church, World and the Christian Life*, 5.
103. Healy, *Church, World and the Christian Life*, 54; see also 5, 39.
104. Healy, *Church, World and the Christian Life*, 53.
105. See Healy, "Practices and the New Ecclesiology," 287–308.
106. Healy, "Practices and the New Ecclesiology," 302. See the glossary for definitions of
immanent Trinity and **economic Trinity**.
107. Healy, "Practices and the New Ecclesiology," 302.
108. Healy, *Church, World and the Christian Life*, 5.
109. See Healy, "Practices and the New Ecclesiology," 302.

misperformance.[110] It follows that there is no sense in which the practices of the church are "ideally intended and performed," or have "sufficiently fixed meanings" such that they can ever be identified exclusively as the activity of the Holy Spirit;[111] and because the practices of the church are distorted and misperformed, the activity of the Holy Spirit can never be collapsed into those practices or understood to be synonymous with them. The Spirit, as John's gospel reminds us, is free to blow wherever the Spirit pleases (John 3:8), both within and without the church, and irrespective of the form that church practice takes. Any account of lived ecclesial life and performed church practice that associates the activity of the Holy Spirit too closely with the church and its practices—or with any one particular form of practice—runs the risk not only of rendering those practices impervious to sin but of limiting in ecclesiological description both the effect of human agency and the divine freedom of the Holy Spirit.[112]

Further, in such an account—or at least in one that is not authorized by a doctrine of God—"it becomes rather too easy," Healy writes, "to interpret the emphasis upon the church and its practices as if it reflects the view that Christianity is all about being Christian, and the gospel is broadly identifiable with the church's practices and doctrines."[113] In other words, the emphasis on lived ecclesial life and performed church practice "threatens to collapse the object of faith into ourselves."[114] Healy continues, "Our proclamation becomes rather too much about us and what we over-optimistically think we do."[115] Put otherwise, Healy is alive to the risk that type 1, empirical ecclesiology, fails to register: the risk of collapsing, in an account of the church, speech about divine action into language about ecclesial human reality.

Still, Healy is adamant that ecclesiological description be oriented toward lived ecclesial life and so reordered to concrete and particular ecclesiological contexts—to the agencies of Christian believers and performed (and misperformed) church practice—as constitutive of what the church is. But this reordering must nevertheless be determined by reference to the life and work of God as the condition of the possibility of church life and action.[116] In conceiving ecclesiology as an "active engagement" between theological

110. See Healy, "Practices and the New Ecclesiology," 292–96.
111. Healy, "Practices and the New Ecclesiology," 292, 295.
112. See Healy, "Practices and the New Ecclesiology," 297–98.
113. Healy, "Practices and the New Ecclesiology," 302.
114. Healy, "Practices and the New Ecclesiology," 302.
115. Healy, "Practices and the New Ecclesiology," 302.
116. Healy, "Karl Barth's Ecclesiology," 287–99, esp. 294.

and nontheological fields of study, then, Healy (like Hauerwas) does not seek an approach to ecclesiology in which theology has no innate disciplinary superiority over—or distinction from—nontheological disciplines. Instead, what Healy seeks is an approach to ecclesiology in which nontheological disciplines are employed as "useful" but never as normative.[117] More specifically, Healy seeks an approach to ecclesiology that uses *theologically qualified* forms of nontheological disciplines, what he calls "theological history," "theological sociology," and "ecclesiological ethnography."[118] He hopes, ultimately, that these theologically qualified disciplines will draw ecclesiological description "back to the confusions and complexities of life within the pilgrim church."[119] This inclination to draw theology and non-theological disciplines together in ecclesiological description finds perhaps its greatest expression among contemporary approaches to ecclesiology in the thought of Daniel Hardy.

The Church as Created Sociality

Hardy's ecclesiology and his theological inquiry, more widely, are driven by his concern that theology is impoverished by the self-limitation of its resources.[120] This concern itself arises out of Hardy's most fundamental theological conviction: that God's presence and activity are in and with the world. Hardy writes, "The truth and purposes of God are 'refracted'—as it were spread like a band of colour—in other forms of life and thought; and the purpose of theology is to rediscover the dynamic of God's life and work in this 'band of colour' and from it."[121] Theology, then, must treat worldly forms of life and thought, and the way in which they understand human life in the world, as loci for understanding the presence and activity of God. Theological inquiry thus proceeds, Hardy argues, as "a symbiotic relation" between theological and nontheological disciplines, such that they interpenetrate or "pass through" one another in interdisciplinary study.[122]

---

117. Healy, *Church, World and the Christian Life*, 155.
118. Healy, *Church, World and the Christian Life*, 184–85. Healy sees Ephraim Radner's *The End of the Church* as representative of theological history. Healy, *Church, World and the Christian Life*, 162; see Radner, *End of the Church*. He sees William T. Cavanaugh's *Torture and Eucharist* as a model form of ecclesiological ethnography. Healy, *Church, World and the Christian Life*, 183; see Cavanaugh, *Torture and Eucharist*.
119. Healy, *Church, World and the Christian Life*, 185.
120. See Hardy, "Magnificent Complexity," 307–56, esp. 308.
121. Hardy, *God's Ways with the World*, 1–2.
122. Hardy, *God's Ways with the World*, 319, 323.

In this way, Hardy seeks to integrate theological truth with the truth of nontheological disciplines, "*unfolding* the former into the latter and *enfolding* the latter into the former."[123] This is not to say that theological truth is identical with the truth of nontheological disciplines, or vice versa. Nor is it to say that theologians are to leave behind the inherited tradition of a Christian **canon** of authoritative scriptural, creedal, and **doxological** texts.[124] It is instead to say that theological and nontheological disciplines must interact with—or "refract"—one another so as to account more fully for the truth and vitality of God in the world.[125] The inherited tradition of orthodox Christian understanding is certainly necessary to this refractive process, according to Hardy, but by itself it is nevertheless "inadequate except as preparatory" for accounting for the fullness of God's vitality and truth that emerges *in* the refraction and *from* it.[126] In this sense, theology is a dynamic discipline that must endeavor to reconstitute and enrich itself by an intentional extension of its resources beyond itself—that is, to theologize *through* art, poetry, music, cosmology, economics, and so on. By doing so, theologians not only treat adequately the magnificent complexity of life lived in situ but also resist the tendency to present abstract theological accounts that stand detached from, and over against, this complexity.[127] Theologians must, in fact, energetically oppose any move toward what Ben Quash describes as "ahistorical completeness,"[128] and thus also any supposition that theology is concerned with the imposition of theological truth contained in a fixed set of governing doctrines from which Christian believers would know how to "act right" (to recall Hauerwas's phrase).[129]

For Hardy, this energetic opposition to any such supposition is demanded of theologians, especially in their speech about the church. As Hardy writes, "The Church was not first an idea or a doctrine but a *practice* of commonality in faith and mission."[130] As such, "the Church is not measured by any fixed standard, because the Church is embodied in its practices and its practices embody a living relationship among its members and the triune persons of God."[131] That the church is a practical embodiment of a living relationship between God and God's people means that ecclesiology necessarily resists

---

123. Hardy, "Magnificent Complexity," 348 (emphasis original).
124. See Hardy, *God's Ways with the World*, 325.
125. See Hardy, *God's Ways with the World*, 324.
126. Hardy, *God's Ways with the World*, 2; see also 324.
127. See Hardy, "Magnificent Complexity," 308.
128. Quash, *Found Theology*, 1.
129. See Hardy, "Magnificent Complexity," 330.
130. Hardy, *Finding the Church*, 29 (emphasis original).
131. Hardy et al., *Wording a Radiance*, 65.

definitive closure as a doctrine. Indeed, as Hardy puts it, "thinking the Church is unlike any other doctrine: it is more a theological and practical engagement with what the Church is and should be."[132] The doctrine of the church, like the discipline of theology, is itself dynamic, or "moving."[133] This means that, in their speech about the church, theologians must also themselves be "moving," theologizing only in relation to what the church is (and should be) in its concrete and particular sociohistorical existence.[134] To conduct "moving ecclesiology," as Hardy describes it, theologians must "move off" their chairs.[135] Theologians of a moving church "wander first," Hardy argues, "and then think theologically and practically in response to what they have found. Whoever or whatever turns up as they walk, whatever they find as they go along, these become the found realities in response to which they think and act."[136] To theologize in this way about the church, then, is to accept not only that there is no fixed doctrine of the church that precedes what the church is in its sociohistorical existence but also that theologians, if they are to "find" the church, must attend to the actual practices of the church and to the many nontheological fields of study that are able to understand the materiality of them.

In Hardy's desire to "find" the church, he is, however, alive to the risk identified in relation to type 1, empirical ecclesiology—that is, to the risk of reducing, in ecclesiological description, either the theological to the empirical or the doctrinal to the cultural. Indeed, Hardy's process of refraction aims neither to dissipate nor to wholly assimilate the discipline of theology into nontheological fields of study. The aim of the refractive process is rather to fulfill the distinct capacity of theology to account for God's truth and vitality in the world—to embrace, as Hardy argues, the vitality and truth of nontheological disciplines within the primary truth and vitality of God.[137] Any attempt to "find" the church in its sociohistorical existence and to attend to actual church practice and lived ecclesial life as the proper object of ecclesiological description must be warranted, then, by an account of God's trinitarian life to which sociohistorical existence, says Hardy, is relative.[138] For Hardy, the space and time in which theologians wander to "find" the church are neither "predetermined" nor "haphazard."[139] The entire creation

132. Hardy, *Finding the Church*, 238.
133. Hardy et al., *Wording a Radiance*, 87.
134. See Hardy et al., *Wording a Radiance*, 87.
135. Hardy et al., *Wording a Radiance*, 86.
136. Hardy et al., *Wording a Radiance*, 86.
137. See Hardy, *God's Ways with the World*, 324.
138. See Hardy, "God and the Form of Society," 131–44.
139. Hardy et al., *Wording a Radiance*, 58.

is instead "measured" by divine "estimation."[140] What Hardy means by this is that God as Holy Trinity is self-structured in an ongoing and dynamic relation with that which God has created and one day will perfect.[141] Basic to this account of God's own life therefore is the "full differentiation" but also the "full relationality" between God and the world.[142] In this differentiated relation the life of God interacts with and "suffuses" the world and human participation in it "energetically," such that God's presence and activity really is *in* and *with* human beings in the being of the world.[143] The relationality and sociality of human beings is thus not only derived (in form) from God, but receives from God its own dynamic energy. As Hardy writes, "Their moving toward themselves and towards others are energized by God."[144]

This energizing relationality that Hardy understands God to be and have with the world ultimately identifies God's being as *directed* being—being that is directed, in other words, toward God's creation and creatures.[145] At the same time, it also identifies the being of creation and creatures as directed toward God.[146] For Hardy, "God creates things toward him," and that which is created is "created to move toward God."[147] Indeed, "The very nature of things *is* towardness."[148] This creaturely ontology of towardness Hardy names "attraction."[149] Everything, Hardy argues, is attracted to move beyond itself and toward God. And by this attraction, creatures (because of their creatureliness) are attracted to move beyond themselves and toward one another. Attraction to others and to God therefore characterizes what Hardy sees as "the inherent sociality of all creation,"[150] or, as he writes elsewhere, "the social transcendental" of created reality.[151] In other words, by virtue of God's own sociality as Father, Son, and Holy Spirit, created reality is social.[152] More acutely, Hardy understands created sociality, in consequence of the double attraction that characterizes it, to be a form of

140. Hardy et al., *Wording a Radiance*, 59.
141. See Hardy, "God and the Form of Society," 142–43.
142. Hardy, *God's Ways with the World*, 16.
143. Hardy, *God's Ways with the World*, 16.
144. Hardy, "God and the Form of Society," 143.
145. See Hardy, *God's Ways with the World*, 25.
146. See Hardy et al., *Wording a Radiance*, 45–49.
147. Hardy et al., *Wording a Radiance*, 46, 47.
148. Hardy et al., *Wording a Radiance*, 47 (emphasis original).
149. Hardy et al., *Wording a Radiance*, 45.
150. Hardy et al., *Wording a Radiance*, 49.
151. Hardy, "Created and Redeemed Sociality," 29; see also 21–47.
152. See Hardy, "Created and Redeemed Sociality," 42.

what he describes—drawing on the thought of Samuel T. Coleridge—as abductive **sociopoiesis**.[153]

For Hardy, this means that God by the Holy Spirit works in and through sociohistorical reality in order, by the human making and shaping of ever-expanding orders of social relation, to draw all of creation beyond itself and into fulfillment in God's kingdom.[154] Sociopoiesis, then, is the human making and shaping of social relations in sociohistorical reality, and its abductive nature is the drawing by God of those relations, and creation itself, transformatively toward Godself. Abduction (as a characteristic of "attraction") thus identifies in Hardy's thought a movement from created to redeemed sociality,[155] a movement by which created sociality moves against "self-attraction" and reengages its "primordial attraction" to God and others.[156] Hardy writes, "Attraction is redemptive because it restores the directionality of things and, thereby, restores the integrity of creation."[157]

What is more, God's attraction is dispersed in three forms—what Hardy describes as "socio-poietic modalities"—of human social life in the world: the nation, global society, and the church.[158] This is critical for Hardy's understanding of what the church is: it is through these three modalities that he sees created sociality being drawn beyond itself by the Holy Spirit into fulfillment in God's kingdom, thereby actualizing redeemed sociality. To be sure, the church, as Christ's body, is a specific form of human social life in the world; the church participates in a particular way in the Spirit's work of drawing created sociality beyond itself into redeemed sociality. Hardy emphasizes: the church is *"the activity of assembling all that needs to be assembled to promote the fullness of human society."*[159] However, politics, education, commerce, and law also play a role. And these are as much a part of abductive sociopoiesis as church form, function, and polity. For Hardy, ecclesial, global, and national aspects of created sociality are all, as David Ford puts it, "oriented towards the attractive and attracting God who has created everything towards himself and works immanently as well as transcendently" through them.[160] Further, the ecclesial, global, and national aspects of each socio-poietic modality are

---

153. See Hardy et al., *Wording a Radiance*, 49. For Coleridge, "abduction" names a "being drawn toward the true center" of all things—that is, God. See Coleridge, *Opus Maximum*, 15:327.

154. See Hardy et al., *Wording a Radiance*, 49–53.

155. See Hardy, "Created and Redeemed Sociality," 47.

156. Hardy et al., *Wording a Radiance*, 47, 51.

157. Hardy et al., *Wording a Radiance*, 47.

158. See Hardy, "Receptive Ecumenism," 428–40, esp. 434.

159. Hardy et al., *Wording a Radiance*, 70 (emphasis original).

160. David F. Ford, "Living Theology in the Face of Death," 124; see also 111–36.

to be understood, Hardy argues, neither apart from one another nor collapsed into one another, but rather as mutually implicating and interpenetrating and as ordered within God's ongoing and dynamic relationship with human social life in the world.[161] In Hardy's construction, the church, then, while vital to abductive sociopoiesis, is itself not sufficient for the actualization of redeemed sociality.

Performative Ecclesiology: An Assessment

Notwithstanding the obvious trinitarian footing of Hardy's ecclesiological thought, with his emphasis on abductive sociopoiesis, the church is, in his own words, "not altogether distinguished from those forms of society that do not explicitly embody God's purposes."[162] Not only is the church unable to find those purposes wholly within itself, but other forms of human social life in the world may well find and begin to realize them in a more vital way than the church.[163] The effect of this, for Hardy, is that those who do find and begin to realize redeemed sociality in this way "may be closer to God than a 'church,'" and they may thereby represent what Hardy describes as a "pre-church."[164] Thus, the church's being is "plastic," according to Hardy, in the sense that it defies any fixed meaning or standard.[165] The effect of this is that Hardy understands the being of the church to be one form among many societal forms in which human social life in the world is lived and by which that life is drawn to the truth of its meaning in God. Put otherwise, the church is but one subspecies of created sociality among others. And in performative ecclesiology, crucially, it is one subspecies of created sociality whose specific human empirical form is constituted ultimately by the agency of Christian believers and performed church practice. In Hardy's words, "The distinctive character of a *church* is that it finds the meaning of society in God, and seeks to bring society into closer and closer approximation to the truth that also frees people to be fully themselves, that is to the truth of God."[166] But that the distinctive character of the church is located in the church *finding* the meaning of society in God might lead the reader to worry that the church is distinguished as a form of society from all other societal forms only by what it believes about God and by the form of social

161. See Hardy, "Receptive Ecumenism," 434–35.
162. Hardy, *Finding the Church*, 39.
163. See Hardy, *Finding the Church*, 40.
164. Hardy, *Finding the Church*, 40.
165. Hardy, *Finding the Church*, 40.
166. Hardy, *Finding the Church*, 240 (emphasis original).

life it maintains and performs in consequence of those beliefs.[167] As Healy contends, in words that might energize this worry, the church is adequately described as *the church*—and thereby distinguished from all other religious and nonreligious communities—on the basis of its beliefs about God: "Its members believe that they, as a community, have been brought into a unique relation to God, who elects them . . . to make known to others something true and of great significance about the way created things are related to what is not part of creation."[168] Or, as Healy puts it elsewhere, what renders the church unique is that unlike all other religious and nonreligious communities, "the church claims that it is orientated towards the ultimate goal of all humanity."[169] This "Spirit-empowered *orientation* to Jesus Christ," or the "unique relation to God" that makes the church distinct, is derivative, however, of what the church believes or claims about God and itself and of how these claims or beliefs subsequently come to shape a specific social identity that "takes concrete form in the web of social practices accepted and promoted by the community as well as in the activities of its individual members."[170]

The distinctiveness of the church as a sociohistorical human community is thus constituted by what Healy describes, alternatively, as the church's "mediating function," its function of drawing its members into relationship with God—that is, into the "quest" of believing Christians to live authentically Christian lives in the world that give witness to Jesus Christ.[171] Another way to put this is to say, as Hauerwas does, that what distinguishes the church as *the church* is "the *kind* of narrative that determines its life."[172] To be sure, that the church is a social ethic certainly means, for Hauerwas, that the church is distinct to all other social bodies in the world, but this distinction is not a metaphysical one; rather, it is an ethical one. As Hauerwas writes, "The only difference between church and world is the difference between agents."[173] In

167. For Hardy, the Eucharist is the prototype of ecclesial social life: "The Eucharist is an embodiment of all the dimensions of human existence in the world—biological, physical and historical circumstances, personal participation, social relations, political configuration, economic exchange and cultural formation—in a forward trajectory anticipating the final good of all people and things. In it, these dimensions are held in social meaning referred to God, by which God is seen as originating, mediating and fulfilling all of them. Seen in such a way, the Eucharist . . . is a comprehensive event or performance of social meaning." See Hardy, *Finding the Church*, 244.
168. Healy, "What is Systematic Theology?," 36–37.
169. Healy, *Church, World and the Christian Life*, 17.
170. Healy, *Church, World and the Christian Life*, 17, 5.
171. See Healy, "Ecclesiology, Ethnography, and God," 182–99, esp. 193, 197–98.
172. Hauerwas, *Community of Character*, 4.
173. Hauerwas, *Peaceable Kingdom*, 101.

other words, the only difference between the church and the world is the difference between the personal, ethical actions of those who believe the story of God's gospel and the personal, ethical actions of those who do not. The difference between the church and the world may not, then, go all the way down.[174]

If performative ecclesiology portrays the church as one subspecies of created sociality among others, one whose distinctiveness is constituted by the agency of Christian believers and embodied in lived ecclesial life and performed church practice based on what the church believes about God and itself, the reader might worry that in this type of ecclesiology there is nothing ontologically distinct about the being of the church per se. In this way, performative ecclesiology might seem to be open to the same critique as type 1, empirical ecclesiology: the critique that it proffers an account of the church that collapses speech about divine action into language about ecclesial human reality.

Performative ecclesiology, however, is cognizant of Karl Barth's fear of forgetting God in its concern to attend to the church's human empirical form as the proper object of ecclesiological discourse.[175] Indeed, the work done in performative ecclesiology to base its account of lived ecclesial life and performed church practice on an account of the life and work of God means that, in contrast to empirical ecclesiology, performative ecclesiology is in fact not open to the critique that it altogether collapses speech about divine agency into speech about human subjectivity.

That said, the distinctiveness of what the church is in performative ecclesiology lies not in a theological account of God's own life and work but in a particular kind of human social life embodied in a particular set of human practices configured in response to a particular set of human beliefs about God. Notwithstanding the desire in performative ecclesiology to account for the church as a creature of God's grace, and as much as it may seem like performative ecclesiology holds together in speech about the church an account of divine and human agency, in accordance with the basic ecclesiological task, the reader may wonder whether this type of ecclesiological approach is nonetheless theologically disordered and disproportionate. After all, when confronted by the actual content of speech about the church in performative ecclesiology, ecclesiological description emerges primarily in the context of lived ecclesial life and performed church practice, and it is about this primary sociohistorical reality and the Christian beliefs in response to which it is configured that theologians subsequently theologize.

174. See Hauerwas, *Work of Theology*, 5.
175. See Barth, *Church Dogmatics* I/2, 794.

Consequently, the account of the church that emerges in performative ecclesiology might be seen to lack an appropriate sense of theological order and proportion because of its emphasis on human agency. While performative ecclesiology does indeed speak to one extent or another about God's immanent life and economic work in constituting what the church is, this speech nevertheless remains, proportionately speaking, a somewhat thin and remote (or presupposed) ecclesial backdrop, against which thicker and denser speech about ecclesial human reality is set. To be sure, in Hardy's ecclesiological speech, and because of his application of trinitarian doctrine within his understanding of created and redeemed sociality, speech about God's immanent life and economic work is more than an ecclesial backdrop. However, it remains the case for Hardy that the actualization of redeemed sociality is not peculiar to the church: the church's being—not only in Hardy's thought, but in performative ecclesiology as a type—is not rendered ontologically distinct as a sociohistorical human community brought into existence and sustained by God and God's gracious acts.

What is peculiar to the church, instead, is its embodied social ethic shaped in response to the agency of God's action. And it is this—what Christian believers *do* in lived ecclesial life and performed church practice in worship of God—that constitutes the being of the church as distinct (but critically not altogether distinct) in performative ecclesiology. Thus the risk in performative ecclesiology is that of presenting an account of the church that is inadequately attentive to the unique nature of the church that God and God's gracious acts create *as* a sociohistorical reality. The church is not just one creaturely reality in creation among others. Rather, as a creature of God's grace, the church is distinct from all other creaturely realities and forms of sociohistorical human community, and ontologically so. Yes, the church is the people of God, and it is such only as a lived sociohistorical reality. But as Paul's appropriation of God's covenantal promise to the church in Corinth (which we explored in chap. 1) makes clear, the church is God's people only because *God* has first determined to be this people's God.

The risk, then, in performative ecclesiology is not only that of forgetting that, in its sociohistorical existence, the church is *uniquely* constituted by the agency of divine action but also that of forgetting to address God and God's gracious acts sufficiently in the attendant ecclesiological description. This risk is a deficiency that places in doubt the ability of performative ecclesiology to perform successfully ecclesiology's most basic task of holding together in speech about the church an account of both divine and human agency in which the former relativizes but does not minimize the latter. Indeed, the reader may worry that in performative ecclesiology the doctrine of the church is again treated—as it was in type 1, empirical ecclesiology—too independently from a doctrine of God. It is this precise worry that stands at the forefront of the third type of contemporary approach to ecclesiology that this book seeks to articulate in its fivefold typology of contemporary approaches to ecclesiology. It is therefore to an articulation and assessment of type 3, communion ecclesiology, that we now turn.

4

Communion Ecclesiology

In the third type of contemporary approach to ecclesiology that I am proposing, the proper object of ecclesiological speech—in contrast to both
type 1, empirical ecclesiology, and type 2, performative ecclesiology—is
not the church's human empirical form but, rather, the life and work of God.
In communion ecclesiology, the church's being is spoken of properly only
when theologians set their ecclesiological descriptions in relation to an account of divine agency indexed to the being of God as triune. The desire in
communion ecclesiology is to account for the unique nature of the church as
a sociohistorical human community with reference to a substantive doctrine
of God's immanent life as Father, Son, and Holy Spirit and, more specifically,
with reference to a **social-trinitarian** framework.[1]

This desire does not mean, however, that to speak in a genuinely theological fashion about what the church is theologians must attend first to
the immanent life and economic work of the divine Trinity. In communion
ecclesiology, description of the life and work of God is not a normative and
necessary foundation of ecclesiology per se. The tendency in contemporary
approaches to ecclesiology to attend either to the church's human empirical
form or to the life and work of God is not stated as an explicit methodological
claim. This tendency is instead seen in communion ecclesiology (as it was in

---

1. The purchase of **social trinitarianism** in contemporary trinitarian theology and ecclesiology owes much to the work of Jürgen Moltmann in *The Trinity and the Kingdom* as well as to
scholars writing in his wake, including John D. Zizioulas, Colin Gunton, Elizabeth A. Johnson,
and Miroslav Volf. See Moltmann, *Trinity and the Kingdom*. For a concise but critical discussion
of social trinitarianism, see Kilby, "Perichoresis and Projection," 432–45.

performative ecclesiology) to be an implicit logical consequence of the account of the church that is proffered. While not built, therefore, on the problematic either/or tendency in contemporary approaches to ecclesiology, communion ecclesiology nevertheless displays it. For what communion ecclesiology seeks to retain to one extent or another in ecclesiological description is what Robert Jenson describes as the "ineradicable materiality" of Christian doctrine.[2] Thus the desire to account for the church's being with reference to God's immanent life and economic work is matched in communion ecclesiology by an equal desire to account for the concrete particularity of the church as it is in its sociohistorical existence. This dual desire is expressed perhaps most obviously and recently in contemporary approaches to ecclesiology by Colin Gunton.

The Church as Anticipation of Communion

Gunton's ecclesiological thought proceeds from his identification of a "manifest inadequacy" in the tradition of ecclesiological inquiry: "The conception of God as a triune community" has "made no substantive contribution to the doctrine of the Church."[3] A secondary (but no less significant) concern for Gunton is what he sees as the overdetermination of ecclesiology by **Christology**, and, in particular, by a "docetically tending" Christology.[4] The effect of this is ecclesiological description that is dogmatically flawed in the sense that it makes too much of the church's divinity and too little of its humanity—too little, that is, of the church's concrete particularity and of the contingency and fallibility of its sociohistorical existence.[5] Gunton, therefore, seeks an account of the church's being that is rooted in the being of God while still belonging to the vicissitudes of the created world.[6]

To construct this account, Gunton makes two moves he considers necessary in speech about the church. First, he seeks to mediate the relationship between ecclesiology and Christology pneumatologically. This Gunton does in order to ensure that the greatest stress in ecclesiology is placed on the economic action of the Holy Spirit, as the divine person who constitutes the church as the church in its sociohistorical existence. As a doctrine, ecclesiology is thereby determined by pneumatology.[7] Second, Gunton seeks to ground the being of the church as a sociohistorical human community in the immanent

2. See Jenson, *Systematic Theology*, 1:19.
3. Gunton, "Church on Earth," 48, 52.
4. Gunton, "Church on Earth," 60; see also 58–65.
5. See Gunton, "Church on Earth," 62.
6. See Gunton, "Church on Earth," 74.
7. See Gunton, "Church on Earth," 58–65.

life of God as triune.[8] Here, Gunton draws specifically on the ontological and trinitarian tradition of the **Cappadocian Fathers**, and in particular the Cappadocian understanding of the oneness of God's being as consisting only in the dynamic of the three divine persons in relation.[9]

This understanding of the Trinity itself rests on the distinction made by the Cappadocians between the Greek words *ousia* and *hypostasis*.[10] Previously thought to be synonymous, ousia is understood by the Cappadocians to mean "essence" or "being," while hypostasis is understood to mean "subsistence" or "individual subject"—a meaning assimilated eventually to the term "person." God as Father, Son, and Holy Spirit is thus thought of by the Cappadocians as one ousia ("being") in three hypostases ("persons"). Each hypostasis of the Trinity shares the ousia of the Godhead in that Father, Son, and Holy Spirit are said to be uncreated, but each hypostasis is nevertheless distinct in terms of the internal relation that they have in being "Unbegotten" (God the Father), "Begotten" (God the Son), and "Proceeded" (God the Holy Spirit). As Basil of Caesarea writes, there is, in the Trinity, "the proper peculiarity of the Persons . . . each of these being distinctively apprehended by His own [hypostatic] notes," but at once "a certain communion indissoluble and continuous."[11] Further, this communion and distinction of the divine ousia and hypostases is such that "the continuity of nature [is] never rent asunder by the distinction of the hypostases, nor the notes of proper distinction confounded in the community of essence."[12] There is in the Godhead instead a "conjoined separation and separated conjunction,"[13] in accordance with which Father, Son, and Holy Spirit have their being "in" or "through" one another. "The Son," Basil writes, "is in the Father and the Father in the Son," and the Holy Spirit is "conjoined . . . to the one Father through the one Son, and through Himself complet[es] the adorable and blessed Trinity."[14] For the Cappadocians, the being of God thus *is* the community of trinitarian persons in mutually constitutive—or *perichoretic*—relatedness. In the Cappadocian tradition, "God," as Gunton notes, "is no more than what Father, Son and Spirit give to and receive from each other in the inseparable communion that is the outcome of their love."[15]

8. See Gunton, "Church on Earth," 65–80.
9. For a helpful overview of the development of Christian orthodoxy in this period, see Irving, *We Believe*. For a detailed exposition of the contribution of each Cappadocian Father to this development, see Behr, *Nicene Faith*, pt. 2.
10. See Basil of Caesarea, *Letter XXXVIII*.
11. Basil of Caesarea, *Letter XXXVIII*, 4.
12. Basil of Caesarea, *Letter XXXVIII*, 4.
13. Basil of Caesarea, *Letter XXXVIII*, 4.
14. Basil of Caesarea, *De Spiritu Sancto*, XVIII.45.
15. Gunton, *Promise of Trinitarian Theology*, 10.

In order to ground the church's being in this communion of the Trinity, Gunton argues for drawing an analogy between the being-in-relation that God is and the being of the church: the human empirical form of the church is called to be an "echo" of the interpersonal communion of the immanent trinitarian life.[16] The account of the church that Gunton develops on the basis of this analogy of echo proceeds, however, with great theological care—and necessarily must do so, Gunton cautions. For what Gunton does *not* intend by understanding the being of the church as analogous to God's own being is a collapse of the all-important ontological distinction in Christian theology between God and that which is not God. As Gunton writes, "All forms of ontological continuity, whether they express an assured link between divine agency and that of a church or the automatic divine involvement in forms of created being, must be excluded."[17] Put otherwise, God, in the order of being, is *other* than what is created, and the being of the church is not synonymous with God's own being—and it must never be treated in ecclesiological description as if it were. In Gunton's speech about the church's sociohistorical existence as analogous to God's own being, Gunton does not intend to lose, then, "the dynamic of what is the essence of economy as theologically construed: a structured though open embracing of time by eternity."[18] What Gunton means by this is that the ontological distinction between God and that which is not God must be maintained securely in Christian theology because only by marking out the being proper to each—to God and to the world, that is—can it be affirmed that there is, indeed, "personal space" between the world and God,[19] and that the world exists only because of God's graciousness in creating out of nothing and sustaining creation continually.[20] For Gunton, this is precisely why ecclesiological description, and theological inquiry more widely, must affirm a doctrine of God's immanent trinitarian life "in *relative* distinction" to God's economic work.[21] It is also why the analogy that Gunton draws in his ecclesiological thought between God's being and the being of the church is indirect in nature: the *echo* of God's interpersonal, eternal communion that Gunton sees the church as is a temporal one.[22]

What is more, the temporality and indirect nature of this analogical echo that is so central to Gunton's ecclesiology is underscored by a particular

16. Gunton, "Church on Earth," 69.
17. Gunton, *The One, the Three and the Many*, 228–29.
18. Gunton, *The One, The Three and the Many*, 161.
19. Gunton, *Intellect and Action*, 103.
20. Gunton, "Church on Earth," 67.
21. Gunton, *Intellect and Action*, 103 (emphasis added).
22. See Gunton, "Church on Earth," 75.

account of how the church comes to "body forth" in its sociohistorical existence the interpersonal communion of God's immanent trinitarian life. For
Gunton, the echo of God's immanent life that is the church is wholly the
outcome of the economic action of the Holy Spirit. The Holy Spirit, as Paul
writes, is the "firstfruits [*aparchēn*]" (Rom. 8:23) of the life everlasting, the
"deposit [*arrabōn*], guaranteeing what is to come" (2 Cor. 5:5). This is to
say that, in Paul's thought, the Holy Spirit is the **eschatological** gift of God,
the one who makes present now the conditions of what will be fully on the
day of Christ's future **parousia**: the redemption of all things.[23] Given this,
"the action of the Spirit," writes Gunton, "is to anticipate, in the present
and by means of the finite and contingent, the things of the age to come."[24]
The church then becomes an echo of the interpersonal communion of God's
immanent trinitarian life only as the Holy Spirit acts on and toward it, and
thereby enables it to *anticipate* that life, proleptically, in its own sociohistorical existence. As Gunton puts it, "The Church is the body called to be the
community of the last times, that is to say, to realise in its life the promised
and inaugurated reconciliation of all things."[25]

Critically, however, it is the Holy Spirit who is the agent of this realization: it
is the Holy Spirit who constitutes, or more precisely "particularizes," Gunton
writes, the church's human empirical form.[26] Put otherwise, the Holy Spirit,
as the perfecting cause of creation,[27] enables the church in its sociohistorical
existence to be concretely and particularly the echo of God's immanent trinitarian life—the form of social life in the world that flows from the action of
the Holy Spirit making real in this particular human community anticipations
of the eternal communion that God is and that, in the life of the age to come,
God will be seen to be.[28] In this way, as Terry Cross puts it, "The *koinōnia*

23. For more about the eschatological tension of God's kingdom and its history of interpretation, see Moltmann, *Coming of God*, esp. 3–46; and from the perspective of biblical studies,
see Dunn, *Christianity in the* Making, 1:383–487.

24. Gunton, "Church on Earth," 61. For the most developed sketch of Gunton's understanding of this action of the Holy Spirit, see Gunton, "God the Holy Spirit," 105–28.

25. Gunton, "Church on Earth," 79.

26. Gunton, "Church on Earth," 61. The pattern of this particularizing action of the Holy
Spirit in relation to the church is true, for Gunton, christologically as well. It is only as a result of
the action of the Holy Spirit on and toward the incarnate, crucified, risen, and ascended Christ
that Christ is the human being He is—that is, without sin (Heb. 4:15)—and that His human
life *is* God's own life. See Gunton, "God the Holy Spirit," 112–19. For a helpful introduction
to the relation of Christology and pneumatology more generally, see Sánchez M., *T&T Clark
Introduction to Spirit Christology*.

27. The conception of the Holy Spirit as "the perfecting cause" of creation is Basil's. See
Basil of Caesarea, *De Spiritu Sancto*, XVI.

28. See Gunton, "Christian Community and Human Society," 119–38.

of the Trinity becomes the basis for the *koinōnia* of the saints assembled."[29] Gunton would doubtless agree. What is more, for Gunton, the being of the church consists in the relations of the assembled saints one to another as they are indwelt by the Holy Spirit.[30] But for the church to be this *koinōnia* (2 Cor. 13:14), this community or fellowship—for the church to be *the church*, that is—"it has constantly to be constituted anew"; it "must, ever and again, take place,"[31] Gunton argues, by the eschatological work of the Holy Spirit (2 Cor. 13:14). Thus, according to Gunton, the church is particularized "from time to time"[32] in created reality as the community of Christ's body in which the purpose of God for the created world is realized, "to bring unity to all things in heaven and on earth under Christ" (Eph. 1:10).

This pneumatological determination of ecclesiological description, by which the church is said to be what it is in the Holy Spirit, is found similarly in the work of Jürgen Moltmann. For Moltmann, the church, likewise, is the concrete fellowship and community of those who have been justified and liberated by Christ.[33] But this community and fellowship of Christ only "comes about 'in the Holy Spirit.'"[34] Accordingly, the church is brought into existence by the Spirit mediating in the here and now the presence of Christ and the future of new creation: "What is called 'the church' is this mediation."[35] That the church *is* because of the eschatological action of the Holy Spirit means, further, that the church is a "happening"—an event of the Holy Spirit that makes the church "the church of Jesus Christ."[36] In turn, this means that theologians cannot ask what the church is by recourse to abstract theological first principles because the dynamic nature of the church as a "happening" evades total absorption into the *concept* of "the church."[37] Moltmann writes, "We cannot therefore say what the church is in all circumstances and what it comprises in itself."[38] Instead of asking *what* the church is, theologians must ask *where* the church is.[39] More precisely, they must ask "*where* the church happens."[40] In a fashion similar to Hardy in type 2, performative ecclesiology, the church, therefore, is to be *found*. And in order to "find" the church, "to

29. Cross, *People of God's Presence*, 205.
30. See Gunton, "Church on Earth," 71.
31. Gunton, "Church," 202, 203; see also 187–205.
32. Gunton, "Christian Community and Human Society," 122.
33. See Moltmann, *Church in the Power of the Spirit*, 33.
34. Moltmann, *Church in the Power of the Spirit*, 33.
35. Moltmann, *Church in the Power of the Spirit*, 35.
36. Moltmann, *Church in the Power of the Spirit*, 122.
37. See Moltmann, *Church in the Power of the Spirit*, 122.
38. Moltmann, *Church in the Power of the Spirit*, 65.
39. See Moltmann, *Church in the Power of the Spirit*, 121–23.
40. Moltmann, *Church in the Power of the Spirit*, 65 (emphasis original).

discover the happening of Christ's presence" that is mediated by the Spirit's eschatological work, theologians must start their ecclesiological search from this pneumatological event.[41] For Moltmann, the church, then, is wherever the Spirit makes the presence of Christ manifest; accordingly, the discipline of ecclesiology must proceed not from the church as it is now, concretely and particularly, but from the church's future, as that future is opened up by the Holy Spirit making Christ's salvation history present.[42]

According to Moltmann, this christological manifestation of the Spirit that the church is nevertheless occurs particularly and concretely in history. More specifically, it occurs as the Holy Spirit mediates the aforementioned "happening" of Christ's presence through the proclamation of God's gospel; in the administration of baptism and the Lord's Supper; in the worship, fellowship, and way of life of the community of Christian believers; and in the poor and suffering.[43] In other words, for Moltmann, the church is brought into existence by the Spirit using what, in Gunton's words, are "earthly, this-worldly means."[44] Indeed, for Gunton, the church becomes an echo of the *koinōnia* of God's trinitarian life by proclaiming the Word of God, celebrating the sacraments, living in light of Jesus's way of being in the world, and being a community of praise.[45]

It is critical, however, that the effectiveness of these concrete or worldly means by which the church becomes, for Gunton, an echo of the life of the Godhead and, for Moltmann, the "happening" of Christ's presence is guaranteed only by the Spirit's eschatological work: the dynamic happening or echo that the church is occurs not because of the means themselves but only as the Holy Spirit graciously and freely makes real in them anticipations of the communion of God's coming kingdom.[46] In this sense, the church, says

41. See Moltmann, *Church in the Power of the Spirit*, 122.
42. See Moltmann, *Church in the Power of the Spirit*, 190.
43. See Moltmann, *Church in the Power of the Spirit*, 122, 206–26, 226–60, 261–88, 126–30.
44. Gunton, "Community of Reconciliation," 179; see also 173–203.
45. See Gunton, "Community of Reconciliation," 178–203.
46. See Gunton, "Christian Community and Human Society," 122; and Moltmann, *Church in the Power of the Spirit*, 24–26, 33–35. The reader should note that while Moltmann and Gunton both determine their ecclesiological description by reference to the free and gracious action of the Holy Spirit, Gunton's account of the Spirit's freedom in relation to the church might be considered more appropriate. Gunton is clear: "It is not . . . that the Spirit is in some way at the disposal of the church, so that what the church does the Spirit is doing." Gunton, "Christian Community and Human Society," 121. There is no sense in which the church, therefore, can claim to "possess" the Holy Spirit automatically. See Gunton, "Christian Community and Human Society," 122. Moltmann, however, might be seen to render the relation between the Spirit and the church in problematic terms. For Moltmann, "The community and fellowship of Christ which is the church comes about 'in the Holy Spirit'"; but, Moltmann adds, "the Spirit is this fellowship." Moltmann, *Church in the Power of the Spirit*, 33. This conflation of the Holy

Moltmann, "lives from the surplus of promise"—that is, in "the possibilities and powers of the Holy Spirit," who is not exhausted by the church's human-empirical form."[47] Or, in Gunton's words, "The concrete means by which the church becomes an echo of the life of the Godhead are all such as to direct the church away from self-glorification to the source of its life in the creative and recreative presence of God to the world."[48] Put otherwise, in the ecclesiological thought of both Gunton and Moltmann, the church exists eccentrically: the church receives its being *from outside itself* as a gracious gift, as the work and person of God the Holy Spirit anticipates in its sociohistorical existence the church's own true being.

The Church as Communion

This eccentric referent in speech about the church, by which the church's true being is said to be realized in its human empirical form by the Spirit's eschatological work, is echoed by Robert Jenson. Like Moltmann and Gunton, Jenson draws on the eschatological category of anticipation in working out his ecclesiological thought. "The church," he writes, "exists in and by *anticipation*."[49] Or, as he puts it elsewhere, "The church is what she is just and only as anticipation of what she is to be."[50] And what the church is to be, or what the church now anticipates in its being, is, in repetition of Gunton's proposal, the interpersonal communion of God's immanent trinitarian life, of which the church's community and fellowship is "sheer *arrabon*."[51] In contrast with Gunton's proposal, for Jenson, the church's own communal way of being also anticipates the church's inclusion in the communion that God is as Father, Son, and Holy Spirit; Jenson imagines the church itself as standing at heaven's gate in the future of the new creation.[52] He writes, "The church exists to be taken into the triune community as the body of the

---

Spirit with the church's fellowship thus seems to include the being of the church in the Godhead per se and to deny the freedom of the Spirit to act independently of or apart from the church.

47. Moltmann, *Church in the Power of the Spirit*, 24, 25.

48. Gunton, "Church on Earth," 79.

49. Jenson, *Systematic Theology*, 2:171 (emphasis original).

50. Jenson, "The Church and the Sacraments," 216.

51. Jenson, *Systematic Theology*, 2:222. As noted above, *arrabōn* is the Greek word that Paul uses of the Holy Spirit in 2 Cor. 1:22, 2 Cor. 5:5, and Eph. 1:14. In classical usage, the word describes a first installment or deposit given in advance to guarantee what later will be bestowed in full.

52. See Jenson, *Systematic Theology*, 2:222. By contrast, Gunton writes, "An inescapable characteristic of the Church . . . is that as part of the creation it, too, is finite and contingent." Gunton, "Church on Earth," 67. For Gunton, the church's finitude and contingency mean that it cannot be standing at heaven's gate in the future.

second person of that community."[53] Thus, for Jenson, the church and Christ together constitute the identity of the second person of the Trinity: "Christ is personally the second identity of God, and the *totus Christus* is Christ with the church."[54] To speak of the relation of Christ and the church in this way is, as David Yeago observes, to locate the church "interior to Christ's *self-identification*."[55] Or else, you might say, there is no Christ—or at least no "whole Christ" (*totus Christus*)—without the church, according to Jenson.[56] Jenson therefore sees the being of the church, as Christ's body, united with the second person of the Trinity in a serious ontological sense. The ontological nature of this unity roots the church's being in the immanent life of God as triune: "The church is God the Logos's body."[57]

In fact, notwithstanding Jenson's reference to the church as the "bride" of Christ (Eph. 5:31–32) and the necessity that the church be understood as in some way distinct from Christ thereby,[58] Jenson argues that the church is united so completely with Christ that "the church is ontologically the risen Christ's human body."[59] According to Jenson, in his description of the church as the body of Christ (1 Cor. 12:27; Eph. 1:23), Paul intends neither metaphorical interpretation nor ontological evasion.[60] As Sergius Bulgakov once suggested, the temptation to transform figuratively the ontological or substantial significance of the unity between Christ and the church that Paul's image affirms should be resisted.[61] That the church is the body of Christ is, as Bulgakov puts it, "an authentic, although mysterious, reality."[62] In Jenson's words, the church is "*truly* Christ's body for us."[63] Indeed, for Jenson, Christ needs no *other* body than the church to be the risen man that He is.[64] The church, then, is what Jenson describes as the object-presence or availability of the risen Christ in the world—the body in the world that the risen Christ is and "as which the risen Christ is available to be found, to be responded to, to be

53. Jenson, "The Church and the Sacraments," 217.
54. Jenson, *Systematic Theology*, 2:167.
55. Yeago, "Church as Polity?," 203 (emphasis original).
56. The *totus Christus* motif was developed by Augustine, initially, in his exposition of the Psalms. See Cameron, "Emergence of *Totus Christus*," 205–26. For a comprehensive overview of the motif itself, see Mersch, *The Whole Christ*.
57. Jenson, *Unbaptized God*, 127.
58. Jenson, *Systematic Theology*, 2:213.
59. Jenson, *Systematic Theology*, 2:213.
60. See Jenson, "The Church and the Sacraments," 212. For a brief but helpful summary discussion of Paul's description, see Hultgren, "Church as the Body of Christ," 124–32.
61. See Bulgakov, *Bride of the Lamb*, 258.
62. Bulgakov, *Bride of the Lamb*, 261.
63. Jenson, *Systematic Theology*, 1:206 (emphasis original).
64. See Jenson, *Systematic Theology*, 1:206.

grasped."[65] Jenson therefore takes in his ecclesiological thought the Catholic side of what Schleiermacher identifies as the basic antithesis between Protestant and Catholic understandings of union and communion with Christ: "The former makes the individual's relation to the Church dependent on his relation to Christ, whereas the latter contrariwise makes the individual's relation to Christ dependent on his relation to the church."[66] In Jenson's thought, because the church in its sociohistorical existence *is* Christ's risen body and as such is united ontologically to the second person of God's immanent trinitarian life, the church necessarily is—with Christ—the instrument of salvation.[67] The being of the church must be considered, therefore, as both prior to and distinct from created reality.

Because the *totus Christus* is Christ *with the church*, there is, then, a clear sense in which Jenson sees the being of the church as **predestined** in God's eternal will to be included in the trinitarian communion of God's coming kingdom—or, as Jenson himself puts it, "to abide, finally in God."[68] Indeed, that the church exists is "dictated," Jenson writes, by "the unmediated and wholly antecedent will that is the Father."[69] Further, being chosen or elected by the eternal will of God in this way means that the church is, in God's intention, both logically prior to the gospel of God and mandated to exist "as something other than the world or the Kingdom."[70] The church, as such, is not an outward work of God in the world (*opus ad extra*) in the same way that creation is.[71]

However, the church that has its being in a way that is distinct to created reality nevertheless is "exactly the one that exists" and has its "historically actual" existence as an outward work of God in creation.[72] The church, in Jenson's thought, is thus describable neither as "simply heaven" nor as "a phenomenon of this age."[73] What the church is cannot be spoken about only in abstract or idealized theological terms ("in the imagery of apocalyptic," as Jenson puts it), but neither can theologians speak about the church only in terms drawn from secular social theory.[74] This is the case for Jenson not only because the being of the church is logically prior to and distinct from created

65. Jenson, "The Church and the Sacraments," 210.
66. Schleiermacher, *Christian Faith*, 103.
67. See Jenson, *Unbaptized God*, 90–103, 125–28.
68. Jenson, *Systematic Theology*, 2:174.
69. Jenson, *Systematic Theology*, 2:173.
70. Jenson, *Systematic Theology*, 2:173; see also 2:168.
71. See Jenson, *Systematic Theology*, 2:167.
72. Jenson, *Systematic Theology*, 2:173, 2:194.
73. Jenson, *Systematic Theology*, 2:172.
74. Jenson, *Systematic Theology*, 2:172.

reality but because of the nature of theological inquiry itself. Theology, Jenson writes, "claims to know elements of reality that are not directly available to the empirical sciences or their predecessor modes of cognition, but that yet must be known—if only subliminally—if such lower-level cognitive enterprises are to flourish. We may press theology's claim very bluntly by noting that theology, with whatever sophistication or lack thereof, claims to know the one God of all and so to know the one decisive fact about all things, so that theology must be either a universal and founding discipline or a delusion."[75]

In a fashion similar to Hauerwas's view (in type 2, performative ecclesiology), here the church's intelligibility is dependent on theological investigation of what the church is. For Jenson, however, the church's intelligibility is dependent on Christian doctrine and **dogma**, which serves in theological investigation to function factually—that is, with objective import in relation to its truth claims—and thereby prescriptively with respect to what is true about God and all things as they relate to God.[76] Given this, and contrary to the trajectory of thought found in type 1, empirical ecclesiology, Jenson argues that theology does not necessarily map lived ecclesial life and church practice, for that practice and life may actually pervert the truth either of the gospel's God or God's gospel.[77] There is thus a need for Christian dogma and doctrine to stand sometimes polemically over against the church and its practices, in order to instruct the church when its practices and life are "speaking Christianese ungrammatically," as Jenson puts it.[78] Or, as Miroslav Volf writes, echoing Jenson's overriding concern, "Only a poor ecclesiology would simply chase after the developmental tendencies of modern societies. . . . The social form of the church must find its basis in its own faith rather than in its social environment."[79] And for the church to find its basis in its own faith, or to receive instruction as to the truthfulness (or otherwise) of its actual life and practice, means that ecclesiology must be rooted in the doctrine of God's triunity. In Jenson's words, "the needed social theory" for the church's intelligibility "is and can only be the doctrine of the Trinity itself."[80]

75. Jenson, *Systematic Theology*, 1:20.
76. See Jenson, *Systematic Theology*, 1:19–20.
77. See Jenson, *Systematic Theology*, 1:20.
78. Jenson, *Systematic Theology*, 1:20. Jenson's language directly echoes Lindbeck's (see chap. 2 on empirical ecclesiology). Drawing on Lindbeck's terminology, theology is described by Jenson as "a sort of *grammar*" that "formulates the syntax and semantics" of the language that the church speaks (i.e., "Christianese"). Christian doctrine and dogma thus function as "accepted rules of proper usage" of Christianese. See Jenson, *Systematic Theology*, 1:18.
79. Volf, *After Our Likeness*, 15.
80. Jenson, *Systematic Theology*, 2:173.

In saying this, Jenson (like Hauerwas and, for that matter, Volf) does not want to deny that social-scientific tools of analysis and the resources of cultural anthropology may sometimes be convenient for theologians to borrow in ecclesiological description. Any such "borrowings from secular theory" must, however, be made to serve theology as the higher-level cognitive enterprise, which, in its claims about God as triune, relativizes the truth claims of all other disciplines.[81] To use Volf's words again, "A theologian should be ready to learn [from other disciplines], even to be told what to learn, but should never give up the prerogative of ultimately deciding when and from whom help is needed and how best to use it."[82] Indeed, the borrowings from nontheological fields of inquiry that Jenson speaks of must be "strictly ad hoc" and carried out with "great circumspection" and "considerable bending of the recruited concepts."[83] It is theology alone—and specifically trinitarian theology—that is able to know, according to Jenson, the one decisive fact about what the church is: that the church, having been predestined by God the Father to be united as Christ's body ontologically with the second person of the Trinity, is, in its sociohistorical existence, the body of the risen Christ. As such, the church is both continuous and discontinuous with created reality, and so certain to persist in the consummated eschaton. And more to the point, the church is thus only by the economic work of the Holy Spirit.

It is the work of the Holy Spirit, Jenson argues, to found the church. As Jenson writes (quoting Luther), "'It is the proper work of the Holy Spirit, to make the church.' And we must add: the Spirit does this by giving himself to be the spirit of this community, by bestowing his own eschatological power to be her liveliness."[84] The Spirit's work in founding the church is thus seen by Jenson to be a work of divine freedom: the Holy Spirit graciously and freely gives the Spirit's own eschatological power to enliven the community of Jesus's disciples to be the church as Christ's body. Put otherwise, the Holy Spirit freely liberates the church from the constraints of its sociohistorical existence, in order that an actual human community might be fit to be united to the second person of God's immanent trinitarian life, and thereby become the body of Christ.[85] Further, "The miracle by which the community of Jesus's disciples and their converts *can* be the body or bride of the risen one is that the spirit of this particular community is identically the Spirit of God. The Spirit founds the church by giving himself to be her spirit and so freeing a

81. Jenson, *Systematic Theology*, 2:172.
82. Volf, *After Our Likeness*, 5.
83. Jenson, *Systematic Theology*, 2:172.
84. Jenson, *Systematic Theology*, 2:197.
85. See Jenson, *Systematic Theology*, 2:179.

community within this age to be appropriate for union with a person risen into the eschatological future."[86]

It is the decisive work of the Holy Spirit, then, in accordance with the electing will of God as Father, to establish the church in its sociohistorical existence as the risen Christ's own body, and in doing so to unite the church as Christ's risen body ontologically to the second person of God's immanent trinitarian life.[87] It is in this strictly pneumatological register that the church, as Susan Wood notes, is "elevated" in Jenson's thought "beyond creaturely status."[88] Indeed, both the triune communion that the church anticipates in its own communal way of being and the communion that the church now has with God's immanent trinitarian life as the risen body of Christ, results only from God's gift of communion with Godself animated by the Holy Spirit.

Put otherwise, the communion that the church is does not result from the communion that its human members have with Christ in common. Jenson writes, "The church is not a plurality of persons held together by common commitment, like a club or an interest group, not even when the commitment is to Christ."[89] Contrary, therefore, to both the trajectory of thought found in type 1, empirical ecclesiology, and the highly individualized theological accounts of what the church is proffered in and following the Reformation, the church, Jenson contends, is not constituted by the autonomous association of individual human wills. There is, without doubt, no church apart from the concrete coming together of individual Christian believers; but the human response to Christian faith evident in Christian believers coming together concretely is preceded by, and completely dependent on, the unmediated and antecedent will of God the Father and the economic work of the Holy Spirit. Jenson is clear: "*We* do not create our communion, moved by our—in itself very real—affinity. We receive one another with Christ and Christ with one another; we at once receive Christ

---

86. Jenson, *Systematic Theology*, 2:182 (emphasis original). To describe the communal spirit of the church as *identical* with God's Spirit, or to say that "the spirit of the church is the Holy Spirit himself," is contentious. Jenson, *Systematic Theology*, 2:196. The reader might worry that Jenson—like Moltmann—conflates the Holy Spirit so completely with the church's being that he risks denying the actuality of divine freedom that is, in fact, critical to the being of the church. The conflation is also made in relation to Jesus Himself: "All Christianity's talk of the Spirit unpacks one simple but drastic experience and claim: the spirit of the Christian community and the personal spirit of Jesus of Nazareth are the same." Jenson, *Visible Words*, 53.

87. See Jenson, *Unbaptized God*, 139.

88. Wood, "Robert Jenson's Ecclesiology," 180.

89. Jenson, *Systematic Theology*, 2:222.

and the church in which we receive him."[90] What is more, this christological reception that the Spirit mediates in accordance with God's eternal will, and by which the church becomes Christ's risen body and the triune communion of God is animated in the church's own life, is indexed by Jenson eucharistically.[91]

Only in the Eucharist, Jenson argues, does the church become what it truly is, because it is in the Eucharist that the Holy Spirit makes the church the risen body of Christ.[92] As the church narrates the story of God's work of salvation in Christ, and does so in the act of receiving broken bread and wine outpoured, the Holy Spirit actualizes in the church's own communal way of being the triune communion of God, such that the church is united ontologically to Christ's resurrected body.[93] In other words, in pointing *to* Christ, the church, according to Jenson, becomes—actually *is*—Christ;[94] that is, the church, and not only the Eucharist, is at once *signa* ("sign") and *res signata* ("the thing signified").[95] In this sense, the church, Jenson avers, is "the event of the remembered Jesus as the presence of the coming one."[96] But the church is this only at the site of the Eucharist. In Bulgakov's words, the Eucharist is "the realization of the body of the Church as the body of Christ."[97] Put otherwise, and in more formal eucharistic terms, only in **anamnesis** and **epiclesis** is the church freed from the constraints of its sociohistorical existence to be Christ's risen and returning body and thus "the gateway of creation's translation into God."[98] Without the work of the Holy Spirit, indeed without the explicit liturgical moment of the epiclesis, by which the eucharistic president summons God the Holy Spirit to come upon the elements of bread and wine and upon the gathered community of Christian believers, there is no church: "If the Spirit did not enliven the assembled church and rest upon the eucharistic elements," writes Jenson, "the risen Christ indeed would not be present."[99]

90. Jenson, *Systematic Theology*, 2:222 (emphasis original).
91. See Jenson, *Systematic Theology*, 2:211–27.
92. See Jenson, *Systematic Theology*, 2:220.
93. See Jenson, *Systematic Theology*, 2:226–27.
94. See Jenson, "The Church and the Sacraments," 212.
95. Classically, this is what a sacrament is in Christian theology. A sacrament consists of a visible sign—water, in the case of baptism, and bread and wine, in the case of the Eucharist—signifying effectively that which it is: the promise of God's grace. As Peter Lombard teaches, "A sacrament is properly so called because it is a sign of the grace of God and the expression of invisible grace; so it bears its image and is its cause." Lombard, *On the Doctrine of Signs*, 4. For a helpful introduction to the Christian sacraments, see Macquarrie, *Guide to the Sacraments*.
96. Jenson, *Systematic Theology*, 2:259.
97. Bulgakov, *Bride of the Lamb*, 287.
98. Jenson, *Systematic Theology*, 2:179.
99. Jenson, *Systematic Theology*, 2:257.

Only in the Eucharist, then, is the being of the church *as* communion actual: "The eucharist does not merely enable or manifest the communion we call church, it *is* that communion."[100] It is the Eucharist that constitutes what Jenson describes as "the ontological heart" of the church's sociohistorical existence, such that the church is the church only in the Eucharist.[101]

The Church as Eucharistic Communion

Jenson's pneumatologically indexed eucharistic determination of what the church is echoes the influential work of John D. Zizioulas. For Zizioulas, "The Church as a communion reflects God's being as communion."[102] Drawing, like Gunton, on the trinitarian and ontological tradition of the Cappadocian Fathers, Zizioulas understands the being of God by definition as a relational being: "God *is* trinitarian . . . a non-trinitarian God is not *koinonia* in his very being."[103] Or, as Zizioulas puts it elsewhere, "The substance of God, 'God,' has no ontological content, no true being, apart from communion."[104] The personal communion that exists between Father, Son, and Holy Spirit, then, becomes the basis for Zizioulas's speech about the church as *koinōnia*. The church, Zizioulas argues, exists in space and time as a "mode of existence" or "*way of being*" that corresponds directly to God's trinitarian being.[105] This is both self-evident, according to Zizioulas, and the consequence of the specific work of the Holy Spirit in the Eucharist.[106] In the Eucharist, it is the Spirit's work to constitute and express the mystery of the church's being as *koinōnia*. This programmatic point in Zizioulas's thought places his ecclesiology firmly in the tradition of the eucharistic ecclesiology developed by Nicholas Afanasiev.[107]

100. Jenson, "The Church and the Sacraments," 215 (emphasis original).
101. Jenson, *Systematic Theology*, 2:260.
102. Zizioulas, "Church as Communion," 8.
103. Zizioulas, "Church as Communion," 6.
104. Zizioulas, *Being as Communion*, 17.
105. Zizioulas, *Being as Communion*, 15 (emphasis original).
106. See Zizioulas, "Church as Communion," 6. Further, he writes, "Ecclesiology must be based on Trinitarian theology if it is to be an ecclesiology of communion." Zizioulas, "Church as Communion," 6.
107. See Afanasiev, *Church of the Holy Spirit*. The reader should note that while Zizioulas consciously places himself in this tradition, he is critical of what he perceives to be its tendency to prioritize in ecclesiology the local or parochial church over the catholic or universal church. See Zizioulas, *Being as Communion*, 23–25, 132–33. The question of whether Zizioulas's critique of Afanasiev is legitimate is, however, a moot one. On the rehabilitation of Afanasiev against Zizioulas, readers should see Wooden, "Eucharistic Ecclesiology of Nicolas Afanasiev," esp. 552; and Wooden, "Limits of the Church," 473–81.

For Afanasiev, the fullness of the church's being is found in the Eucharist precisely because the Holy Spirit creates in the elements of bread and wine *koinōnia* with "the full reality" of the body and blood of Jesus Christ.[108] "The Church," Afanasiev writes, "is where Christ is, but Christ is always present in the fullness of the unity of his Body in the Eucharist."[109] Christ, then, comes in the Eucharist in the Holy Spirit, and the church of the Holy Spirit is where the Eucharist is celebrated.[110] Further, that the church is *of* the Holy Spirit means that the *eschata* abide in the midst of the church as *Christ's* body.[111] Following the general trajectory of Afanasiev's thought here, and more basically the trajectory of Pauline pneumatology noted above, Zizioulas contends that the Holy Spirit is, therefore, "the *beyond* history" who brings into history the *eschata*.[112] In doing so, the Holy Spirit confronts the process of history both with its consummation and with its transformation, as the Spirit makes present now the conditions of what will be fully on the day of Christ's future parousia.[113] For Zizioulas, what is critical in this economic action of the Holy Spirit, by which the *eschata* are brought into history and the historical process is transformed, is that "the Spirit does not vivify a pre-existing structure; He *creates* one; He changes linear historicity into a *presence*."[114] What Zizioulas means by this is that the historical sequence of past, present, and future is synthesized and thereby transcended by the Spirit eschatologically. As Zizioulas writes, "The *arrabon* of the Kingdom which is the presence of the Spirit in history, signifies precisely the synthesis of the historical with the eschatological."[115] Further, he argues this moment of synthesis that is the Spirit's presence, and according to which history no longer is understandable in terms of past, present, and future, occurs archetypally in the Eucharist.[116] In the Eucharist, the extensive layers of sociohistorical existence are conjoined by the intensive action of the Holy Spirit and thus copresent.[117] Or, as Zizioulas himself describes it, in consequence of the li-

---

108. The point is made by Afanasiev in *The Lord's Supper*, published as Трапеза Господня (*Trapeza Gospodnia*) in 1952, and, as far as I am aware, is still today available only in Russian. I am indebted therefore to Anastacia K. Wooden for this reference. See Wooden, "Limits of the Church," 474.

109. Afanasiev, *Church of the Holy Spirit*, 4.

110. See Afanasiev, "Das allegemeine Priestertum in der orthodoxen Kirche," esp. 337.

111. See Afanasiev, *Church of the Holy Spirit*, 7.

112. Zizioulas, *Being as Communion*, 130 (emphasis original).

113. See Zizioulas, *Being as Communion*, 180.

114. Zizioulas, *Being as Communion*, 180 (emphasis original).

115. Zizioulas, *Being as Communion*, 186.

116. See Zizioulas, *Being as Communion*, 187–88.

117. I borrow the language of "extensity" and "intensity" from Hardy. See Hardy, *Finding the Church*, 243–44.

turgical epiclesis and the Spirit bringing the *eschata* into the present thereby, the church's anamnesis acquires "the *memory of the future.*"[118] The result of this acquisition is the recognition that the church's being itself resists any move to historicize completely what the church is as *the church.*[119] What the church is, is instead to be found in the sacramental coincidence of past and future; that is, in the history of Christ's first and final advents, which at once is present in the Eucharist by the work of the Holy Spirit.

What is more, this making present of Christ's past and future history is the precise work of the Spirit that enables the church to be a "*way of being*" or "mode of existence" that corresponds, according to Zizioulas, directly to God's own trinitarian being.[120] For it is only as the Holy Spirit transcends the linearity of history in the Eucharist eschatologically that the church in its sociohistorical existence acquires what Zizioulas describes alternatively as a "*eucharistic hypostasis.*"[121] In other words, in the Eucharist, because of the eschatological transcendence of past and future effected by the Spirit, the church is freed from the constraints of history by the presence of the *eschata* and given the taste of the eternal life of the Trinity.[122] And critically, here, not merely a *foretaste* of God's eternal life, but *the taste*: "In every [eucharistic] celebration, the Kingdom *in its entirety*," contends Zizioulas, "enters into history and is realized *here and now.*"[123] With the eternal life of God said to be realized entirely in every Eucharist, the church accordingly is set free in "eucharistic mysticism" to exist as the "image" (*eikōn*) of God's triune being.[124] Thus is the true being of the church made manifest. Indeed, only in the eucharistic epiclesis does the church become, by the action of the Holy Spirit, conjoined with the One who *is* "the image [*eikōn*] of the invisible God" (Col. 1:15). While the church's anamnesis therefore offers "the historic 'guarantee' of Christ's real presence" in the Eucharist, "the invocation of the Spirit is necessary for this presence to happen."[125] And in making the Christ-event in history happen, the Holy Spirit "makes real *at the same time* Christ's personal existence as a body or community."[126] As the Holy Spirit makes the eschaton real in the eucharistic epiclesis, then, the eucharistic anamnesis

---

118. Zizioulas, *Being as Communion*, 180 (emphasis original).

119. See Zizioulas, *Being as Communion*, 20.

120. Zizioulas, *Being as Communion*, 15 (emphasis original).

121. Zizioulas, *Being as Communion*, 59 (emphasis original).

122. See Zizioulas, *Being as Communion*, 21 and 188.

123. Zizioulas, "L'eucharistie: quelques aspects bibliques," 68n52 (emphasis original). I owe this reference to Miroslav Volf.

124. Zizioulas, *Communion and Otherness*, 297.

125. Zizioulas, *Communion and Otherness*, 295n33.

126. Zizioulas, *Being as Communion*, 111 (emphasis original).

becomes "a *re*-presentation"[127] of Christ's actual body, and the church the body *of Christ* thereby.

This becoming of the church as Christ's body by the action of the Holy Spirit is "so strong" or "complete," according to Zizioulas, that it actually negates any separation or distinction between Christ and the church.[128] In the Eucharist, church and Christ are identical, such that "Christology without ecclesiology is inconceivable"[129] and the church "is part of the definition of Christ."[130] The result of this identification—indeed, coinherence—of Christ and the church is that the church in its sociohistorical existence acquires its "*eucharistic hypostasis*," or what Zizioulas describes again alternatively as its "iconic" existence.[131] This existence enables the church's being to become in the Spirit an *eikōn* of the Trinity itself.[132] Volf, in light of his own discussion of Zizioulas's ecclesiology, puts the matter thus: "The Spirit unites the gathered congregation with the triune God and integrates it into a history extending from Christ, indeed, from the Old Testament saints, to the eschatological new creation. This Spirit-mediated relationship with the triune God and with the entire history of God's people—a history whose center resides in Jesus' own proclamation of the reign of God, in his death and in his resurrection—constitutes an assembly into a church."[133]

Indeed, for Zizioulas, that the *true* being of the church as the *eikōn* of God's trinitarian being is manifested in the Eucharist means that the church's being must be understood in two different dimensions. First, it must be understood as that which is instituted or "historically *given*."[134] The historical givenness of the church—its human empirical form, you might say—is seen in the concrete and particular *koinōnia* of God's people "coming together" (*epi to auto*; Acts 2:1 and 1 Cor. 11:20) to celebrate the Eucharist.[135] This "altogetherness" or "assembly," as Volf describes it in the quote above, can therefore be considered, in Alexander Schmemann's words, as "the first and

---

127. Zizioulas, *Being as Communion*, 161 (emphasis original).

128. Zizioulas, "Le mystère de l'église," 328 (my trans.). The French here reads, "Le Fils, le Christ, s'est identifié lui-même si fortement avec la communauté ecclésiale que toute séparation, ou même distinction . . . rendrait ces prières [eucharistiques] sans signification et sans fruit." The English version was published as "The Mystery of the Church in Orthodox Tradition."

129. Zizioulas, "Mystery of the Church," 299.

130. Zizioulas, "Ecclesiological Presuppositions," 68.

131. Zizioulas, "Mystery of the Church," 300.

132. See Zizioulas, "Pneumatological Dimension," 75–90, esp. 79.

133. Volf, *After Our Likeness*, 129.

134. Zizioulas, *Being as Communion*, 22 (emphasis original).

135. The Greek phrase "*epi to auto*" appears also in Matt. 22:34; Luke 17:35; Acts 1:15, 2:44, 4:26; and 1 Cor. 7:5, and 14:23. It emphasizes meeting or gathering all together in the same place or on the same ground.

basic" eucharistic act of the church, the purpose of which is "to reveal, to realize, the Church."[136] According to Schmemann, "When I say that I am going to church, it means I am going into the assembly of the faithful in order, together with them, *to constitute the Church.*"[137] Second, for Zizioulas, the church must be understood as *constituted* by the work of the Holy Spirit *in* the Eucharist—that is, the church is manifested as the Eucharist is celebrated, as that which "is constantly realized as an event of free communion, prefiguring the divine life and the Kingdom to come."[138] As Zizioulas goes on to write, "Christ and history give to the Church her being, which becomes *true being* each time that the Spirit con-stitutes the eucharistic community as Church."[139]

In Zizioulas's estimation, therefore, the church receives what might be described as its "biological" existence from the human social response to Christ's life, death, and resurrection in history. This "biological" existence is received as the people of God gather together to celebrate the Eucharist. However, this existence becomes what might be described as "ecclesial" existence (the church's *true* existence) only as the Holy Spirit constitutes the church as the *eikōn* of God's trinitarian being in the actual event of the eucharistic **synaxis.**[140] Understood in these two different dimensions, the church, then, "*constitutes the Eucharist while being constituted by it.*"[141] And the church without the Eucharist is not, therefore, the church.

That the church's being is conditioned exclusively by the pneumatological event of the Eucharist excludes in ecclesiological discourse any presupposition of the church's priority over the Eucharist.[142] Put otherwise, the Eucharist is not the liturgical event of an already existing church; rather, it is itself the event that constitutes the church's actual existence, "enabling the Church to *be*" as an *eikōn* of the Holy Trinity.[143] For Zizioulas, it is therefore a mistake in ecclesiological description to conceive of the Eucharist as a sacrament that is produced by an ontologically prior church, already instituted concretely and particularly.[144] The Eucharist is instead the liturgical event that

136. Schmemann, *Eucharist*, 11, 15.

137. Schmemann, *Eucharist*, 23 (emphasis original).

138. Zizioulas, *Being as Communion*, 22.

139. Zizioulas, *Being as Communion*, 22.

140. The church might be described in terms of these two modes of existence because Zizioulas employs the notion of a contrasting movement between "biological" and "ecclesial" existence first and foremost in his theological anthropology, and correspondingly in his understanding of the essence of Christian salvation. See Zizioulas, *Being as Communion*, 49–65.

141. Zizioulas, "Ecclesiological Presuppositions," 68 (emphasis original).

142. See Zizioulas, *Communion and Otherness*, 296; and Zizioulas, "Ecclesiological Presuppositions," 68.

143. Zizioulas, *Being as Communion*, 21.

144. See Zizioulas, "Ecclesiological Presuppositions," 68.

pneumatologically qualifies the ontology of the church per se. In Schmemann's words, "The Eucharist . . . [is] the very manifestation and *fulfilment* of the Church in all her power, sanctity and fulness."[145] To speak in ecclesiological description of the Holy Spirit enlivening or animating a church that already exists is thus likewise mistaken, argues Zizioulas. For in the Eucharist it is precisely the Holy Spirit who "makes the Church *be*."[146] And, critically, this making be "happens every time as a new event, *as if it did not have to happen*" in *each* eucharistic celebration: the *eschata* are realized by the Holy Spirit in the repeated event of the Eucharist itself, and thereby the eucharistic communion of God's gathered people ever again becomes the church.[147]

Communion Ecclesiology: An Assessment

Given the emphasis in communion ecclesiology on the church receiving its own true being from outside itself in consequence of the Holy Spirit realizing the *eschata* in the church's human empirical form, the reader might worry that communion ecclesiology is at risk of marginalizing what the church is as a sociohistorical reality. This is because the church's lived sociohistorical existence might be seen, in communion ecclesiology, to be nothing more than an "empty space" or "crater" (to borrow Karl Barth's provocative imagery) that is filled, so to speak, by the *eschata* occasionally—again and again—and thereby made to be the church by the pneumatologically and eucharistically mediated *koinōnia* of God's immanent trinitarian life.[148] There is thus a sense in which the being of the church—or at least the "true" being of the church—might be seen to be fleeting. Indeed, for Zizioulas, the church (in terms of its true identity at least) can only be thought of—in a fashion similar to the arguments of Jenson, Moltmann, and Gunton—as "an event that takes place ceaselessly anew."[149]

The worry, in other words, is that communion ecclesiology is open to the critique that it introduces into ecclesiological description what might be described as something of a problematic occasionalism. In communion ecclesiology, the church's "true" being is constituted or realized *only* as the Spirit

145. Schmemann, *Eucharist*, 24.

146. Zizioulas, *Being as Communion*, 132.

147. Zizioulas, *Communion and Otherness*, 295 (emphasis original).

148. In his commentary on Romans, Barth describes the relationship between the church and the gospel of God in terms that depict church activity as "no more than a crater formed by the explosion of a shell and seeks to be no more than a void in which the Gospel reveals itself." See Barth, *Epistle to the Romans*, 36.

149. Zizioulas, "Le Mystère de l'Église," 333 (my trans.). The French here reads, "L'Église est un événement qui a lieu sans cesse à nouveau, et non une société structurellement instituée de manière permanente."

works to mediate within the church's human empirical form the interpersonal *koinōnia* of God's triune life, and *only* as the Spirit does this prototypically in the Eucharist. This occasional emphasis in speech about the church might give the reader pause for thought, therefore, as to the extent to which it negates or diminishes the ability of communion ecclesiology to construe what the church is with *full* reference to its concrete and particular sociohistorical existence. To what extent, for example, can the "true" being of the church be said to exist in the time between eucharistic celebrations? Or similarly, to what extent can the church's "true" being be said to exist in the time between the moments when the *eschata* are realized in the human empirical form of the church by the Spirit's work?

Notwithstanding the desire to account in communion ecclesiology for the materiality of the church as it is in its sociohistorical existence, the risk of marginalizing the being of the church as a lived sociohistorical reality is thus a clear and present danger. In communion ecclesiology, there is, in fact, proportionately very little speech about the church's particular and concrete sociohistorical existence and lived ecclesial life. Irrespective of communion ecclesiology's rightly ordered desire to set ecclesiological description in relation to an account of divine agency indexed to God's triune being, the reader may wonder whether this type of ecclesiological approach is still not theologically disordered and disproportionate. After all, when confronted by the actual content of speech about the church in communion ecclesiology, the church's human empirical form is somewhat swallowed up by the thick theological account of God's own immanent life and economic work. Communion ecclesiology's account of divine agency indexed to the being of God as triune might then be seen to diminish or negate its ability to account adequately for the church as a sociohistorical reality and for how human empirical forms and church practices integrate with the work of God the Holy Spirit in bringing the church into being. This deficiency, in turn, places in doubt the ability of communion ecclesiology to perform successfully the basic ecclesiological task of holding together in speech about the church an account of both divine and human agency in which the former relativizes but does not minimize the latter. The reader might worry that, in direct contrast to type 2, performative ecclesiology, the account of the church that emerges in communion ecclesiology lacks an appropriate sense of theological order and proportion because its disproportionate emphasis on *divine* agency works not only to minimize human agency but in fact to marginalize it.

Further, the mode of accounting for the church's being subsequent to what often in communion ecclesiology is a social understanding of God's immanent trinitarian life might itself be seen to be theologically precarious. What I mean by this is that the use of social-trinitarian terms—such as "relation" and "re-lational," or "person" and "personal"—to help describe the immanent life of God as Father, Son, and Holy Spirit perhaps permits communion ecclesiology to move all too easily and freely between God's own being and the being of church, and to do so without first safeguarding adequately either the contingent nature of the church as a creature of God's grace or the church's unqualified difference from God's own immanent trinitarian life. Another way to put this is to say that, in the emphasis on the correspondence and even coinherence of the church's own communal way of being and the triune *koinōnia* of God, communion ecclesiology betrays in its speech about the church what John Webster describes as "a drift into divine immanence."[150] This drift is perhaps seen most clearly in the tendency of communion ecclesiology to overidentify the being of the church as Christ's body with Christ Himself.[151]

This tendency is such that, notwithstanding the explicit pneumatological qualification and eucharistic determination of what the church is, communion ecclesiology threatens to collapse the church into Christ without remainder, and thus to absorb the church as a sociohistorical human community into the person of Christ. As noted above, the identification between Christ and the church as Christ's body is, for Zizioulas, complete in the Eucharist. This completeness is such that "*all separation* between Christology and ecclesiology vanishes in the Spirit."[152] In Jenson's thought, the ontological identification of the church with either the body of God the Logos or the risen Christ's human body is likewise complete in the Eucharist. And, for Moltmann, the church in the Spirit's power is "the happening of Christ's presence."[153] This happening of Christ's presence that the church is means that Christ is the primary subject of both Christology and ecclesiology. "Every statement about the church," Moltmann avers, "will be a statement about Christ."[154] And

---

150. Webster, *Holiness*, 55. I explore Webster's ecclesiological thought in the articulation of type 4, ideal ecclesiology, in chap. 5.

151. The reader will note in what follows the absence of reference to Gunton as an example of this tendency. This is because there is a profound hesitation in Gunton's thought about using Paul's description of the church as the body of Christ. For Gunton, the doctrine of the ascension serves "to remind us that we are concerned with the absent Jesus." Gunton, "Christian Community and Human Society," 121. Jesus's absence—the fact that He is risen and ascended and, in the words of the Apostles' Creed, "seated at the right hand of the Father"—means that the church cannot claim automatically to be Christ's body: "The risen Lord is made present only by the Father's Spirit, and any institution claiming either in some sense automatically to mediate—let alone be—the presence of Christ or automatically to be in possession of the Spirit is in danger of subverting its own [pneumatological] constitution." Gunton, "Christian Community and Human Society," 122.

152. Zizioulas, *Being as Communion*, 111 (emphasis added).

153. Moltmann, *Church in the Power of the Spirit*, 122.

154. Moltmann, *Church in the Power of the Spirit*, 6.

thus, as Moltmann goes on to write, "Ecclesiology can only be developed from Christology, as its consequence and in correspondence with it."[155] This impulse in communion ecclesiology to coordinate ecclesiology, ultimately, with Christology (either to the point of coinherence or otherwise), and the associated overidentification of the church as Christ's body with Christ Himself (to a greater or lesser extent), is perhaps best reflected in the words of Avis, echoing the claim of Origen of Alexandria: "If Jesus Christ is *autobasileia*, the kingdom itself, he is also *autoekklēsia*, the church itself."[156]

To suggest such coinherence of Christ and the church as these words of Avis and the arguments of Moltmann, Jenson, and Zizioulas do is, to one extent or another, certainly to display in speech about the church the drift into divine immanence that Webster fears. The reader might worry, further, that this drift in fact threatens to collapse—notwithstanding Gunton's appeal to the indirect nature of the correspondence between triune *koinōnia* and ecclesial communion—the ontological distinction between God and that which is not God. The drift is such that the overidentification of the church as Christ's body with Christ Himself might even risk denying the contingent nature of the church as a creature of God's grace. It might also risk collapsing the transcendence of God in the risen and ascended Jesus Christ into the immanence of the church's human empirical form. Where type 2, performative ecclesiology, may treat ecclesiology too independently from a doctrine of God, the worry here is that communion ecclesiology associates its doctrine of the church too closely with a doctrine of God. It is this worry that, in part, motivates the fourth type of contemporary approach to ecclesiology that this book seeks to articulate in its fivefold typology of contemporary approaches to ecclesiology. But before turning in the next chapter to the articulation of type 4, ideal ecclesiology, a corollary of this worry in relation to communion ecclesiology should be registered in order to underscore these points.

The subclause on ecclesiology in the Nicene Creed, "We believe one holy catholic and apostolic Church," emerges under the clause on the person and work of the Holy Spirit: "We believe in the Holy Spirit, the Lord, the giver of life." The subclause on ecclesiology does not emerge under the clause on the person and work of Jesus Christ ("We believe in one Lord, Jesus Christ, the only Son of God").[157] To determine or coordinate ecclesiology christologically

155. Moltmann, *Church in the Power of the Spirit*, 66.
156. Avis, *Theological Foundations*, 1:212; see also 1:45. Origen, as Avis notes, is the first to suggest that Jesus is the kingdom in person (*autobasileia*).
157. For more on this point, see Emerton, "Jesus Christ: The Centre of the Church," 244–46; and Emerton, *God's Church-Community*, 64. Quotations from the Nicene Creed have been taken from the Archbishops' Council, *Common Worship*, 173. The subclause on ecclesiology

is thus, creedally speaking, to mislocate the doctrine of the church under the second article of the creed. The doctrine properly falls under the third article. What is more, scripturally speaking, the narrative of the Acts of the Apostles (specifically, Acts 2) gives witness to the creation of the church as a sociohistorical human community not by Jesus Christ but by the coming of God the Holy Spirit at Pentecost. As F. F. Bruce writes, "The Holy Spirit, promised by the Lord, . . . comes upon the disciples on the Day of Pentecost." The Spirit enables them "to speak with tongues, to proclaim the Good News with convicting effect and to perform 'signs and wonders' in the Name of Christ, and, above all, uniting them into one Body, the Church."[158]

To be sure, Jesus certainly is the *foundation* of the church: the church, after all, is chosen in Christ from and for all eternity (Eph. 1:4); and the foundational truth upon which the church is built, as Bruce notes, is that God has made the crucified Jesus both Lord and Messiah (Acts 2:36).[159] But, as Avis well establishes, Jesus is not the *founder* of the church.[160] In Avis's words, "Jesus had no intention of 'founding' a church of any kind."[161] At least, Jesus did not intend or foresee the organization or institution of the church that came after his announcement of God's kingdom.[162] The sociohistorical human community that the church is—and in whatever institutional or organizational form it orders itself—is founded at Pentecost by God the Holy Spirit. Following the witness of Acts 2 and the dogmatic trajectory delineated by the creed, the church is the creation of the Holy Spirit of God. It is the Holy Spirit who is the founder of the church, *not* Jesus Christ. Thus, the reader might worry that an overidentification of the being of the church as Christ's body with Christ Himself, amounting to a determination of ecclesiology christologically—as in communion ecclesiology—will occlude this central dogmatic truth. It is this worry that, in part, motivates the fifth type of contemporary approach to ecclesiology that this book seeks to articulate in its fivefold typology of contemporary approaches to ecclesiology. But before turning to that articulation in chapter 6, I will turn to an articulation and assessment of type 4, ideal ecclesiology.

---

has been modified by omitting the creedal preposition *in* because of the argument rehearsed in chap. 1, note 19.

158. Bruce, *Acts of the Apostles*, 30. I explore the significance of Acts 2 for any consideration of what the church is further in the articulation of type 5, ecclesiological ecclesiology, in chap. 6.

159. See Bruce, *Acts of the Apostles*, 96.

160. See Avis, *Theological Foundations*, 1:13–81.

161. Avis, *Theological Foundations*, 1:77.

162. See Avis, *Theological Foundations*, 1:77. My turn of phrase here recalls the oft-quoted sentiment of Alfred Loisy who, in his 1902 work, *L'Évangile et l'Église*, writes, "Jesus announced the kingdom, and it was the church that came." Loisy, *The Gospel and the Church*, 145.

5

Ideal Ecclesiology

As I noted in the previous chapter, the fourth type of contemporary approach to ecclesiology that this book seeks to articulate is motivated, in part, by a concern to guard ecclesiological description against drifting into divine immanence, and thereby associating ecclesiology too closely with a doctrine of God. Put alternatively, in ideal ecclesiology a theology of God's aseity works against the overidentification or conflation of the church's being with the triune *koinōnia* of God, and thereby against a social-trinitarian frame of reference in which ecclesial sociality is seen to be like the sociality of God's immanent life as Father, Son, and Holy Spirit. In ideal ecclesiology, there is thus a desire to safeguard in speech about the church both the contingent nature of the church per se and the non-necessity of creation, as expressions of the doctrine of *creatio ex nihilo*.[1]

This desire itself is derivative, however, of a more fundamental concern to establish in ecclesiological description a normative and necessary foundation for ecclesiology per se. In contrast to type 3, communion ecclesiology—and to both type 2, performative ecclesiology, and type 1, empirical ecclesiology— what is methodologically paramount in ideal ecclesiology is an account of divine agency indexed to a theology of God's aseity. In other words, in ideal ecclesiology, the tendency in contemporary approaches to ecclesiology to attend either to the church's human empirical form or to the life and work of God is stated as an explicit methodological claim in order to make a theology of God's aseity the normative and necessary foundation of any and all speech

---

1. See "Church and Covenant," in chap. 1 above.

about the church. It is for this reason that communion ecclesiology might be seen—as I noted in the introduction—as a soft form of ideal ecclesiology.

In ideal ecclesiology, theologians speak properly of what the church is only if they attend *first* to the immanent life and economic work of God and thereby set their speech about the church under a doctrine of God and God's gracious acts. For in ideal ecclesiology, theologians set their ecclesiological descriptions categorically against the prevailing tide of contemporary ecclesiological accounts in which the church's human empirical form is considered to be either the normative and necessary foundation of all ecclesiological speech (as it is in empirical ecclesiology) or the proper object of such speech (as it is in performative ecclesiology). Ideal ecclesiology instead seeks to treat God's immanent life and economic work as the proper object of speech about the church and thereby to account fully for the church as a creature of God's grace. It is from this foundation that theologians will best understand the church's being and have proper grounds for accounting theologically, in an ordered and proportionate way, for what the church is. In the field of contemporary ecclesiology, this type of approach is perhaps evidenced most obviously by the ecclesiology of John Webster.

The Church as Movement Moved by God

In what might be seen as a summary statement of his ecclesiological thought, Webster writes, "A theology of the church is not simply a phenomenology of ecclesial social history but an inquiry into that history's ontological ground in the being and works of the church's God."[2] Or, as he puts it elsewhere, "The church is not constituted by human intentions, activities and institutional or structural forms, but by the action of the triune God, realized in Son and Spirit."[3] The doctrine of the church is thus an extension of the doctrine of God, and ecclesiological description must be wholly referred to speech about God's being and action. This is because the subject matter of Christian theology itself is most properly "God, and everything else *sub specie divinitatis*."[4] That all things other than God have their being relative to God and therefore are understandable only "from the standpoint of divinity" (*sub specie divinitatis*) ensures that Christian doctrine as a whole, and any

2. Webster, "'In the Society of God,'" 200.
3. Webster, *Word and Church*, 195.
4. Webster, *Holy Scripture*, 43. Webster echoes here the thought of Thomas Aquinas who proposed that the subject matter of theology is God and all things understood as being in relation to God, as their beginning and end. See Aquinas, *Summa Theologica*, 1.1.3, 1.90.3.

individual doctrine apart from the doctrine of God, is seen by Webster as a corollary of the doctrine of God exclusively. What needs to be said about the being of the church, therefore, must be drawn from God's own triune life as the principal topic of Christian doctrine.[5] In Webster's own words, "A doctrine of the church is only as good as the doctrine of God which underlies it."[6] Theologians cannot, then, work toward their accounts of the church inductively, from ethnographic investigations of the church's human empirical forms. Rather, they must arrive at their accounts from "Trinitarian deduction."[7]

In describing this deduction, Webster is careful to distinguish his work from the deductive methodology of social trinitarianism and, in particular, from the kind of trinitarianism that enables an analogy to be drawn between the relations of Father, Son, and Holy Spirit in God's immanent trinitarian life and the church community, and to see the former as "echoed" in the latter.[8] This echo, and the analogy on which it is predicated, is problematic, Webster contends, because it fails to safeguard adequately the contingent nature of the church and its unqualified difference from God's own life.[9] Consequently, he writes, "The connection between theology proper and ecclesiology is best explicated not by setting out two terms of an analogy but by describing a sequence of divine acts both in terms of their ground in the immanent divine being and in terms of their creaturely fruits."[10] This sequence of divine acts Webster describes in three moves.[11] First, the church exists because of the loving intent of God the Father, who eternally begets the eternal Son and (with the Son) spirates the eternal Spirit; and who purposes in love, "before the creation of the world" (Eph. 1:4), creaturely and ecclesial existence as a reality other than God the Holy Trinity. Second, the church exists because this divine purpose is effected in space and time through the eternally begotten Son taking flesh obediently and acting as reconciler of sinful creatures, thereby restoring their fellowship with God. God's purpose for fellowship with God's creatures is then realized, third, by the Holy Spirit: the Holy Spirit consummates the incarnate Son's reconciling work, completing the works

5. See Webster, *God without Measure*, 1:4.

6. Webster, "On Evangelical Ecclesiology," 12.

7. Webster, "'In the Society of God,'" 205.

8. Webster, "'In the Society of God,'" 206. See chap. 4, on communion ecclesiology, for a fuller description of this view.

9. See Webster, "'In the Society of God,'" 206. For Webster this critique also applies with equal force to ecclesiologies that affirm the *totus Christus*. See Webster, "'In the Society of God,'" 206.

10. Webster, "'In the Society of God,'" 205. See the glossary for a definition of **theology proper**.

11. See Webster, "'In the Society of God,'" 207–13.

of God toward God's creatures by enabling those creatures to attain their proper end as God's children and further enabling the church to take human empirical form. As Webster puts it, "Through the Spirit it comes about that there exists a temporal, cultural, bodily reality in fulfilment of the divine appointment: 'You shall be my people.'"[12] The very possibility of the church's being is therefore deduced by Webster from this threefold movement, which he describes as the "self-moved" life of God.[13]

Only after describing God's self-movement both apart from the world, in the eternal relations of paternity, filiation, and **spiration**, and in the world, through Christ and the Holy Spirit, can theologians turn to consider the being of the church in its sociohistorical existence.[14] Webster thus seeks to secure that "ecclesiology has its place in the flow of Chistian doctrine from teaching about God to teaching about everything else in God."[15] And only after securing the primacy of **theology proper** in ecclesiological description in this way does Webster proceed to consider the church's human empirical form. For Webster, it is clearly important that, in their speech about the church, theologians do indeed proceed in this way. He writes, however, "This emphasis on the priority of divine action over the church as an act of human association should not be allowed to eclipse the 'visibility' of the church."[16]

Webster's account of the church's visibility proceeds in relation both to the fundamental forms by which the church is structured in its sociohistorical existence as movement moved by God, and to the modes of action that characterize the church as such. With respect to the former, Webster notes (by way of example), first, that the church is a form of association or human assembly "in the Lord" (*en kyriō*; Eph. 2:21); second, that this assembly is gathered by and around the divine Word to hear Holy Scripture and Christ's address in it; and third, that the gathered assembly exists in a distinctive order administered, primarily, by Scripture and the sacraments but, derivatively, by creeds and confessions, canon law, and a publicly authorized ministry, which together sanctify lived ecclesial life.[17] Typical of the modes of action that characterize the church as a human assembly "in the Lord" is that the acts of the church are creaturely, excessive, and obscure: creaturely, because

12. Webster, "'In the Society of God,'" 213.
13. Webster, "'In the Society of God,'" 206.
14. While it is commonplace in Christian theology to appropriate particular outward works of God to particular persons of the Godhead (the doctrine of appropriations), the Trinity acts in the world indivisibly as one divine being. This is affirmed in the Latin axiom *opera Trinitatis ad extra indivisa sunt* ("the works of God on the outside are indivisible").
15. Webster, "'In the Society of God,'" 205.
16. Webster, *Word and Church*, 196.
17. See Webster, "'In the Society of God,'" 216–20.

divine agency is their efficient and sustaining cause; excessive, because, in their creatureliness, they point beyond themselves to God's own triune life; and obscure, because, in pointing beyond themselves, ecclesial acts necessarily display their divine causality with ambiguity.[18] For Webster, the church's human empirical form and its modes of action are thus visible only spiritually.[19] This means that what the church is, "is not exhausted in its phenomenal surface, because the church is constituted by the presence and action of God 'who is invisible' (Heb. 11:27)."[20] More specifically, "The 'phenomenal' form of the church is . . . the phenomenal form of the *church* only in reference to the Spirit's self-gift."[21] Only by the perfecting work of the Holy Spirit do the fundamental forms of ecclesial life and the modes of action that characterize it come to indicate God's presence, and thereby constitute the church as a sociohistorical reality.[22]

Put otherwise, and in more formal terms, the sociohistorical phenomena of the church do not constitute what the church is *ex opere operato*—that is, simply by virtue of the work of those phenomena having been performed or done, as it were. Such is the force of Paul's *en kyriō* in Ephesians 2:21: only "in the Lord" is the church constituted as *the church*; and only because of the agency of the Holy Spirit as Lord and giver of life can the church's fundamental forms and modes of action be known as phenomena *of the church*.[23] As Webster writes, "'in the Lord' (Eph. 2:21)" is "no mere rhetorical flourish through which the ethnographer penetrates to some more primary natural level," but is rather "metaphysically irreducible."[24] Consequently, the spiritual visibility of the church means that the church's being is known only through the eyes of Christian faith, in the knowledge that comes in the wake of divine revelation, and according to which "the church steps out of the obscurity and indefiniteness of an historical phenomenon and becomes fully and properly visible as the creature of the Spirit."[25]

Webster's primary concern in all of this is thus to deny that in ecclesiological description "the real is the social-historical" and "the church is the people of God because certain events occur within a group of human beings."[26]

18. See Webster, "'In the Society of God,'" 214–16.
19. See Webster, "'In the Society of God,'" 215–16; see also Webster, "On Evangelical Ecclesiology," 24–34.
20. Webster, "'In the Society of God,'" 215.
21. Webster, "On Evangelical Ecclesiology," 26 (emphasis original).
22. See Webster, "On Evangelical Ecclesiology," 26–27.
23. See Webster, "On Evangelical Ecclesiology," 27.
24. Webster, "'In the Society of God,'" 217.
25. Webster, "On Evangelical Ecclesiology," 27.
26. Webster, "'In the Society of God,'" 202.

The causal ordering in these two ecclesiological convictions is dogmatically flawed, Webster contends; it is flawed because the ordering confuses what Webster describes as "the proximate *res* of ecclesiology" with its "principal *res*"[27]—that is, it confuses the church's human empirical form with God's immanent life and economic work, treating the former as the proper object of ecclesiological speech.

Webster sees this ecclesiological confusion as a symptom of "severe *doctrinal* disarray" in the discipline of Christian theology itself.[28] The disarray is evident in presentations of Christian theology whose material doctrinal content is "seriously under-determined" by the Christian doctrine of God.[29] These result from the discipline's "failure of theological nerve" in the context of the modern Western university.[30] Webster writes, "The theological disciplines have, in effect, been 'de-regionalized,' that is, they have been pressed to give an account of themselves in terms drawn largely from fields of enquiry other than theology, fields which, according to prevailing criteria of academic propriety more nearly approximate to ideals of rational activity."[31] The result of this rise in "de-regionalization" is the decline of what Webster describes as "theological theology," or a working understanding of the discipline's proximate and principal objects. Webster summarizes the resultant confusion thus: "Since the object of Christian theology is the *economy* of God's works as creator and reconciler of humankind, then theology should naturally direct its attention to the *temporal and social* as the sphere of God's presence and activity."[32]

The assumption that God's outward works in the world are the proper object of Christian theology leads to the conclusion that what is social and temporal is causal—a conclusion that, in turn, funds ethnographic investigation of the church's human empirical form on the basis of the mistaken belief that the social and temporal *is* what is "real" about the church. And the belief is mistaken because that which is social and temporal exists only *ex nihilo*. As Webster writes, "Time and society are derivative realities, and that derivation is not simply a matter of their origination; it is a permanent mark of their historical condition."[33] What "the real" is in ecclesiological description is not the sociohistorical; it is instead the triune life of God as creator, sustainer, and reconciler of derivative, or creaturely, reality.

27. Webster, "'In the Society of God,'" 202. The Latin noun *res* means the object or subject matter of something.
28. Webster, *Holy Scripture*, 11 (emphasis original).
29. Webster, *Holy Scripture*, 11.
30. Webster, "Theological Theology," 17.
31. Webster, "Theological Theology," 22.
32. Webster, "'In the Society of God,'" 202–3 (emphasis added).
33. Webster, "'In the Society of God,'" 203.

For Webster, Paul's assertion in 2 Corinthians 5:18 that "all this is from God [*de panta ek tou theou*]" is a signal and "utterly proximate" one; "It does not merely furnish the ultimate backcloth against which other more immediate or available or manageable realities may stand out in relief."[34] The effective force of Paul's *ek tou theou* indeed requires theologians to offer "most of all" in their speech about the church a theology of God's aseity as it manifests itself in God's work of creation, reconciliation, and redemption.[35] Created reality—including the reality of the church—is neither self-generated nor self-sustaining; it has its being as a gift "from God." Only because God as Father, Son, and Holy Spirit moves Godself to establish a reality other than the immanent trinitarian life by gracious economic action does created reality and the reality of the church exist.[36] To study this reality, then, "it is necessary first to study the one by whom it comes to be."[37] Webster is insistent: in both theological inquiry and ecclesiological description, theologians must speak of God as agent *before* anything else.[38]

To index speech about the church to the doctrine of God in this way is to set ecclesiological description firmly under "the metaphysics of grace."[39] This means that, absent the specific order whereby a theology of God's aseity and an account of divine agency is methodologically paramount in ecclesiology, any account of what the church is will fail to attain its proper object. Indeed, absent such order, ecclesiological description misperceives the divine motion to which it must be directed and thereby is deficient in its account of the human empirical form of the church as movement moved by God.[40] What is more, this means that if speech about the church is to obtain its proper object, it must be subject, Webster contends, to "a proper hierarchical arrangement" of two different types of investigation: first, a dogmatic type that investigates "the principal *res*" of ecclesiology and offers an account of the church from trinitarian deduction; second, a phenomenological type that investigates (in the light of the first account) ecclesiology's "proximate *res*" and concerns itself with the church's human empirical form.[41]

It is critical for Webster that in any speech about the church the first type of investigation precedes *and* governs the second type. By respecting this hierarchy of method, theologians resist presenting what Webster describes

34. Webster, *Word and Church*, 215.
35. Webster, *Word and Church*, 215.
36. See Webster, "On Evangelical Ecclesiology," 17–18.
37. Webster, *God without Measure*, 1:9.
38. See Webster, "Theological Theology," 23.
39. Webster, "'In the Society of God,'" 203.
40. See Webster, "'In the Society of God,'" 221.
41. Webster, "'In the Society of God,'" 221.

as "naturalized ecclesiology."[42] In "naturalized ecclesiology," or what I have described as type 1, empirical ecclesiology, the second (phenomenological) type of investigation either interrupts or overtakes the first (dogmatic) type. Or results from the second type are understood to be synonymous with those of the first. Either way, "naturalized ecclesiology" relegates the proper object of ecclesiology to the shadows, says Webster, and fails to have particular concern for what ecclesiological description most properly should articulate: the fundamental priority of God's immanent life and economic work for accounting for what the church is, and thus the asymmetry of divine and human agency in the church's being.[43]

The Church as the Peaceful Time of God

Webster's resounding call for a more theological ecclesiology that is clearly and methodologically set under the **metaphysics** of God's grace is without doubt expressed by others in contemporary approaches to ecclesiology. For example, Webster's concern that theological inquiry and ecclesiological description have both been "de-regionalized," and therefore need to be re-regionalized, is reminiscent of what John Milbank describes as the tendency of nontheological disciplines to "polic[e] the sublime."[44] For Milbank, the very pathos of Christian theology as a discipline is indeed its "false humility" before the analytical and critical gaze of social-scientific fields of inquiry.[45] This humility, says Milbank, is in fact "a fatal disease," because it positions Christian theology relative to secular reason; by being so positioned, Christian theology surrenders its claim as a meta-discourse that positions all other discourses, and secular reason becomes its "ultimate organizing logic."[46] Milbank's move "beyond secular reason" in theological inquiry is motivated, therefore, by his desire to make it clear that no reality—not least sociohistorical reality—is more real than the theological, and to claim, derivatively, that Christian theology *is* "the discourse of non-mastery."[47] To suppose that the critical tools of social-scientific analysis are better equipped than theology to make sense of, or speak more authoritatively about, sociohistorical reality is thus a denial of God as creator and a denial of theological truth thereby.[48] Milbank writes, "Either it idolatrously con-

42. Webster, "'In the Society of God,'" 221.
43. See Webster, *Word and Church*, 195–96.
44. Milbank, *Theology and Social Theory*, 101.
45. Milbank, *Theology and Social Theory*, 1.
46. Milbank, *Theology and Social Theory*, 1.
47. Milbank, *Theology and Social Theory*, 6.
48. See Milbank, *Theology and Social Theory*, 390.

nects knowledge of God with some particular immanent field of knowledge—
'ultimate' cosmological causes, or 'ultimate' psychological and subjective needs.
Or else it is confined to intimations of a sublimity beyond representation, so
functioning to confirm negatively the questionable idea of an autonomous
secular realm, completely transparent to rational understanding."[49]

For Milbank, there is no secular realm that is completely transparent to
rational understanding because there is no realm that is autonomous of God
and God's gracious acts as creator. There is, in other words, no vantage point
from which secular reason can take priority over Christian theology that
would require Christian theology to either submit to the social sciences or
borrow diagnoses of sociohistorical reality from those social-scientific disciplines.[50] Another way to put this is to say, as Milbank does, that there can be
only "*theology, tout court*"[51]—that is, theology and nothing else, theology
that stands "as a gaze at once above, but also alongside, (with or against)
other, inherited human gazes,"[52] and thus without mediation or qualification
by nontheological fields of inquiry. And this is true especially when it comes
to accounting for what the church is.

Taking up Augustine's distinction between the *civitas terrena* (the "earthly
city") and the *civitas Dei* (the "city of God"), Milbank develops his account
of what the church is in light of his desire to move "beyond secular reason,"
but in relation to what he understands as two competing orders of being that
mark created reality: an earthly ontology of violence and a heavenly ontology of peace.[53] The former Milbank associates with life lived strictly within
the confines of human agency. It is an order of being marked by self-love and
self-assertion, and therefore by violent power over others—by sin, in other
words. The earthly ontology of violence is thus synonymous, ultimately, with
life lived in denial of God. In contrast, Milbank associates the latter (ontology
of peace) with life lived in acceptance of God. This life is liberated from sin
and its violent succession of power, domination, and pride, and thus is open
to divine agency and ordered according to God's peaceful reign and rule. This
way of being in peace and its way of working in the world to harmonize all
difference in the knowledge of "the fact that there is a true way for things to
be and a way things eternally are"[54] is what Milbank calls "church."[55] The

49. Milbank, *Theology and Social Theory*, 1.
50. See Milbank, *Theology and Social Theory*, 250–53.
51. Milbank, *Theology and Social Theory*, 251 (emphasis original).
52. Milbank, *Theology and Social Theory*, 253.
53. See Milbank, *Theology and Social Theory*, 391–95.
54. Milbank, "Ecclesiology," 136; see also 105–37.
55. Milbank, *Theology and Social Theory*, 394.

question of the church, therefore, is the question of "collective peace"[56]—or, as he conceives it elsewhere, the question of "the assembly of humanity as such in order that it might govern itself in love."[57] This peaceful consensus that is the church is established, however, only by the truth of Christ as the Word of God, and as this truth is revealed and given to humanity as the Holy Spirit's self-gift of peace.[58]

The peace that is the church is not, then, a peace that human agency is able to construct or achieve, according to Milbank; it is instead a peace that is already and divinely given.[59] And, for Milbank, this peace is "given, super-abundantly, in the breaking of bread by the risen Lord, which assembles the harmony of the peoples then and at every subsequent eucharist."[60] Paradoxi-cally, however, the peace that God gives superabundantly in the Eucharist as a gift to be received is not a peace that is realized upon reception. This is because "the body and blood of Christ only exist in the mode of gift, and they can *be* gift (like any gift) only as traces of the giver and promise of future provision from the same source."[61] There is, then, a promissory aspect to the ontology of peace that God establishes as the church on the site of the Eucharist, one that necessitates its outworking by the church in the world. The Eucharist, Milbank avers, positions us "as fed" and "assimilates us to the food we eat, so that we, in turn, must exhaust ourselves as nourishment for others."[62] The church, then, is composed of those "who, unrecorded, have gone away from receiving the Eucharist and loved and forgiven their neighbour."[63] In doing so, the church embodies a peaceful ontology in the world that "re-articulates [Christ's] earthly performance" and foreshadows the realized peace of God's eternal reign.[64] To be and to begin to realize this peace, however, requires re-ception of the Eucharist itself, and thereby the peaceful self-gift of the Holy Spirit who gifts the truth of Christ to humanity as the divine power necessary for the church to be *the church*.

56. Milbank, "Ecclesiology," 109.
57. Milbank, "Stale Expressions," 273.
58. See Milbank, "Ecclesiology," 106.
59. See Milbank, "Enclaves," esp. 342.
60. Milbank, "Enclaves," 342.
61. Milbank, "Enclaves," 342 (emphasis original).
62. Milbank, "Enclaves," 342.
63. Milbank, "On Theological Transgression," 168. It is for this reason that Milbank (some-what ironically) rejects the idea that the church should move out into or toward the world: "The idea that the Church should 'plant' itself in various sordid and airless interstices of our contemporary world, instead of calling people to "come to church," is wrong-headed, because the refusal to come out of oneself and *go to* church is simply the refusal of Church *per se*." Milbank, "Stale Expressions," 271.
64. Milbank, "Enclaves," 342.

In Milbank's account of what the church is, there is thus a clear sense in which the source of the church is the Eucharist. The church, Milbank writes, "is not a given, but arrives endlessly, in passing,"[65] and it does so "on the site of the eucharist."[66] Critically, however, and again paradoxically, the site of the Eucharist is itself "not a site, since it suspends presence in favour of memory and expectation."[67] What Milbank means by this is that the Eucharist remembers the peace that God gives in the body and blood of Jesus Christ (Rom. 5:1), but ceaselessly expects the Holy Spirit's self-gift to realize this peace in the world until "the Lord of peace" (2 Thess. 3:16) comes again in glory. Accordingly, the church exists, Milbank maintains, not as "an ideal *presence* real or imagined," but as "something more like an 'ideal transmission' through time," or "serious fiction,"[68] enacted eucharistically. The church most truly is not, then, a site that is spatially identifiable in sociohistorical existence, in the sense of being a physical place at which one might arrive;[69] rather, "the Church, like grace, is everywhere," says Milbank.[70] Indeed, as an ontology of peace and its outworking in the world, the church exists "not in time, but *as* time."[71] And, more specifically, it exists as the transmission through time of what is perhaps best described as *peaceful* time—a time of "gift and promise,"[72] one that arrives endlessly in (receiving) the Eucharist and derivatively in the eucharistic practice of loving and forgiving one's neighbor.

That the church's being is said by Milbank to arrive endlessly in this way does not mean, however, that the church is not able to be located as a sociohistorical reality. While the church is (like grace) "everywhere" and thus endlessly arriving, "it also truly is in all its physicality and placement in *cathedrae*."[73] Given this, says Milbank, ecclesiological description must be "rigorously concerned with the actual genesis of real historical churches, not simply with the imagination of an ecclesial ideal."[74] This then requires that theologians be concerned with offering what Milbank describes as "critical narratives of the (endless) genesis of the Church," as well as "judicious

---

65. Milbank, "Ecclesiology," 105.
66. Milbank, "Enclaves," 341.
67. Milbank, "Enclaves," 342.
68. Milbank, "Enclaves," 342 (emphasis original).
69. See Milbank, "Enclaves," 341.
70. Milbank, "Grace," 138.
71. Milbank, "Enclaves," 342 (emphasis added).
72. Milbank, "Enclaves," 342.
73. Milbank, "Ecclesiology," 135. How this claim and the prior metaphysical claim are both true *at once* remains somewhat unspecified in Milbank's thought, however.
74. Milbank, *Theology and Social Theory*, 380.

narratives of ecclesial happenings."[75] These judicious narratives—which Milbank admits to being "rather minimal"[76] in his own ecclesiological thought (at least as he developed it in *Theology and Social Theory*)—can never be complete, however. This is not only because Milbank's endlessly arriving church exists in passing, but because the church exists in this way as a result of God's prior sacramental and gracious action. This action of God itself demands in ecclesiological description what Douglas Farrow describes as an "epistemological rebound,"[77] a negative **epistemological** moment, you might say, that arises in consequence of the fact that there is something more to the church's being than its human empirical form.

For Farrow, this something more results from the Eucharist itself—or, more precisely, from the central christological paradox that the Eucharist introduces, and according to which the church ever again becomes the body of Christ.[78] In the Eucharist, the body and blood of Jesus Christ exist by the Holy Spirit's self-gift as both present and absent. In the words of Joseph Ratzinger, the church is "received from a source where she already exists and really exists: from the sacramental communion of [Christ's] Body as it makes its way through history."[79] To recall Milbank's language, Christ's body and blood exist in the mode of gift and promise: in the Eucharist, "the Church is always about to receive again its own body from without."[80] Therefore, the being of the church, because the church receives its own *true* being into itself from outside itself "is *defined*," says Milbank, "by its surplus over itself."[81] Or as Henri de Lubac puts it, "By her very essence," the church "carries herself, as it were, above herself."[82] Thus, as Farrow writes (affirming what Roman Catholic theology has long maintained), "The church itself is established only by 'the upwards call of God in Christ Jesus,' and that call is made concrete precisely in the eucharistic liturgy. *Sursum corda!* is the cry that heralds the possibility of ecclesial being, and to that possibility ecclesiology is naturally bound."[83]

75. Milbank, "Enclaves," 343, 344.
76. Milbank, "Enclaves," 344.
77. Farrow, *Ascension and Ecclesia*, 6.
78. See Farrow, *Ascension and Ecclesia*, 3.
79. Ratzinger, *Church, Ecumenism, and Politics*, 20.
80. Milbank, "On Theological Transgression," 166.
81. Milbank, "On Theological Transgression," 166 (emphasis added).
82. De Lubac, *Church*, 27.
83. Farrow, *Ascension and Ecclesia*, 2. See the glossary for a definition of *sursum corda*. In de Lubac's words, "Literally speaking, therefore, the Eucharist makes the Church. It makes of it an inner reality. By its hidden power, the members of the body come to unite themselves by becoming more fully members of Christ, and their unity with one another is part and parcel of their unity with the one single Head." De Lubac, *Corpus Mysticum*, 88.

The Church as the (Unmakeable) Mystery of God

To be bound in speech about the church to this eucharistic possibility is to admit that the church's being participates in what Emil Brunner once described as "the special character of the holy, the numinous, the supernatural, in the hallowing presence of God."[84] In other words, it is to admit that the church's being participates in God's being to such an extent that—perfectly united to Christ as Christ's body—the being of the church can be said to be "all-holy and all-sanctifying."[85] To be bound to this eucharistic possibility is, further, to admit that the church's being is neither determined by, nor reducible to, its own human empirical form. The moment that ecclesiological description attends only to this form, to that which is "publicly accessible," as Farrow puts it, ecclesiology becomes divorced from both its divine foundation and its actual possibility: God's gracious and sacramental action. In fact, at this moment, says Farrow, ecclesiological labors "cease to be churchly and hence to be Christian."[86] For ecclesiology to be bound to this eucharistic possibility of ecclesial being is to admit ultimately, then, that the church, as Brunner insisted, is "unintelligible from a purely sociological standpoint."[87] In point of fact, the church is intelligible only when theologians seek to understand it with reference to what T. F. Torrance describes as its "dimension of depth" in God's own trinitarian life.[88]

As Torrance writes, the church is "the empirical community of men, women and children called into being through the proclamation of the Gospel, indwelt by the Holy Spirit in whom it is united to Christ and through him joined to God. Far from being a human institution it was founded by the Lord himself and rooted in the Holy Trinity."[89] For Torrance, the true being of the church is found only in the triune being of God and the economic actions of Father, Son, and Holy Spirit. What is more, the economic acts of God, because they are *God's* acts, "are not acts which can be reduced to the phenomenal level."[90]

---

84. Brunner, *Misunderstanding of the Church*, 12.
85. De Lubac, *Church*, 24. See also de Lubac, *Splendour of the Church*, 112. To describe the church as *all*-holy and *all*-sanctifying, and thus as the continuation of the incarnation—as de Lubac also does (see de Lubac, *Church*, 24)—is contentious. In light of the concern registered in chap. 4 in relation to type 3, communion ecclesiology, and its overidentification of the being of the church with Christ Himself, the reader might worry that de Lubac too makes this misstep, and in doing so denies the reality of ecclesial sin. On this (possible) denial, see the discussion below in this chapter.
86. Farrow, *Ascension and Ecclesia*, 7.
87. Brunner, *Misunderstanding of the Church*, 12.
88. See Torrance, *Preaching Christ Today*, 57.
89. Torrance, *Trinitarian Faith*, 253.
90. Torrance, *Theology in Reconciliation*, 291.

Theologians, in their accounts of the church, must therefore look beyond the church's sociohistorical existence to what Torrance describes as its "inner dogmatic form" and speak first about God's triune being, whose operation it is to bring the church into existence.[91] Only by looking and in speaking in this way, Torrance contends, are theologians able to perceive the "controlling centre of reference for a doctrine of the Church founded and rooted in the self-communication of the Holy Trinity."[92] Central to this self-communication is the economic work of Christ and the Spirit that flows from the eternal purpose of God the Father to be one with humanity.

For Torrance, God's eternal self-determination to be God "for us" takes concrete form in the person of Christ and in the coming of the Holy Spirit. The Holy Spirit works to actualize subjectively in human beings what is realized objectively in Christ's incarnation: that is, the union of humanity with Christ, and thus humanity's participation in the life of the Godhead through Christ's own intrinsic relation to the Father and the Holy Spirit.[93] By this divine work, the eternal, loving *koinōnia* that God is as Father, Son, and Holy Spirit comes to interpenetrate sociohistorical existence in such a way, says Torrance, as to generate the church.[94] He writes, "The self-giving of God [in Christ] actualises itself in us as the Holy Spirit creates in us the capacity to receive it and lifts us up to participate in the union and communion of the incarnate Son with the heavenly Father."[95] This participation in the eternal *koinōnia* of God by individual Christian believers on a vertical axis has, as its corollary, a creaturely *koinōnia* between those who have been united with Christ—and thus with one another—on a horizontal axis.[96] This horizontal, creaturely *koinōnia* is the church, Torrance says. The church, then, is a community of loving, interpersonal relations that participates in, and is actualized and sustained by, God's own *koinōnia* and that, further, reflects that *koinōnia* in its lived ecclesial life.[97]

However, this is not to say that what the church is as a sociohistorical human community can be seen (as it is by some social trinitarians) to be "like" the communion of love that God is in God's own eternal being as Father, Son, and Holy Spirit; neither is it to say that an analogy can be drawn deductively from the eternal *koinōnia* of God's immanent Trinitarian life to

91. Torrance, *Royal Priesthood*, 71.
92. Torrance, *Trinitarian Faith*, 263.
93. Torrance, *Trinitarian Faith*, 264.
94. See Torrance, *Reality and Scientific Theology*, 181–83.
95. Torrance, *Theology in Reconciliation*, 100.
96. See Torrance, "What Is the Church?," 6–21.
97. See Torrance, *Reality and Scientific Theology*, 182.

the church in its sociohistorical existence, so as to permit theologians to see the former "echoed" in the latter.[98] Such is the force of Torrance's concept of participation in his understanding of what the church is: it is God in Christ through the Holy Spirit who *lifts up* human beings to participate in God's own divine life as an act of sheer, gratuitous grace. The fundamental distinction between God as creator and that which God creates *ex nihilo* thus "sets limits to the reciprocity he establishes between us."[99] Indeed, God's "transcendent objectivity," writes Torrance, "prevents us from including him within our own subjectivity."[100] In ecclesiological description, then, theologians must resist the temptation either to collapse speech about divine action into language about ecclesial human reality, or to project the creaturely content of lived ecclesial life into God's own life. At the same time, theologians must also constantly safeguard the contingent nature of the church and the nonnecessity of creation. Notwithstanding God's self-determination in love to exist as God "for us," God is absolutely free from creation and creatures in God's own divine life. The human empirical form of the church and its interpersonal relations of love can only be understood properly, therefore, "*from* the Communion of Love in God which is both their source and their goal."[101] Or, put otherwise, the creaturely, horizontal *koinōnia* that the church is, is wholly dependent for its existence on a prior vertical participation in God's own *koinōnia*, which itself is wholly dependent on the being of God and God's gracious acts. As Torrance writes, "It is only through vertical participation in Christ that the Church is horizontally a communion of love. . . . It is only as we share in Christ Himself that we share in the life of the Church."[102] And conversely, it is only as we share in the life of the church—"with all saints in their relation to Christ"—that we participate (by our prior union with Christ) in the life of God.[103]

It is for these reasons that, for Torrance, the "controlling centre of reference" for a doctrine of the church grounded in the Holy Trinity's self-communication is Paul's expression "the body of Christ."[104] But to speak of

98. See chap. 4 on communion ecclesiology.
99. Torrance, *Reality and Scientific Theology*, 181.
100. Torrance, *Reality and Scientific Theology*, 181, 179.
101. Torrance, *Reality and Scientific Theology*, 178 (emphasis added).
102. Torrance, "What Is the Church?," 9–10.
103. Torrance, "What Is the Church?," 10. Torrance's thought here is echoed by Ratzinger when he speaks of the Holy Spirit effecting in the giving and receiving of Christ's body both a vertical unification of human beings with the triune love of God and a horizontal unification of otherwise disparate and divided human beings. See Ratzinger, *Called to Communion*, 76. For Ratzinger, as for Torrance, "Only by the impulse power of vertical unification can horizontal unification . . . also successfully take place." Ratzinger, *Called to Communion*, 76.
104. See Torrance, *Trinitarian Faith*, 263.

the church as Christ's body is to insist, Torrance contends, that the weight
of theological emphasis in ecclesiological description is always placed on
"*of Christ*" and *not* on "body."[105] In its twofold participation in Christ on a
vertical and horizontal axis, the church, above all, is "of Christ." Indeed, for
Torrance, "The advantage of this expression [the body of Christ] is that it does
not focus our attention upon the Church as a sociological or anthropological
magnitude, nor upon the Church as an institution or a process, but upon the
Church as the immediate property of Christ which He has made His very
own and gathered into the most intimate relation with Himself."[106] What
is more, this relation that Torrance sees as existing between Christ and the
church as Christ's body expresses a profound ontological truth: "Through the
communion of the Holy Spirit the Church is united to Christ and grounded
in the hypostatic union of God and man embodied in him."[107] Torrance thus
finds and roots the church's being by the operation of the Holy Spirit in the
body of Christ. This means not only that the church exists *in* Christ prior
to Christian believers being incorporated into it but that apart from Christ
the church has no independent existence: "It is what it is," writes Torrance,
"because of what Christ, the incarnate and risen Son of God is; it is what
it is because of its indissoluble bond with him who will not be without it."[108]
Indeed, for Torrance, the church in its sociohistorical existence cannot be
thought of as having any life or being of its own: it is nothing at all "apart
from what is unceasingly communicated to it through its union and communion with Christ who dwells in it by the power of the Spirit and fills it with
the eternal life and love of God himself."[109] Put otherwise, the church derives

105. Torrance, "What Is the Church?," 7 (emphasis original).
106. Torrance, "What Is the Church?," 7.
107. Torrance, *Trinitarian Faith*, 278. See the glossary for a definition of **hypostatic union**.
108. Torrance, *Theology in Reconstruction*, 205. The reader might worry whether Torrance
overidentifies here, in a fashion similar to de Lubac, the being of the church with Christ Himself. While Torrance affirms that "Christ is the Church," he at once *denies* that the "Church is
Christ." Torrance, "What Is the Church?," 9. This is because Christ, by His ascension, "has
removed His body from us," and thus the church, even as the body of Christ, is still "other than
Christ." Torrance, *Royal Priesthood*, 45, 46. The worry therefore might be mitigated. What is
not mitigated, however, is the concern that Torrance occludes, in a fashion similar to type 3,
communion ecclesiology, the central dogmatic truth that the church is founded not by Christ
but by the Holy Spirit. While the operation of the Spirit is certainly evident in Torrance's speech
about the church, his ecclesiology is determined, ultimately, christologically: "The Church did
not come into being with . . . the pouring out of the Spirit at Pentecost. That was not its birth
but its new birth. . . . Jesus Christ had already gathered and built the nucleus of the Church
round himself." Torrance, *Theology in Reconstruction*, 204. This christological determination
of ecclesiology, for Torrance, is such that "the doctrine of the Spirit is really Christology . . .
applied to the Church as the Body of Christ." Torrance, *Royal Priesthood*, 25.
109. Torrance, *Theology in Reconstruction*, 205.

its life and being not "from below" in its individual human members but only "from above," as a gift, in the trinitarian life of God.[110] Therefore, what the church is "cannot be known or interpreted out of itself."[111]

In this way, Torrance's concern in speech about the church prefigures the concern of Webster: "the real" in ecclesiological description is not found in the church's sociohistorical existence, but only in the immanent life and economic work of God, in whose being the being of the church is grounded, actualized, and sustained. This "transcendent dimension of the church" (to use Farrow's words) requires theologians to accept in their speech about the church "an internal and strictly doxological engagement for its interpretation," and to admit that "it is not *vis-à-vis* the world's own social, religious or scientific communities that the truth about the Christian communion is ultimately to be uncovered."[112] Any notion that ecclesial truth is to be uncovered in relation to such communities or that ecclesiology *requires* the social sciences to account for what the church is (to recall Milbank's argument) always therefore implies what Milbank describes as "the displacing of the Christian metanarrative."[113] It implies the displacing of the fact that the church, in de Lubac's words, is first and foremost "of God," and as such "a mysterious extension in time of the Trinity."[114] Or, as Torrance himself conceives it, any such notion risks relegating to the periphery of ecclesiology the central dogmatic truth that the doctrine of the Trinity *is* "the dynamic grammar" of Christian theology.[115]

To claim this is not to say, however, that for ideal ecclesiology the human empirical form of the church should not offer itself up to investigation by social-scientific fields of inquiry, or that "secular paths" to understanding what the church is are devoid of insight.[116] But it is to say that there is *always* something more to what the church is than its sociohistorical existence. As

110. Torrance, *Theology in Reconstruction*, 192.
111. Torrance, *Theology in Reconstruction*, 192.
112. See Farrow, *Ascension and Ecclesia*, 2n5.
113. Milbank, *Theology and Social Theory*, 249.
114. De Lubac, *Splendour of the Church*, 71; De Lubac, *Church*, 24. De Lubac traces the mystery at the ground of the church's being to God's immanent Trinitarian life—specifically, to the eternal divine processions (de Lubac, *Splendour of the Church*, 71)—and, subsequently, to God's economic work, which he describes as the "free designs" of God to become "for us" in Christ and to sanctify us by the Holy Spirit (de Lubac, *Church*, 14; and de Lubac, *Splendour of the Church*, 14). De Lubac's account might be seen to be conceived in a fashion similar to those of both Torrance and Webster, therefore, even though his account of divine agency is indexed in more strictly Catholic terms to a eucharistic doctrine of the mysterious union of Christ as head to the church as His body.
115. See Torrance, *Christian Doctrine of God*, 10.
116. Farrow, *Ascension and Ecclesia*, 2n5.

Torrance notes, the communion that the church and its members have with God's immanent trinitarian life "extends infinitely above and beyond us"; it "reaches out into the sheer infinity and eternity of God."[117] To participate in this communion, then, is for the church and its members to participate in and be constituted by a level of reality that is beyond every phenomenal level of existence: the reality, that is, of "the mystery of God."[118] And because of the reality of God's trinitarian mystery, the church, as de Lubac notes, "mysteriously transcends the limits of her visibility."[119] Or, as he writes elsewhere, "The Church is not a this-worldly-reality such as lends itself to exact measurement and analysis."[120] In fact, the true being of the church is always anterior and superior to its human empirical form, and thus eludes mastery by human reason: "The Church is a mystery for all time out of grasp because, qualitatively, it is totally removed from other objects of knowledge that might be mentioned."[121] To reduce the church's being to what Ratzinger has described as "the level of the makeable"[122]—to the level of an empirical, this-worldly reality—is thus to deny what, in de Lubac's words, the church is "as God made her, in the mystery of her supernatural being."[123]

Indeed, the church, Ratzinger avers, is not a makeable object. It is not "an inner-worldly association."[124] Nor, as he puts it elsewhere, is it "a contrivance or an apparatus"; it is "not merely an institution or one of the usual sociological entities" that is internal to the world and that can be self-made by human willing or deciding.[125] Rather, the church exists only as a creature of God and God's gracious acts, and thus as the gift that God gives that reaches—to recall Torrance's language—infinitely above and beyond the church's own sociohistorical existence. The being of the church as a mystery is, in other words, irreducible to its human empirical form. What is thus needed in ecclesiological description is "not a more human, but a more divine Church."[126] The truth of what the church is cannot be "made" or simply read off in an obvious way from its phenomenal surface by social-scientific or nontheological fields of inquiry. At every step of the ecclesiological way, theologians must ensure that their accounts of the church work to resist the naturalization of ecclesiology

117. Torrance, *Theology in Reconciliation*, 292.
118. Torrance, *Theology in Reconciliation*, 292.
119. De Lubac, *Church*, 27.
120. De Lubac, *Splendour of the Church*, 4.
121. De Lubac, *Church*, 14; see also de Lubac, *Splendour of the Church*, 76.
122. Ratzinger, *Called to Communion*, 139.
123. De Lubac, *Splendour of the Church*, 9.
124. Ratzinger, *Called to Communion*, 139.
125. Ratzinger, *Church, Ecumenism, and Politics*, 28.
126. Ratzinger, *Called to Communion*, 146.

by sociological reduction and affirm, with Torrance, that without God the church is nothing.[127]

The Church as the Eventful Act of God

This forceful dogmatic corrective to ecclesiology—and the priority in ecclesiological description of an account of divine agency indexed to a theology of God's aseity, upon which it rests—is evident also in the ecclesiological thought of Torrance's theological mentor, Karl Barth. As Barth develops his ecclesiology in the context of his *Church Dogmatics*, he certainly sees the church as a concrete and particular sociohistorical human community: "It is," Barth writes, "a phenomenon of world history which can be grasped in historical and psychological and sociological terms like any other."[128] Or, as he describes it further, the church is "a definite human fellowship" that "never has been and never is absolutely invisible."[129] This denial of "ecclesiastical Docetism," as Barth describes it, is matched, however, by a denial of what might be described as ecclesiastical **Ebionitism**: while the church exists in Barth's thought visibly as a sociohistorical human community "whose history involves from the very first, and always will involve, human action," what the church is most truly, for Barth, is nevertheless not reducible to its human empirical form.[130] This is because the church's human empirical form exists only by the agency of *God's* action.[131] Barth therefore proceeds to elaborate his ecclesiological thought in terms of what he describes, contrastingly, as "apparent church" (*Scheinkirche*)—or "the mere semblance of a Church"—and the "true church" (*wirkliche Kirche*).[132] The former, Barth says, is what the human empirical form of the church is, or seems to be, in itself, as a visible human phenomenon.[133] However, the latter is, in a sense, invisible. It arises, or becomes visible, says Barth, only as God is at work in that human phenomenon

127. See Torrance, *Theology in Reconstruction*, 192.

128. Barth, *Church Dogmatics* IV/1, 652. Barth's mature ecclesiological thought is found primarily in *Church Dogmatics* IV/1, 643–739 (§62); *Church Dogmatics* IV/2, 614–726 (§67); and *Church Dogmatics* IV/3.2, 681–901 (§72). For more on the development of his thought from his early ecclesiology, see Bender, *Karl Barth's Christological Ecclesiology*.

129. Barth, *Church Dogmatics* IV/1, 653. See also de Lubac's comment that the mystery that the church is "is not of some purely spiritual ideal or invisible reality, without a tangible structure, but is a communion that at least in one of the qualities that constitutes her is a visible society." De Lubac, *Church*, 34.

130. See Barth, *Church Dogmatics* IV/1, 653.

131. See Barth, *Church Dogmatics* IV/2, 616; see also 616–17.

132. Barth, *Church Dogmatics* IV/2, 617; see also 614–17. See also Barth, "Real Church," 337–51.

133. See Barth, *Church Dogmatics* IV/2, 616–17.

in accordance with God's will and in the power of God's act.[134] In this way, Barth subordinates his speech about the church wholly to a doctrine of God.

Barth grounds this doctrine, first, in God's absolutely free, eternal decision to be God's own Word, Jesus Christ, and in Christ, to be God "for us."[135] God's divine will to elect Jesus Christ and to be gracious toward humankind in Christ is thus seen by Barth as the foundation of God's work of creation, reconciliation, and redemption.[136] This work, further, is fulfilled or has its center, Barth says, in the atonement.[137] Barth grounds his doctrine of God, second, in the power of the act of God completed in Christ's atoning sacrifice. What is more, this divine, reconciling work is itself realized subjectively, says Barth, by "the awakening power of the Holy Spirit."[138] For it is the work of the Holy Spirit to call forth the sociohistorical reality of the church as "the perfect form" of the community of humankind elected by God in Christ.[139] As Barth writes, "The work of the Holy Spirit as this awakening power is the historical reality of the community."[140] When humankind is awakened by the Spirit to "the Word spoken by the Lord," as Barth puts it, "there is in their inner fellowship and there arises in their outward assembly a new humanity within the old. A new history within world-history. A new form of fellowship is quietly founded amongst other sociological forms."[141] This new sociological form of fellowship is the church—the Spirit-awakened body of Christ. It is by the work of the Holy Spirit, then, that the church as Christ's body takes on human empirical form, but it does so in accordance with what "it is by God's decree from all eternity and as it has become in virtue of His act in time."[142]

For Barth, ecclesiological thought must therefore stand on "the firm ground which is none other than the Church's eternal divine election" and proceed from this election to the doctrine of reconciliation worked out in connection to the power of the Holy Spirit as "the quickening power of the Living Lord Jesus."[143] There is thus a need in speech about the church to recognize that the church's being is "of divine origin" and that this divine origin renders the

---

134. See Barth *Church Dogmatics* IV/1, 657; and Barth, "Real Church," 338.

135. Barth's extended discussion of the doctrine of election as christologically conditioned is found in §32, §33, §34, and §35 of the second part of the second volume of his *Church Dogmatics*.

136. See Barth, *Church Dogmatics* II/2, 91.

137. See Barth, *Church Dogmatics* IV/1, 3.

138. Barth, *Church Dogmatics* IV/1, 661.

139. See Barth, *Church Dogmatics* II/2, 211.

140. Barth, *Church Dogmatics* IV/1, 151.

141. Barth, *Church Dogmatics* IV/1, 151.

142. Barth, *Church Dogmatics* IV/1, 667.

143. Barth, *Church Dogmatics* II/2, 84; and Barth, *Church Dogmatics* IV/2, 617.

human empirical origin of the church "an insignificant origin" with regard to what the church truly is.[144] Put otherwise, the true being of the church has no "natural vitality" of its own:[145] "It is not created, formed and introduced by individual [human beings] on their own initiative, authority and insight,"[146] and therefore its existence cannot be considered "a human production" or thought to be secured "from below"—that is, "from the side of its human members."[147] Rather, the church's true being comes into existence only "from above," in consequence of God's own divine act: only as the church "is gathered together, as an act coming down from heaven, from God's eternal throne and out of the secret of the triune God, and coming forth upon earth," writes Barth, does the church exist truly.[148]

More precisely, the true being of the church exists only "as the *event* of this *gathering together*," and thus "by *happening*."[149] In other words, the true church "*is* when it takes place."[150] And the church truly takes place, or "happens," *only* when the Holy Spirit of God works to occasion and fashion the true church from within the church's human empirical form.[151] Put alternatively, for Barth, the human empirical form of the church exists as the true church only as it is divinely and dynamically constituted thus as an "ever-new event."[152] Barth therefore sees the being of the true church as being held, ultimately, "in the hand of God."[153] It is in this sense that the true being of the church is, for Barth, invisible, and therefore "not unequivocally represented" in its sociohistorical existence.[154] What the church truly is cannot be wholly derived, then, from empirical study of its human empirical form. As Barth puts it, "The truth of its existence in space and time is not a matter of a general but a very special visibility."[155] "It cannot be perceived," he concludes, "but only believed."[156] In other words, the truth of what the church is, is visible only to the eyes of Christian faith. For it is the eyes of Christian faith, Barth avers, that enable theologians to see what he describes as the "third dimension" of

144. Barth, *Church Dogmatics* IV/2, 616; and Barth, *Church Dogmatics* IV/1, 151.
145. Barth, *Church Dogmatics* I/2, 689.
146. Barth, *Church Dogmatics* I/2, 213.
147. Barth, *Church Dogmatics* I/2, 221; and Barth, *God Here and Now*, 68.
148. Barth, *God Here and Now*, 62.
149. Barth, *God Here and Now*, 62.
150. Barth, *Church Dogmatics* IV/1, 652.
151. Barth, *Church Dogmatics* IV/2, 617.
152. Bender, *Karl Barth's Christological Ecclesiology*, 156–57.
153. Barth, *Church Dogmatics* IV/1, 657.
154. Barth, *Church Dogmatics* IV/1, 657.
155. Barth, *Church Dogmatics* IV/1, 654.
156. Barth, *Church Dogmatics* IV/1, 657.

the church's existence, the dimension in which the true being of the church becomes visible by the eventful act of God the Holy Spirit.[157]

Ideal Ecclesiology: An Assessment

By appealing to this "third dimension" of the church's existence, Barth voices the concern of ideal ecclesiology to resist the naturalization of ecclesiological description and to insist, instead, that "the real" in speech about the church is found only in God and God's gracious acts. Indeed, these acts, and the truth claims of the Christian faith to which they refer and which Christians confess in the creed, are, for Barth, as Ingolf Dalferth observes, "the standards by which we are to judge what is real, not vice versa."[158] These acts and claims, in other words, "have ontological and criteriological priority over the experiential reality which we all share."[159] Sociohistorical existence is not, therefore, its own autonomous reality independent from God, and the need exists in ecclesiology to maintain the fundamental asymmetry of divine and human agency in the church's being. Ideal ecclesiology does this by setting its ecclesiological description clearly and methodologically under a metaphysics of God's grace and attending first to the immanent life and economic work of God as the condition for the possibility of the church's sociohistorical existence. By doing so, ideal ecclesiology's methodology serves to remind theologians that ecclesiology is not—and must not be treated as if it were—"a separate fourth article" of the creed, independent, so to speak, of the doctrine of God.[160]

This is precisely the concern of ideal ecclesiology: that "ecclesiological hypertrophy," as Webster puts it, results in ecclesiological discourse that, because of its disproportionate emphasis on the church's sociohistorical existence, becomes "too humanly solid," and therefore "insufficiently transparent" toward God and God's gracious acts.[161] Another way to put this is to say that type 1, empirical ecclesiology, and type 2, performative ecclesiology, both obscure—at least from the perspective of ideal ecclesiology—the act and activity of God as the church's originating and sustaining cause. The call of ideal ecclesiology to make paramount in speech about the church an account of divine agency indexed to a theology of God's aseity is therefore sounded to keep

---

157. Barth, *Church Dogmatics* IV/1, 655; see also Barth, "Real Church," 338.
158. Dalferth, "Christology and Reconciliation," 22.
159. Dalferth, "Christology and Reconciliation," 22.
160. Greggs, "Proportion and Topography in Ecclesiology," 98.
161. Webster, "On Evangelical Ecclesiology," 11; and Webster, *Word and Church*, 225.

alive in ecclesiological description the all-important ontological distinction between uncreated and created being, and to remind theologians, further, of the church's contingent nature as the gracious creation of God external to its sociohistorical existence.[162]

This call of ideal ecclesiology to treat God's immanent life and economic work as the proper object of ecclesiological description, and thereby to account fully for the church as a creature of God's grace subsequent to a doctrine of God, must certainly be heard by theologians if they want to speak about what the church is in a genuinely theological fashion, given the most basic ecclesiological task. In light of this task, to hold together in speech about the church an account of both divine and human agency in which the former *relativizes* the latter, it is axiomatic that theologians must *first* speak about the church as a creature of God's grace and treat God and God's gracious acts as the proper object of ecclesiological description. The church is not created and sustained in its sociohistorical existence by human agency, and what the church is cannot be understood on the basis of its human empirical form alone. However, ecclesiology's most basic task is not concerned only with appropriate *order* in ecclesiological description but also with appropriate *proportion*. The account of divine agency, therefore, and the associated theology of God's aseity that theologians make paramount in their speech about the church must not *minimize* the church's human empirical form or the agency of human action in accounting for what the church is. "Divine action," as Ratzinger observes, "is always theandric, that is, divine-*human* action."[163] Or, as Barth conceives it, God acts and exists in God's togetherness with humanity always as the absolutely superior partner, but God nevertheless exists and acts in that togetherness as humankind's *partner*.[164] In other words, the desire to account fully for the church as a creature of God's grace and to treat God and God gracious acts as the proper object of ecclesiological discourse must be matched by an *equal* desire to account fully for the church as the sociohistorical human community that God creates the church to be. If this desire is not present in ecclesiological description, or if it is not sufficiently attended to therein, then the ecclesiological description may in fact do precisely what type 1, empirical ecclesiology, seeks to guard against—that is, it may present in somewhat theoretical or abstract terms an overly idealized account of the church that is disconnected from the experience of lived ecclesial life and neglectful of the church's human empirical form.

---

162. See Webster, "'In the Society of God,'" 221; and Greggs, "Proportion and Topography in Ecclesiology," 95.

163. Ratzinger, *Church, Ecumenism, and Politics*, 125 (emphasis original).

164. See Barth, *Humanity of God*, 45.

The question that needs to be asked at this point is whether ideal ecclesiology is open to this precise critique. The reader may wish to consider, for example, the extent to which the lived experience of the church as a sociohistorical human community is, in fact, described and accounted for in ideal ecclesiology; or what, in reality, ideal ecclesiology says about the church's habits and practices, and about the nature of the church as it exists fallibly and particularly; or how the act and activity of God as the condition for the possibility of the church's existence is related in ideal ecclesiology to this particular and fallible existence. Is it sufficient to limit material treatment of the reality of ecclesial sin to an empirical distortion of the church's true theological identity, as ideal ecclesiology has a tendency to do? As Webster writes, "The acts of the church . . . are movements moved by God,"[165] and "all the acts of the holy Church must demonstrate a reference to the work of the One who alone is holy."[166] To follow the trajectory of Webster's thought here is—if I understand his thought correctly—to affirm either that God is the movement that moves all acts of the chuch, *including sinful acts*, or that all sinful acts of the church somehow remain detached from the true reality of what the church is because they are acts of individual Christian believers. Of course, the latter affirmation is the more appropriate one, and one which de Lubac, for example, makes explicit: "At one and the same time the Church is without sin in herself and never without sin in her members."[167] However, readers might call into question the ability of ideal ecclesiology to account fully for the church in its sociohistorical existence when the sinful acts of individual Christian believers remain detached from what the church truly is—and thus from God's own being and action as the actual possibility of the church's human empirical form.[168]

In fact, the reader may wonder what church ideal ecclesiology is actually speaking of. Where is such a church?[169] As John Swinton observes, it may be correct to suggest (as Milbank does) that the church is not definable as a particular place, or to suggest (as Torrance, de Lubac, and Ratzinger do, each in his own way) that the church is a mystery because it derives its true being from beyond itself.[170] "But, at the same time," writes Swinton, the church "is

165. Webster, "'In the Society of God,'" 215.
166. Webster, *Holiness*, 63.
167. De Lubac, *Splendour of the Church*, 80. De Lubac's claim trades specifically on the Catholic concept of the sinlessness of the church as Christ's body and thus the problematic overidentification of the church's being with Christ Himself noted above.
168. See Brittain, "Why Ecclesiology Cannot Live by Doctrine Alone," 5–30.
169. See Swinton, "'Where Is Your Church?'"
170. Swinton, "'Where Is Your Church?,'" 74.

very much a place!"[171] And in comparison to the eucharistic doctrine of the mysterious union of Christ as head to the church as His body, "the practice of the Eucharist is much less mysterious."[172] Swinton continues, "Someone had to bake the bread and ferment the wine. Someone had to place the elements in their right order. Some real community had to decide on the meaning of this practice and its weighting within the ministries of that particular community."[173]

When confronted by the actual content of speech about the church in ideal ecclesiology, the reader might worry, then, that the proffered account of divine agency and associated theology of God's aseity so fills the ecclesiological horizon that human agency and the church's human empirical form are all but eclipsed. We must ask, Does ideal ecclesiology, by setting ecclesiology clearly and methodologically under a metaphysics of God's grace, in its rightly ordered desire to guard ecclesiological description against drifting into divine immanence, thereby succumb to Barth's fear of forgetting human existence?[174] Where the worry about type 3, communion ecclesiology, may be that it associates the doctrine of the church too closely with the doctrine of God, the worry about ideal ecclesiology may be that it introduces into ecclesiological description too great a distinction between the church's human empirical form and God's immanent divine life and economic action in constituting and sustaining that form. The reader may well worry, therefore, that ideal ecclesiology is, in fact, open to the critique of presenting in somewhat abstract or theoretical terms an overly idealized account of the church that is disconnected from the experience of lived ecclesial life and neglectful of the church's human empirical form.

What is more, the reader might worry that in ideal ecclesiology the church's sociohistorical existence is not just eclipsed by an account of divine agency and associated theology of God's aseity, but is actually at risk of being dissolved by it, so to speak. What I mean by this is that the sheer force that ideal ecclesiology places on the event of God's act to bring the church into existence—by recourse either to a eucharistic doctrine of the church as Christ's mystical body or (in more strictly Protestant terms) to a doctrine of reconciliation traced to the doctrine of election—has a tendency to deny that the human empirical form of the church has any *true* validity *distinct* from the act and activity of God. For instance, in relation to the order of the church in its sociohistorical existence, Torrance writes, "The purpose of this order is to make room in

171. Swinton, "'Where Is Your Church?,'" 74.
172. Swinton, "'Where Is Your Church?,'" 73.
173. Swinton, "'Where Is Your Church?,'" 74.
174. See Barth, *Church Dogmatics* I/2, 794.

the midst for the presence of the risen Christ so that the Church's fellowship *becomes* the sphere where the resurrection of Christ is effectively operative here and now."[175] Indeed, such is the force of the agency of divine action in ideal ecclesiology that the church's human empirical form seems to lack *true* being and is left with only the *possibility* of such being, given that the church becomes what it *truly* is only in the eventful act of God. As Barth avers, "The Church has no history in the strict sense, but only . . . a status of continual self-renewal."[176] The true being of the church, in other words, might be seen in ideal ecclesiology, at worst, to have no real, enduring sociohistorical existence, or, at best, to come into existence only ever again in passing (to recall Milbank's argument), through the agency of God's act in time.

The risk, then, is that, in adopting ideal ecclesiology, theologians may be construing the being of the church in what Welch once described as "an occasionalist sense,"[177] which works not just to marginalize the church's being as a sociohistorical reality (as in type 3, communion ecclesiology) but to dissolve it thoroughly into the act and activity of God. In this way, ideal ecclesiology may be open to the accusation that its account of the church is undergirded by a methodological docetism (Barth's protests to the contrary notwithstanding). Ultimately, the worry in ideal ecclesiology is that it too presents an account of the church that lacks an appropriate sense of theological order and proportion because of its disproportionate emphasis on divine agency. In ideal ecclesiology, the church is essentially what God does, and what the church is might be understood on the basis of divine agency alone.

175. Torrance, *Royal Priesthood*, 67 (emphasis added).
176. Barth, *Church Dogmatics* II/2, 342.
177. Welch, *Reality of the Church*, 66n1.

6

Ecclesiological Ecclesiology

Thus far I have been concerned to present and assess four types of approach to contemporary ecclesiology. The presentation and assessment has proceeded in relation to a basic theological grammar for accounting for what the church is derived from Paul's description of the church in Corinth as *God's* people and *the people* of God—a description that is rooted in God's covenantal promise. Given this grammar, the presentation and assessment has proceeded in relation to the most basic ecclesiological task: the task of holding together in speech about the church an account of both divine and human agency, such that the former relativizes but does not minimize the latter, in order that theologians may speak about the church as both creature of God and sociohistorical human community, but with due concern for the asymmetrical relationship of divine and human togetherness in the church's being. In the course of the presentation, and in the context of the indicative assessments offered in relation to each type of ecclesiological approach, I have also been concerned to demonstrate a fundamental problem in contemporary approaches to ecclesiology: the problem of attending either to the church's human empirical form or to the life and work of God. In doing so, I have sought to suggest, further, how each type of ecclesiological approach might therefore be seen to be deficient to one extent or another in its ability to perform the most basic ecclesiological task successfully, notwithstanding the ways in which each might be seen dialogically to correct the problematic either/or tendencies of the other.

I have suggested that the theological deficiency in type 1, empirical ecclesiology, is ecclesiological description that risks the naturalization, or de-theologization, of ecclesiology per se. As a consequence of the right desire to account fully for the church as a lived sociohistorical reality, empirical ecclesiology is liable to collapse divine agency into human subjectivity, or speech about divine action into language about ecclesial human reality, and to do so to such an extent that it evacuates from speech about the church the agency of God's action as the church's originating and sustaining cause. This tendency in ecclesiological description to treat the doctrine of the church too independently from a doctrine of God, without an appropriate sense of theological order and proportion, is echoed in type 2, performative ecclesiology. While speech about God's activity is not evacuated from ecclesiological description by performative ecclesiology, this type of ecclesiology's disproportionate emphasis on the church as a social body, whose distinctiveness is understood to be constituted by the agency of Christian believers in lived ecclesial life and performed church practice, means that the agency of God's action is nevertheless at risk of being obscured as the originating and sustaining cause of what the church is as a unique sociohistorical reality in creation.

In contrast to both performative and empirical ecclesiology, it was then suggested that the theological deficiency in type 3, communion ecclesiology, is that it treats the doctrine of the church too closely with the doctrine of God. As a consequence of the right desire to account for the unique nature of the church as a creature of God's grace, but because of a disproportionate emphasis on the *koinōnia* of God's immanent trinitarian life, which is understood to realize what the church truly is as the Holy Spirit mediates that life (most effectively in the Eucharist) within the church's own life, communion ecclesiology is liable to overidentify the church's being with the being of God. The overidentification is such that communion ecclesiology marginalizes in speech about the church both the church's human empirical form and the agency of human action in constituting that form. This tendency in ecclesiological description to attend disproportionately to the life and work of God is echoed, it was suggested, in type 4, ideal ecclesiology. While the being of the church is not overidentified with God's own being by ideal ecclesiology, the density and force of its account of divine agency and its associated theology of God's aseity means that the church's sociohistorical existence is not just marginalized in ecclesiological description but eclipsed, and, further, put at risk of being dissolved into the act and activity of God to such an extent that the human empirical form of the church has no true validity distinct from the agency of God's action. I suggested that the theological deficiency in ideal ecclesiology is speech about the church that risks the idealization of ecclesiology per se and the theoretical abstraction of the church's being from the sociohistorical experience of lived ecclesial life; ideal ecclesiology runs this risk by introducing too great a distinction between God's own immanent life and economic work and the life of the church in its sociohistorical existence.

Given these deficiencies in ecclesiological description, the question that is raised is whether there is a way to resolve or at least begin to mitigate them. This is the concern of this final chapter. Put otherwise, the concern of this chapter is to propose a fifth type of contemporary approach to ecclesiology that to one extent or another might provide a corrective to the theologically disordered and disproportionate ecclesiological speech of the first four types of ecclesiological approach. The hope in this chapter, therefore, is to move toward the articulation of a reparative theological grammar for ecclesiology per se—one that, in light of the most basic ecclesiological task, works to resist the tendencies in empirical, performative, communion, and ideal ecclesiology to pry apart in ecclesiological description the asymmetrical relationship of divine and human togetherness in the church's being; the concern thus, derivatively, is to provide a reparative theological grammar, too, for an account of divine and human agency.

As I noted in chapter 1, in this fifth type of contemporary approach to ecclesiology that I am proposing, there is a desire to ameliorate the problematic either/or tendency in contemporary approaches to ecclesiology by holding together in speech about the church *both* the life and work of God *and* the church's human empirical form. In contrast to the first four types of ecclesiological approach, in ecclesiological ecclesiology, description of both the sociohistorical human community that the church is and the gracious divine acts of God that create and sustain the church as that community is the normative and necessary foundation of all ecclesiological speech. More specifically, and critically for the construction of this foundation, an account of divine agency indexed to a theology of God's aseity is methodologically paramount in ecclesiological ecclesiology—in contrast to empirical, performative, and communion ecclesiology. In ecclesiological ecclesiology, theologians speak properly of what the church is only if they first speak about the church as a creature of God's grace and—in a fashion similar to ideal ecclesiology— thereby set their ecclesiological speech under a doctrine of God and God's gracious acts. It is from this foundation of the agency of divine action that theologians will best understand the church's being and have proper concern for accounting theologically for what the church is in an appropriately ordered way. In other words, by treating God and God's gracious acts as the proper object of ecclesiological discourse, theologians will give voice in their speech about the church to the asymmetrical relationship of divine and human togetherness in the church's being and give due concern for ecclesiology's most basic task—that is, they will give an account of divine agency that relativizes their descriptions of the church's human empirical form while safeguarding both the contingent and unique nature of the church as a creature of God's grace. In contrast to ideal and communion ecclesiology, however, in ecclesiological ecclesiology theologians speak properly of what the church is only if they *subsequently* speak about it as the sociohistorical reality that God and God's gracious acts create and sustain the church to be. In ecclesiological ecclesiology, theologians best understand the church's being and have proper concern for accounting theologically for what the church is only if they *also* account for it in a *proportionate* way. In other words, only by ensuring that their ecclesiological speech does not *minimize* the church's human empirical form, or the agency of human action in constituting that form (in a fashion similar to empirical and performative ecclesiology), will a theologian's speech about the church be genuinely theological.

Indeed, a genuinely theological account of the church will account fully for the church as a creature of God's grace, but in doing so it will account fully for the being of the sociohistorical human community that God graciously creates and sustains the church as and the associated human empirical forms and practices that attend to it. The church is, after all, *God's* people and *the people* of God. As the force of Paul's appropriation of God's covenantal promise to the church in Corinth makes clear, the church is at once a divine and a human reality, and the need exists to hold together in ecclesiological description the agency of divine and human action according to the order and proportion of the asymmetrical relationship of divine and human togetherness in the church's being. Following the witness of Acts 2 and the dogmatic trajectory delineated by the creed,[1] ecclesiological ecclesiology seeks to attend to this need by setting the doctrine of the church clearly and methodologically under a doctrine of the person and work of God the Holy Spirit, and thereby establishing the fundamental priority of pneumatology over ecclesiology as a doctrine. In ecclesiological ecclesiology it is the Holy Spirit of God who is the condition for the church's existence, for it is the Holy Spirit alone who creates and sustains the unique nature of the church as *both* creature of God *and* sociohistorical human community. In the field of contemporary ecclesiology, this type of approach might be seen to have its impetus in the work of Dietrich Bonhoeffer.[2]

1. See "Communion Ecclesiology: An Assessment," in chap. 4 above.
2. The reader should note that it is not self-evident that Bonhoeffer's ecclesiology is determined by pneumatology. The critique that in Bonhoeffer's theology pneumatology is, at worst, absent or, at best, underdeveloped is rehearsed frequently by Bonhoeffer scholars. The tendency among Bonhoeffer scholars is to index his theology (including his ecclesiology) to Christology. Offering a corrective to this indexation and characterization of Bonhoeffer's theology (at least

The Church as the Human Community of God the Holy Spirit

Bonhoeffer's ecclesiological thought proceeds in relation to what he sees as two approaches to understanding what the church is: "*one historicizing and the other religious.*"[3] In the first, the "*historicizing*" approach, the church is confused, contends Bonhoeffer, with a human empirical "*religious community*," and, in its overemphasis of "the 'religious motives'" of Christian believers to join themselves together as that community, it presents what Bonhoeffer later describes as a "materialistic-secular" ecclesiology.[4] In the second, the "*religious*" approach, the church is confused instead with "*the Realm of God*," and, in failing to emphasize appropriately the historicity of divine revelation and of human beings themselves, it presents what Bonhoeffer later describes as an "idealistic-docetic" ecclesiology.[5] For Bonhoeffer, both of these approaches for understanding what the church is are problematic.

They are problematic because in accounting for the church in either decidedly sociohistorical terms (in a fashion similar to both empirical and performative ecclesiology) or in a way that threatens to theologically bypass the church's human empirical form (in a fashion similar to both communion and ideal ecclesiology) both approaches misunderstand what the church is—which, as Bonhoeffer states, "is simultaneously a historical community and one established by God."[6] Accordingly, what the church is "can only be said," argues Bonhoeffer, "if we say both what it is from the viewpoint of human beings and what it is from the standpoint of God."[7] Or, as Hans Küng conceives it, what the church is, is *both* "the summons of the God calling from above and the community of summoned people from below,"[8] such that "the essence of the Church is therefore always to be found in its historical form, and the historical form must always be understood in the light of and with reference to the essence."[9] In other words, the divine essence of the church

---

in the context of his ecclesiology) is a concern of my earlier work on Bonhoeffer. For my in-depth consideration of these themes, see Emerton, *God's Church-Community*, esp. chaps. 2, 3, and 4. The following paragraphs are a significantly reworked version of ideas articulated there.

3. Bonhoeffer, *Sanctorum Communio*, 125 (emphasis original).

4. Bonhoeffer, *Sanctorum Communio*, 125 (emphasis original). For the later description, see Bonhoeffer, "Visible Church," 435–36.

5. Bonhoeffer, *Sanctorum Communio*, 125 (emphasis original). For the later description, see Bonhoeffer, "Visible Church," 435. For more on Bonhoeffer's identification of these two approaches in order to understand what the church is, see Mawson, *Christ Existing as Community*, 15–30.

6. Bonhoeffer, *Sanctorum Communio*, 126.

7. Bonhoeffer, "What Is Church?," 262.

8. Küng, *Structures of the Church*, 12 (emphasis altered).

9. Küng, *Church*, 6.

and its human empirical form belong inseparably together. As Bonhoeffer writes, "It is in this dual nature that [the church] exists."[10] Put otherwise, the church exists as both creature of God and sociohistorical human community; and, for Bonhoeffer (and, for that matter, for Küng too), the church exists in this way only because of the agency of God's action: "God, not we, makes the church into that which it is."[11] In Küng's words, the church is "something *given by God*," and as a work of God "the *congregatio fidelium* [congregation of the faithful] exists only as *con-vocatio Dei* [assembly of God], the *communio sanctorum* [communion of saints] exists only as *institutio Dei* [institution of God]."[12] That the church is summoned or established by God means, then, that the church exists only through God's own act.[13] The church is thus prior to the agency of human action, according to Bonhoeffer: "It has not been made by human beings!"[14] Or, in Küng's words again, "The beginnings of the Church do not lie with [people] as individuals. The Church is not composed by the free association of individuals."[15] But, as Bonhoeffer argues, that the church exists only through the act of God means that the church has being at once in space and time as a sociohistorical reality—that is, as the place where the will of God to be God as God of a people is made concrete and particular—and through the agency of individual church members to create and sustain what the church is in its sociohistorical existence.[16] And further, for Bonhoeffer, as the concrete and particular people of God, the church is established by God as a sociohistorical human community that is ontologically and sociologically distinct from all other creaturely realities and forms of human community, but nevertheless as one that remains fallible and sinful, precisely because of the agency of human action.[17] Thus, in critique of the "*historicizing*" and "*religious*" approaches for understanding what the church is, "one must speak," says Bonhoeffer, "of the being and act of the church together."[18] Put otherwise, in their speech about the church, theologians must remember both the being of the church in its sociohistorical existence (including that, in this existence, the church is sinful and fallible) and the act and activity of God as the originating and sustaining cause of

---

10. Bonhoeffer, "What Is Church?," 262.
11. Bonhoeffer, "What Is Church?," 264.
12. Küng, *Church*, 75 (emphasis original), 86.
13. Bonhoeffer, "Nature of the Church," 306. See also Küng, *Church*, 76.
14. Bonhoeffer, "Nature of the Church," 306.
15. Küng, *Church*, 86.
16. See Bonhoeffer, *Sanctorum Communio*, 141.
17. See Bonhoeffer, *Sanctorum Communio*, 177, 213–14, and 264; see also Küng, *Church*, 28, 168–69, and 320.
18. Bonhoeffer, "Nature of the Church," 274.

the church's human empirical form. Indeed, as Küng maintains, because "*the real essence of the real Church is expressed in historical form*," theologians must resist either retreating into "harmless theologumena, remote from real life, about the 'essence' of the Church" or concerning themselves simply "with the present form of the Church, becoming absorbed with ecclesiastical activity."[19] Instead, in Bonhoeffer's view, theologians must start and end their ecclesiological descriptions by affirming that the church is, at the same time, both *God's* church and *the church* of God.[20]

To draw out the force of this point of departure for ecclesiology further, Bonhoeffer proceeds to construct his account of what the church is within what might be described as his realization-actualization paradigm. This paradigm means that, for Bonhoeffer, the church, on the one hand, is realized (or elected) in Christ from eternity.[21] In this essential sense, the church, Bonhoeffer contends, is established by God's own act, and (eschatologically speaking) is "*already completed in Christ*."[22] Another way to put this is to say that in Christ, because of Christ's own redemptive history, there exists the realized possibility of the creation of the church as the body of Christ. This possibility is a realized one because, for Bonhoeffer, the possibility of the church *not* taking on human empirical form is, in fact, an *impossibility* considering the historical nature of God's revelation in Christ.[23] As Bonhoeffer writes, "In the resurrection of Jesus Christ his death is revealed as the death of death itself, and with this the boundary of history marked by death is abolished, the human body becomes the resurrection-body, and the humanity-of-Adam has become the church of Christ."[24] But what here is realized in the death and resurrection of Christ—that is, the being of the church as an ontological reality—is not yet actualized in human empirical form.[25] In Bonhoeffer's ecclesiological thought, there is no doubt that Jesus is "*the foundation of the church*," but as Bonhoeffer goes on to write, He is "*not the founder*."[26] Indeed, the church that is already completed in Christ "*is to be built within time upon Christ as the firm foundation*."[27] In this empirical sense, therefore, the church (eschatologically speaking) is "in the process of growing" toward

19. Küng, *Church*, 5 (emphasis original).
20. See Bonhoeffer, *Sanctorum Communio*, 126.
21. See Bonhoeffer, *Sanctorum Communio*, 145–57; see also 137.
22. Bonhoeffer, *Sanctorum Communio*, 142 (emphasis original).
23. See Bonhoeffer, *Sanctorum Communio*, 144; cf. Bonhoeffer, *Act and Being*, 90–91.
24. Bonhoeffer, *Sanctorum Communio*, 151–52.
25. See Bonhoeffer, *Sanctorum Communio*, 152.
26. See Bonhoeffer, "Nature of the Church," 301 (emphasis original); see also the discussion of this point in "Communion Ecclesiology: An Assessment," in chap. 4 above.
27. Bonhoeffer, *Sanctorum Communio*, 153 (emphasis original).

that which it is in Christ perfectly.[28] Bonhoeffer's realization-actualization paradigm, then, means that the church must be actualized in space and time; and it is the Holy Spirit, Bonhoeffer argues, who actualizes the church as Christ's body in its sociohistorical existence.[29]

Bonhoeffer writes, "In order to build the church as the community-of-God [*Gemeinde Gottes*] in time, God reveals God's own self as *Holy Spirit*."[30] For Bonhoeffer, the church is created and sustained as Christ's body *only* as the Holy Spirit actualizes in space and time that which is realized in Christ. In relation to this aspect of Bonhoeffer's thought, Christopher Holmes puts the matter thus: "The Spirit actualizes the new humanity accomplished in Christ and does so in the church, the church being the social and temporal co-ordinate of the Spirit's activity. . . . Put differently, the new humanity whose ontological reality is Christ becomes socially and historically real in the community of the church by the work of the Holy Spirit."[31] More specifically, however, this work of the Holy Spirit by which the being of the church is actualized as Christ's body is described by Bonhoeffer in what might be seen as three moves.[32]

First, the Holy Spirit "is the will of God that gathers individuals together to be the church-community."[33] It is the Holy Spirit, in other words, who brings Jesus Christ into individual human hearts and transposes those hearts from being "in Adam" to being "in Christ." By mediating within human hearts Christ's presence and that which is realized in Christ (that is, the being of the church as an ontological reality), the Holy Spirit creates faith, and in faith a *new* human being.[34] This new—or, better yet, *ecclesial*—human being, in being "in Christ" in the church, is ordered away from herself and toward God

28. Bonhoeffer, *Sanctorum Communio*, 139.
29. See Bonhoeffer, *Sanctorum Communio*, 157–208. In light of the concern registered in chap. 4 in relation to type 3, communion ecclesiology, and chap. 5 in relation to de Lubac, the reader might worry whether Bonhoeffer too is at risk of overidentifying the being of the church with Christ Himself in the context of his realization-actualization paradigm. While Bonhoeffer affirms that the church is "Christ existing as church-community," any coinherence of Christ and the church that this affirmation suggests is qualified with reference to Christ's ascension and future *parousia*. These events mean that "a complete identification between Christ and the church cannot be made." Bonhoeffer, *Sanctorum Communio*, 141, 140. More categorically, Bonhoeffer renders the qualification with reference to the Holy Spirit: "*Through the Holy Spirit*, the crucified and risen Christ exists as the church-community." Bonhoeffer, *Discipleship*, 220 (emphasis added). The worry therefore might be mitigated.
30. Bonhoeffer, *Sanctorum Communio*, 143 (emphasis original).
31. Holmes, "Holy Spirit," 173.
32. The reader should note that these moves are not explicitly delineated by Bonhoeffer himself. Each move is my own summary construction of the theological argument that Bonhoeffer presents primarily in chapter 5 of *Sanctorum Communio*. For my more in-depth considerations of Bonhoeffer's argument, see Emerton, *God's Church-Community*, 75–109, 115–37.
33. Bonhoeffer, *Sanctorum Communio*, 143.
34. See Bonhoeffer, *Sanctorum Communio*, 165.

and other human beings in love, such that, by her love of God and neighbor, she now embraces God's rule and will.[35] In this way, the work of the Holy Spirit is to actualize in time and space that for which Christ's redemptive history is effected—community with God and thereby community with other human beings. Indeed, for Bonhoeffer, human social community (and the actuality of human personhood on which it depends) is established in and through community with God: "*The concepts of person, community, and God*," Bonhoeffer writes, "are inseparably and essentially interrelated."[36] These concepts are interrelated and inseparable not in the sense that human social community is subsequent to community with God, but rather that neither exists without the other.[37] And both exist only because of the actualizing work of the Holy Spirit: "The Holy Spirit establishes the relationship between God and human being and between human being and human being."[38]

In doing so, Bonhoeffer contends, the Holy Spirit renders the ontic-social relations of the church and its sociohistorical ontology unique. Thus, in the second move, Bonhoeffer understands the Holy Spirit mediating, in order to create *as* unique the "community of love" (*Liebegemeinschaft*) that the church is,[39] what he describes as the "vicarious representative action" (*Stellvertretung*) of Jesus Christ.[40] This action is displayed archetypally in Christ's redemptive history. This history not only identifies the being of Jesus as relatedness—as a "being-for" others,[41] as Bonhoeffer otherwise conceives it—but also defines the church likewise: as the body of Christ, the church's being is defined by the church and its members acting "with-" and "for-the-other" after the pattern of Christ Himself, such that the agency of this human action, through the Holy Spirit, actualizes the rule and will of God in the world.[42] Indeed, the church is *the church*, notes Bonhoeffer, only when it acts for others.[43] For Bonhoeffer, such action (at least as he presents it in the context of *Sanctorum Communio*) includes active love for one's neighbor, intercessory prayer, and the mutual forgiveness of sins.[44] However, the actual possibility of these socio-ecclesial

35. See Bonhoeffer, *Sanctorum Communio*, 165.
36. Bonhoeffer, *Sanctorum Communio*, 34 (emphasis original).
37. See Bonhoeffer, *Sanctorum Communio*, 63.
38. Bonhoeffer, "Visible Church," 456.
39. Bonhoeffer, *Sanctorum Communio*, 191.
40. Bonhoeffer, *Sanctorum Communio*, 155–56.
41. Bonhoeffer, "Lectures on Christology," 314.
42. Bonhoeffer, *Sanctorum Communio*, 182–83.
43. See Bonhoeffer, "Outline for a Book," 499–504, esp. 503.
44. See Bonhoeffer, *Sanctorum Communio*, 184–92. In the context of his later reflections on Christian community, Bonhoeffer speaks of the action of pastoral or spiritual care (*Seelsorge*), which encompasses the service of listening (including hearing the confession of another); active (or practical) helpfulness; bearing the burden of another's dispositions and sins; forgiveness;

acts, which, according to Bonhoeffer, constitute the church's ontology and sociological structure uniquely as a community of love, rests entirely in the Spirit's prior work of turning the human heart outward toward God and other human beings in love, and in mediating the *Stellvertretung* of Christ Himself.

The implications of these first two moves by which Bonhoeffer describes the work of the Holy Spirit by which the church is actualized are drawn out further in Bonhoeffer's later reflections on what he sees as the event of the church's founding at Pentecost.[45] It is with the coming of the Holy Spirit (Acts 2), and out of the assembled group of disciples (Acts 1), that the church is created, Bonhoeffer says.[46] The assembled group of disciples "itself is not already" the church "but becomes such only through the Spirit."[47] For Bonhoeffer, the church is created by the Spirit in this way because the Spirit, in an act of new creation, leads the church *into community*—into community in and with Christ, and through Christ (because of Christ's own *Stellvertretung*) into community in and with the world.[48] As Bonhoeffer observes, the Holy Spirit comes upon the assembled group of disciples "in words understandable to *everyone*" (see Acts 2:6–8); Peter witnesses to Christ through the Spirit (see Acts 2:14–36) and "summons *the people*" to repentance and new life;[49] and, by the Spirit's active power, the assembled group of disciples "break into" (*Einbruch*) the world and "engage in *missionary* activity" (see Acts 2:43–47).[50] Put otherwise, as an act of the Holy Spirit at Pentecost, the assembled group of disciples is turned out toward the world with a desire to implement in the world "God's will toward the new creation."[51] In this outward turn, the church, Bonhoeffer says, is created. It is this "eccentric existence" of the church, according to which the church's being consists in its being ordered by the Holy Spirit ultimately toward the world, that further constitutes the church uniquely as a community of love.[52] As the new creation

---

and speaking God's Word of comfort and admonition, one to another. See Bonhoeffer, *Life Together and Prayerbook*, 98–107.

45. See Bonhoeffer, "Visible Church," 438–46.

46. See Bonhoeffer, "Visible Church," 438. The importance of the demarcation between Acts 1 and Acts 2 for ecclesiological description is expressed similarly but more fully by Greggs. See Greggs, *Dogmatic Ecclesiology*, 1:li–liii, 1:12–21; and the discussion of Greggs's ecclesiological thought below.

47. Bonhoeffer, "Visible Church," 438.

48. See Bonhoeffer, "Visible Church," 441–42.

49. See Bonhoeffer, "Sichtbare Kirche im Neuen Testament," 427, 429 (emphases added).

50. Bonhoeffer, "Konkrete Ethik bei Paulus," 724.

51. Bonhoeffer, "Visible Church," 442.

52. I am borrowing the phrase "eccentric existence" from Kelsey, *Eccentric Existence*. As Bonhoeffer himself puts it, the church "does not, therefore, exist just for itself, but its existence is already always something that reaches far beyond it." Bonhoeffer, *Ethics*, 63.

of the Holy Spirit, the church exists in the world with what Bonhoeffer describes as "a double divine purpose"—"namely, being oriented toward the world, and, in this very act, simultaneously being oriented toward itself as the place where Jesus Christ is present."[53] The characteristic of the church as "a distinct polity" (*Gemeinwesen*), then, can be described as follows: "within the de*limited*ness of its own spiritual and material domain [the church] gives expression to the *un*limitedness of the message of Christ, and it is precisely the unlimitedness of the message of Christ that calls the world back into the limitedness of the church-community."[54] Or, as Küng observes, in somewhat more straightforward terms perhaps, only the church as the creation of the Holy Spirit is in receipt of the Spirit as the firstfruits and guarantee of salvation, and only the church can therefore make "demonstration of the Spirit's power" (1 Cor. 2:4).[55] For Küng, the presence of God's power in the Spirit is what constitutes "the essential difference" between the church and all other religious and nonreligious communities, and thus the church's unique nature, or what Küng describes as its "charismatic structure," in distinction to all other creaturely realities and forms of human community.[56] Bonhoeffer would doubtless agree, not least because Küng sees the church's charismatic structuring as being defined, in part, by the principle of *"with one another for one another"* in the way of service and love.[57]

What is more, that the church is in this way (for Küng) a strictly "pneumatic reality,"[58] and (for Bonhoeffer) a loving community of and in the Spirit (*Geistgemeinschaft*),[59] means that ecclesiological description, in Bonhoeffer's words, "cannot consist in the question of the empirical association of people and their psychological motivation."[60] This is not to say that the church in its sociohistorical existence cannot become the object of what Bonhoeffer calls "a sociological morphology," or that sociology and other related nontheological disciplines might not be of service to theologians in accounting for what the church is.[61] Indeed, because the church is, in Küng's words, "unavoidably

---

53. Bonhoeffer, *Ethics*, 405.
54. Bonhoeffer, *Ethik*, 409 (my trans.; emphasis follows original).
55. See Küng, *Church*, 150–203, esp. 168–69.
56. Küng, *Church*, 168, 179; see also 179–91. "Charismatic" is used here by Küng to refer not to a particular form or style of Christian worship but to the charisms or gifts of grace (*charismata*) given by the Holy Spirit to build up the church (1 Cor. 14:12) in whatever way it practices its worship. Each and every church is, in this sense, charismatic.
57. Küng, *Church*, 189 (emphasis original).
58. Küng, *Church*, 179.
59. See Bonhoeffer, *Sanctorum Communio*, 266.
60. Bonhoeffer, *Sanctorum Communio*, 152.
61. Bonhoeffer, *Sanctorum Communio*, 126. The reader should note that Bonhoeffer's own speech about the church (at least in *Sanctorum Communio*) employs insights from sociology

rooted in history, psychology and sociology," to understand what the church is and (recalling the concern of type 1, empirical ecclesiology) to ensure that ecclesiology does in fact serve the church's life and mission in the world today, theologians must certainly offer "sociological, psychological and historical analyses" of the church in their ecclesiological descriptions.[62] Bonhoeffer's claim is, instead, that ecclesiological description must always proceed on the basis that the church is not, and must never be treated by theologians as if it were, in Küng's words, "a free association of like-minded religious people,"[63] or, in Bonhoeffer's own words, a community of "pious people" or religiously and ethically motivated "kindred spirits," such that what the church is might be seen to be derived from, or produced by, its individual members and their socio-ecclesial acts.[64] Because the church is realized in Christ from eternity, and actualized in its sociohistorical existence by the Holy Spirit who, first, creates ecclesial human beings and, second, renders the church's ontology and sociological structure unique, the church, Bonhoeffer contends, is "fundamentally 'prior'" to both its members and their socio-ecclesial acts of being with and for the other.[65] As Bonhoeffer elaborates, the church is *"willed by God 'prior' to any human will for community."*[66] Consequently, "there is no sociological concept of the church, which is not theologically founded";[67] thus, the fundamental basis for ecclesiological description must always remain a theological account of what the church is as a creature of God the Holy Spirit.

However, as Bonhoeffer elaborates, further, the church is *"real only as human will for community."*[68] This concomitant concern to attend to the agency of human action in accounting for what the church is thus leads Bonhoeffer to develop his speech about the church in relation to the sociological concept of "objective spirit" (*der objektive Geist*).[69] As Bonhoeffer employs

---

and social philosophy positively, but in such a way that the fruitfulness of those insights is limited by Christian theology: "In this study social philosophy and sociology are employed in the service of theology." Bonhoeffer, *Sanctorum Communio*, 21. For more on Bonhoeffer's engagement with sociology and social philosophy in his description of the church in *Sanctorum Communio*, see Mawson, *Christ Existing as Community*, 39–55; and Emerton, *God's Church-Community*, 68–72, 77–95.

62. Küng, *Church*, 35, 484. See also chap. 2 on empirical ecclesiology.

63. Küng, *Church*, 126.

64. Bonhoeffer, "Nature of the Church," 306.

65. Bonhoeffer, *Sanctorum Communio*, 277.

66. Bonhoeffer, *Sanctorum Communio*, 278 (emphasis original).

67. Bonhoeffer, "Graduation Theses," 440; see also 439–41.

68. Bonhoeffer, *Sanctorum Communio*, 278 (emphasis original).

69. The concept of objective spirit has its roots in the work of Georg Hegel and refers to what today might be described as the culture of a given social group. Where acts of the individual willing human spirit unite, willing together and with one another in sociality, objective spirit is said to be generated. Bonhoeffer claims such spirit has "an active will of its own that

the concept in his ecclesiological thought, the socio-ecclesial acts of the willing human spirits of individual church members are said to unite in the church to generate the church's objective spirit. The objective spirit of the church is thus part of history and as such is fallible and sinful;[70] what is more, Bonhoeffer underscores that the objective spirit of the church exists empirically in this way in certain historical or "sociological forms and functions"—in assembling for worship, in preaching, in the sacraments of baptism and the Eucharist, in the priestly office, and in pastoral care.[71]

For Bonhoeffer, it is through these concrete and particular forms and functions of the church's objective spirit that the Holy Spirit works to actualize the church as Christ's body in its sociohistorical existence. This is, finally, the third move by which Bonhoeffer describes the work of the Holy Spirit by which the church is actualized. Bonhoeffer writes, "The Holy Spirit uses the objective spirit [of the church] as a vehicle for its gathering and sustaining social activity."[72] Critically, the Holy Spirit does this just as the church's objective spirit exists sinfully and fallibly in its human empirical forms and functions. The being of the church is therefore "subject to the historical ambiguity of all profane communities" and is sinful and fallible in its objective spirit, according to Bonhoeffer, but in such a way that it does not hinder the Holy Spirit's actualizing work: "We have, on the one hand," writes Bonhoeffer, "the ever-changing, imperfect, sinful, objective human spirit; on the other hand we have the Holy Spirit who bears this human spirit."[73]

To illustrate Bonhoeffer's point here with just one of the forms and functions of the church's objective spirit that he seeks to account for fully in its concrete and particular sociohistorical existence, he notes that the word *preached* is spoken as a human word and as such is necessarily fraught with

---

orders and guides the wills of the members who constitute it and participate in it, and that takes shape in specific forms." Bonhoeffer, *Sanctorum Communio*, 209; see also Bonhoeffer, *Sanctorum Communio*, 97–105; and Hegel, *Encyclopedia of the Philosophical Sciences*, 241–56.

70. See Bonhoeffer, *Sanctorum Communio*, 214–15.

71. Bonhoeffer, *Sanctorum Communio*, 226; see also 226–50.

72. Bonhoeffer, *Sanctorum Communio*, 215.

73. Bonhoeffer, *Sanctorum Communio*, 216; and Bonhoeffer, *Sanctorum Communio*, 215. The reader should note that to describe the relationship between the Holy Spirit and the objective spirit of the church in this way is to insist—in a fashion similar to the argument of Healy in type 2, performative ecclesiology, but contrary to the arguments of Moltmann and Jenson in type 3, communion ecclesiology—that any conflation of the Holy Spirit with the church's being or any given form or practice of the church in ecclesiological description is wholly inappropriate. As Bonhoeffer puts it categorically, "The objective spirit is not the Holy Spirit." Bonhoeffer, *Sanctorum Communio*, 216. Bonhoeffer's point is echoed by Küng: "It would be dangerous to try and identify the Church and the Holy Spirit; for the Holy Spirit is the Spirit of God, not of the Church; hence the fundamental *freedom* of the Holy Spirit." Küng, *Church*, 173 (emphasis original).

"contingency, imperfection, and sin."[74] But this human word, the preached word, Bonhoeffer says, is nevertheless a divine word because it is "the *bearer of the social activity of the Holy Spirit*" that builds up the church's human empirical form by carrying the promise of God's own word.[75] As Bonhoeffer observes elsewhere, "Every *concretum* of human words remains an *abstractum* when the Holy Spirit has not said them."[76] In other words, only the Holy Spirit enables the word preached as a *human* word to be efficacious as the *divine* word of God. The Spirit's efficacy is such that the Holy Spirit not only builds up the church as a sociohistorical human community by using the church's objective spirit in this way but, in doing so, sanctifies it as well. Bonhoeffer explains: "The objective spirit does not bear these forms as one would carry a sack on one's back; rather it is itself sanctified *through the load*. . . . This is of course true only insofar as the Holy Spirit does the carrying within it."[77] In Bonhoeffer's thought, then, preaching, as a form and function of the church's objective spirit, can be spoken of in a genuinely theological fashion only if theologians attend to it as a fallible and sinful human activity that constitutes what the church is in its sociohistorical existence in and by the Holy Spirit's work.[78]

For what Bonhoeffer also affirms in his speech about the church in relation to its objective spirit, is that this spirit is not just *used* by the Holy Spirit to actualize the church as Christ's body in space and time, but that the Holy Spirit actually *produces* the church's objective spirit, and, in fact, *plants into it* its forms and functions as they exist empirically.[79] As Bonhoeffer suggests in his reflections on the event of the church's founding at Pentecost, this implanting and production might be seen to take place precisely as the church is created by the Holy Spirit as an act of new creation, for in this act "the beginnings and indications" of the empirical forms and functions of the church are found, notes Bonhoeffer (see Acts 2:42–47; 4:32–35).[80] In other words, the Holy Spirit

74. Bonhoeffer, *Sanctorum Communio*, 233.
75. Bonhoeffer, *Sanctorum Communio*, 233 (emphasis original).
76. Bonhoeffer, "On Karl Heim's *Glaube und Denken*," 255 (emphasis original); see also 243–58.
77. Bonhoeffer, *Sanctorum Communio*, 216 (emphasis added).
78. The same is true for Bonhoeffer in relation to each of the other forms and functions of the church's objective spirit. For example, the sacraments of baptism and the Eucharist "are acts of the church-community and, like preaching, they unite within themselves the objective spirit of the church-community and the Holy Spirit who is operating through it." Bonhoeffer, *Sanctorum Communio*, 240. For more about the theandric nature of the forms and functions of the church's objective spirit in Bonhoeffer's thought, see Mawson, *Christ Existing as Community*, 161–69; see also Emerton, *God's Church-Community*, 128–37.
79. See Bonhoeffer, *Sanctorum Communio*, 216.
80. Bonhoeffer, "Visible Church," 443.

guarantees not only the efficacy of these forms and functions but also their actual sociohistorical existence.[81]

Indeed, the existence of these forms and functions cannot be understood in any way independent of the agency of the Spirit's action, such that they might be accounted for on the basis of human agency alone, or in purely sociological terms. As Bonhoeffer later writes in relation to the breaking of bread (Acts 2:42), specifically, "The grace of the Lord's Supper can be received only by those who are 'able to distinguish' (1 Cor. 11:29) between the true body and blood of Christ for the forgiveness of sins, and some other meal which may have a symbolic meaning or some other kind of character."[82] Put otherwise, and in more general terms, what the church is in its sociohistorical existence is understandable only from *within* the church and, further, only by those who, having stepped into the church, bow in faith to the church's claim to be "God's church-community."[83] And while, for Bonhoeffer, the socio-ecclesial acts of individual church members certainly unite in the church to generate its objective spirit, this unity of willing human spirits is not in the first instance produced by the agency of (common) human action. The unity instead is produced by a *divine* unity that itself is the consequence of the Holy Spirit first creating ecclesial human being and then rendering the church's ontology and sociological structure unique as a community of love. As Bonhoeffer writes, quoting Luther, "The point is not 'unanimity in spirit,' but the 'unity of the Spirit.'"[84] Bonhoeffer is clear: the Holy Spirit alone establishes the unity of the church's objective spirit, uniting "from above," before the socio-ecclesial acts of the willing human spirits of individual church members unite "from below," the multitude of these members within the church as Christ's body.[85] As Yves Congar observes, nothing less than the Spirit *of God* is needed to effect such unity.[86] Thus, for Bonhoeffer, only as the Holy Spirit produces and works through the unity of the church's objective spirit in its concrete and particular forms and functions is the church as Christ's body made actual in time and space.

81. See Bonhoeffer, *Sanctorum Communio*, 216.

82. Bonhoeffer, *Discipleship*, 270.

83. Bonhoeffer, *Sanctorum Communio*, 33, 127; see also Küng, *Church*, 30: "The Church cannot be properly judged from outside, from the viewpoint of a neutral observer, but only from within, by those who live in and with the Church."

84. Bonhoeffer, *Sanctorum Communio*, 193.

85. See Bonhoeffer, *Sanctorum Communio*, 193, 199. Bonhoeffer's point is echoed by Küng thus: "The unity of the Church is a spiritual entity. It is not chiefly a unity of the members among themselves, it depends finally not on itself but on the unity of God, which is efficacious through Jesus Christ *in the Holy Spirit*." See Küng, *Church*, 273 (emphasis added).

86. See Congar, *I Believe in the Holy Spirit*, 2:17.

It is by this threefold movement of the work of the Holy Spirit—creating ecclesial human being, rendering the church's ontology and sociological structure unique, and producing and working through the unity of the church's objective spirit—that Bonhoeffer understands the church as Christ's body to be actualized in its sociohistorical existence. He thereby seeks to take seriously in ecclesiological description the unique nature of what the church is as *both* creature of God *and* sociohistorical human community. As such, Bonhoeffer avers, "*The day of the founding of the actualized church remains Pentecost.*"[87] The importance of this emphasis on the event of Pentecost for description of the church's human empirical form, and for the strictly pneumatological determination of ecclesiology that it proffers, is echoed but finds greater and more specific definition in the emerging work of Tom Greggs.[88]

The Church as an Event of the Holy Spirit's Act

Central to Greggs's speech about the church is the demarcation between Acts 1 and 2 noted above. Indeed, for Greggs it is vital that theologians heed this demarcation if they want to speak about what the church is in a genuinely theological fashion. As Greggs draws the contrast, there is in the first chapter of Acts a description of "the church so-called."[89] What Greggs means by this is a sociohistorical human community "with the *semblance* of a church."[90] After all, what Luke describes in Acts 1 is a group of faithful followers of Jesus gathered together to pray and worship (Acts 1:13–14), hear a sermon (Acts 1:16–17), and read aloud from Scripture (Acts 1:20); there is even a membership count (Acts 1:15) and the equivalent of a meeting of the board of elders or parochial church council for the purpose of electing Matthias to a place of leadership (Acts 1:21–26).[91] Put otherwise, there is in Acts 1 "a phenomenological and loosely empirical account of the form of the church which describes its officers, liturgy, and polity."[92] And, as Greggs observes further, it is a description of the church's human empirical form that is so

87. Bonhoeffer, *Sanctorum Communio*, 152 (emphasis original).

88. I say "emerging" because the account of the church that Greggs offers is proposed as a three-volume set that, once complete, is intended to be read as a whole. My engagement with Greggs's ecclesiological thought in what follows is thus limited to the first volume of his *Dogmatic Ecclesiology*.

89. See Greggs, *Dogmatic Ecclesiology*, 1:lii–liii, 12; see also 13.

90. Greggs, *Dogmatic Ecclesiology*, 1:lii.

91. Greggs, *Dogmatic Ecclesiology*, 1:lii; see also 12.

92. Greggs, *Dogmatic Ecclesiology*, 1:lii.

often considered by theologians to be the proper object of ecclesiological discourse, or at least its primary concern: "Much in ecclesiology is in effect an account of the church as spoken of in Acts 1."[93]

But the problem Greggs identifies in an approach to ecclesiology that is concerned to attend primarily to lived ecclesial life and performed church practice, through either empirical description or practical discussion, is that the church spoken of in Acts 1 is precisely "the church so-called." In other words (and in an echo of Bonhoeffer's own reflection), for Greggs, the gathered group of faithful followers of Jesus in Acts 1 is *not yet* the church; what makes this gathering the church—what causes the church to come into being, that is—is the coming of God the Holy Spirit in Acts 2.[94] At Pentecost, the church so-called becomes the church, says Greggs, "by an event of the act of the Holy Spirit."[95] Without the agency of this divine action "the church (so-called) remains a shut-away society in an upper room."[96] "But with the Spirit," continues Greggs, "the church becomes the church—that body which is propelled outwards and which internally and corporately is orientated not only towards God but also towards the human others and the rest of creation."[97]

In a fashion similar to Bonhoeffer, therefore, Greggs conceives of the act of the Holy Spirit that creates the church in connection with the Spirit's redeeming and reordering work. For Greggs, it is the particular work of the Holy Spirit to mediate within space and time the reconciling work of God in Jesus Christ, in order to make the human community of the church truly Christ's body.[98] In this mediating work, the Spirit takes the fallen, self-oriented human heart and turns it out toward God, on a vertical axis, and out toward other human beings and other creatures, on a horizontal axis.[99] In this turning outward, the Christian believer is incorporated into the life of Christ, thereby coming to participate in the eternal life of love between Father and Son (the vertical axis), and also into "the way of God's grace *for* the world" (the horizontal axis).[100] The Spirit's work of "catching up" Christian believers, both in the movement of divine love *ad intra* and in the gracious movement of that love out toward the world *ad extra*, is what establishes the church

---

93. Greggs, *Dogmatic Ecclesiology*, 1:12.

94. See Greggs, *Dogmatic Ecclesiology*, 1:12–13.

95. Greggs, *Dogmatic Ecclesiology*, 1:lii.

96. Greggs, *Dogmatic Ecclesiology*, 1:13.

97. Greggs, *Dogmatic Ecclesiology*, 1:13.

98. See Greggs, *Dogmatic Ecclesiology*, 1:23.

99. See Greggs, *Dogmatic Ecclesiology*, 1:34; see also 21–39. For more about the problematic temptation to limit creation to human beings in Christian theology, see Clough, *On Animals*.

100. Greggs, *Dogmatic Ecclesiology*, 1:31 (emphasis original).

as *the church*. "In the church, one lives towards God and towards the given neighbour *simultaneously*."[101]

What the church is as an event of the Holy Spirit's act is thus "a community of hearts turned *outwards*"—a community that God gives in God's redeeming grace to be the (one) human community in the world that, in other words, is being dispossessed of the *cor incurvatum in se* (that is, the heart turned in on itself, or the heart of sin).[102] In this sense, the community of the church, says Greggs, is "a community of salvation" in which the fall and its effects are seen to be reversed: in the work of the Spirit in the church's life humanity is redeemed from the heart turned in on itself by being returned at once to communion with God in Christ (vertically) and to communion with one another (horizontally); and, for Greggs, as for Bonhoeffer, there is no communion in the former sense without communion in the latter sense.[103] Further, this simultaneous reordering work of humanity in the church in its horizontal and vertical directions "is not only internal to the church itself," says Greggs, "but is also the ordering *of the church as a corporate body*."[104] In other words, in the act of the Holy Spirit establishing the church as an event, individual hearts of Christian believers are turned out toward God and humanity but so too is the church's corporate heart. As Greggs writes, "What takes place on the level of individuals in relation to each other in the church takes place simultaneously in relation to the corporate identity of the church in relation to the world."[105] It is in this "twofold dynamism" of the Spirit's "two-directional" reordering and redeeming work that Greggs locates the salvific significance of the church more precisely in a twofold sense.[106]

First, the human other internal to the life of the church is given to the Christian believer as a gift of the Spirit's continuing work of salvation on the horizontal axis of sociohistorical existence.[107] This is to say that by our love of another Christian believer within the church we continue to work out our salvation in fear and trembling because the (God-given) otherness of

---

101. Greggs, *Dogmatic Ecclesiology*, 1:103 (emphasis original).

102. See Greggs, *Dogmatic Ecclesiology*, 1:31 (emphasis altered), see also 31–34. As Greggs writes (following Luther), "Sin is the prioritization of the self . . . over the divine and created others," see Greggs, *Dogmatic Ecclesiology*, 1:34. On Luther's definition of sin, see "A Reformation Legacy?," in chap. 3 above.

103. Greggs, *Dogmatic Ecclesiology*, 1:45; see also 1:36–39.

104. Greggs, *Dogmatic Ecclesiology*, 1:129 (emphasis original).

105. Greggs, *Dogmatic Ecclesiology*, 1:129; see also Greggs, "*Communio* Ecclesiology," 347–66, esp. 363.

106. Greggs, *Dogmatic Ecclesiology*, 1:129.

107. See Greggs, *Dogmatic Ecclesiology*, 1:39–46.

that human other—"even in the other's weakness, fallenness, and propensity to sin, from which we can suffer"—is essential for the possibility of dispossessing the human heart of its self-orientated, sinful identity.[108] This means not only that the church community is itself instrumental for the Christian believer to live a sanctified life,[109] but that human otherness, or difference between human beings, is constitutive of what the church is as a community of salvation. In other words, difference and otherness is both the theater and the means for the work of the Holy Spirit to establish the church in its life of love.[110] This itself is clear in the narrative of Acts 2, observes Greggs: the linguistic difference and cultural otherness of the "God-fearing Jews from every nation" (Acts 2:5) is not denied by the coming of the Holy Spirit; rather, that difference, that otherness, is brought by the Spirit to unity in the actuality of that otherness and difference—that is, each God-fearing Jew is enabled by the Spirit to hear in their *own* vernacular language the wonders of God that the Galilean disciples declare (Acts 2:4–8). The point is made likewise in relation to socioeconomic difference: in consequence of the act of the Holy Spirit, individual, self-orientated ownership of material goods is reordered such that within the church property and possessions are not only held in common but also sold to give to anyone who has need (Acts 2:44–45).[111] This is why, according to Greggs, as an event of the Spirit's act, the church is not and can never be a homogeneous community or a community of the merely like-minded, who associate or are bound together because of common human agreement or shared ethnic, political, or social identity.[112] It is the Holy Spirit who binds the community of the church together and who does so precisely in and through the context of human otherness and difference. In this, the church is distinct from all other creaturely realities and forms of sociohistorical human community in the world.[113] For Greggs, it follows that "churches that are focused on 'types' or classes of people with shared interests and even worldviews should be distrusted as they fail to see the Spirit's work of grace in the creature who is being redeemed by turning in the horizontal as well as the vertical plane away from self and towards the other *in the other's otherness to the self*."[114]

---

108. Greggs, *Dogmatic Ecclesiology*, 1:41.

109. See Greggs, *Dogmatic Ecclesiology*, 1:368; see also Greggs's extended discussion of the corporate nature or "non-interior form" of sanctification at 1:368–401, esp. 390–401.

110. See Greggs, *Dogmatic Ecclesiology*, 1:45, 402–25. Love (of God and humanity) is thus the concrete form of the sanctified life.

111. See Greggs, *Dogmatic Ecclesiology*, 1:45–46.

112. See Greggs, *Dogmatic Ecclesiology*, 1:331.

113. See Greggs, *Dogmatic Ecclesiology*, 1:331.

114. Greggs, *Dogmatic Ecclesiology*, 1:44 (emphasis original).

In the same vein, churches that are self-referential or self-interested—that is, constantly concerned with their own life or institutional survival—should also be distrusted as churches, as these fail to see (to follow the trajectory of Greggs's thought) the Spirit's work of grace that enables the church to turn its heart (corporately, as a community) away from itself and out toward the otherness of the world.[115] Second, then, the life of the church is given as a gift of the Spirit's continuing work of salvation on the horizontal axis of sociohistorical existence *for the sake of the world*—that is, to represent and mediate in and to the world the assurance of God's gospel.[116] By the Spirit, the church lives to proclaim that, for the sake of the world's salvation, "God has made this [crucified] Jesus . . . both Lord and Messiah" (Acts 2:36). As Greggs writes, "It is a living for the world which is essential for the existence of the church."[117] And, for Greggs, the specific form that ecclesial life lived for the world takes, such that the church is demarcated as *the church*, is what he describes as the "priestly form" of Christ's own life and person, the essence of which is a life lived out perfectly and fully toward God and the human other for the sake of the world.[118]

This essence of Christ's priesthood is subsequently identified by Greggs as being embodied in seven active modalities: divine-human (and human-human) mediation; self-sacrifice; bearing iniquity; intercession; obedient and faithful oblation (in the form of thanksgiving and praise); blessing; and holiness.[119] It is these modalities of the priesthood of Christ that are then said by Greggs to take form in the church in both its internal and external relationality as the Spirit's reordering work of grace enables the church to participate actively in Christ's priestly life *as the body of Christ*.[120] But because the being of Christ is

115. See Greggs, *Dogmatic Ecclesiology*, 1:134.

116. See Greggs, Dogmatic Ecclesiology, 1:133.

117. Greggs, *Dogmatic Ecclesiology*, 1:134. The reader should note that to describe the existence of the church in relation to the world in this way is to deny—in contrast to the argument of Jenson in type 3, communion ecclesiology—that the church exists eternally. When God is "all in all," (1 Cor. 15:28) and in the end there is only God, the church itself will end because no world will exist for which the church can live. See Greggs, *Dogmatic Ecclesiology*, 1:130–31.

118. See Greggs, *Dogmatic Ecclesiology*, 1:68.

119. See Greggs, *Dogmatic Ecclesiology*, 1:68–81. A helpful summary of the priesthood of Christ can also be found in Tomlin, *Widening Circle*, 9–50.

120. See Greggs, *Dogmatic Ecclesiology*, 1:114–15. In affirming this, Greggs is at once clear that no direct identification between the being of the church as Christ's body and Christ Himself can (or should) ever be made: "The body of Christ is not a replication of the incarnate person of Christ or even a continuity of it. . . . Christ is not replaced by the church; nor does the church continue something Christ started; nor can there be direct identity between the church and Christ." Greggs, *Dogmatic Ecclesiology*, 1:86. This is because Christ is the *head* of the body, the church (Col. 1:18), and His body is ascended and seated in heaven at the right hand of the Father (Acts 2.33–35; Col. 3:1). See Greggs, *Dogmatic Ecclesiology*, 1:51.

a being lived for others (to recall Bonhoeffer's language), the church becomes Christ's body more fully, Greggs says, when it lives not toward itself but toward those others outside itself for whom it exists.[121] In other words, "The church is priestly precisely where it meets that which is not the church."[122] Or, as he elaborates further, "Where the church intercedes for the world, mediates for the world, offers oblation for the world, makes sacrifices for the world, confesses the sins of the world, seeks to bring reconciling peace within the people of the world, prays God's blessing on the world, and ministers to the world, there the church's priesthood is most intensely present."[123] But all of this is possible only because of the Spirit's redeeming and reordering work of salvation inaugurated at Pentecost. Only with the coming of the Holy Spirit in Acts 2 does the capacity exist in the world for humanity to be individually and corporately ordered not toward itself but toward God and the world in love;[124] and this capacity, as a gift of the Spirit's continuing work of salvation on the horizontal axis of sociohistorical existence, is the life of the church as a human community.

For Greggs, it is imperative therefore that ecclesiological description is focused first and foremost on the act of God the Holy Spirit who brings the church (of Acts 2) into being as an event in space and time, rather than on empirical description or practical discussion of the church so-called (of Acts 1). Indeed, for Greggs, speech about the church that starts with practical discussion or empirical description of the church's human empirical form, and presents an account of the church in predominantly phenomenological or functionalist terms, will fail to see—in a fashion similar to both empirical and performative ecclesiology—that the church is a creature of the saving grace of God the Holy Spirit, and thereby, as the body of Christ, ontologically and sociologically distinct from all other human communities in the world.[125]

However, in wanting to prioritize the agency of the Spirit's action in speech about the church and to establish in this way that the doctrine of the church is a "highly derivative" doctrine that "exists formally a long way downstream" from more foundational Christian doctrines,[126] Greggs is not seeking to put forth an account of the church that, proportionately speaking, overemphasizes—in a fashion similar to both communion and ideal

---

121. See Greggs, *Dogmatic Ecclesiology*, 1:116.
122. Greggs, *Dogmatic Ecclesiology*, 1:117.
123. Greggs, *Dogmatic Ecclesiology*, 1:145.
124. See Greggs, *Dogmatic Ecclesiology*, 1:43.
125. See Greggs, *Dogmatic Ecclesiology*, 1:xxxi–xxxii.
126. See Greggs, *Dogmatic Ecclesiology*, 1:xxxi. See also "The Church as a Topic of Systematic Theology," in chap. 1 above.

ecclesiology—God's immanent trinitarian life. This is not only because in such accounts "little materially about the church itself ever emerges" but because the act of God always takes place (from the perspective of human-kind, at least) *within space and time*, which God creates *ex nihilo* in God's self-determination to be God "for us" and for God's eternal purposes to be fulfilled in and through the church.[127] As Greggs writes, "In the sheer magnificent plenitude of God's being, God has determined Godself for all eternity to be for creation and to be the God who makes Godself known as being *pro nobis* for the world by being *pro nos* within God's community of the church."[128] In other words, God cannot now be God without a relationship to that which is not God—a relationship that God establishes with humanity in the person of Jesus Christ but also, as Greggs says, "with the church in the person of the Holy Spirit."[129] The force of this latter affirmation is such that, for Greggs, there is no sense in which the being of the church can ever be considered fleeting or dissolvable in an occasionalist sense.[130] Notwith-standing the weight of emphasis that ecclesiological ecclesiology places on the Holy Spirit's actualizing work to create the church *as the church*, that the Holy Spirit is the Spirit *of God* means that the Spirit always acts constantly and faithfully according to Godself.[131] And if God has determined Godself such that (from humankind's perspective) there is "no God aside from the God of the church,"[132] and if what the church is, is the community in space and time where the revelation of God's Word is known through the Spirit's work,[133] then the Spirit always acts faithfully and constantly to create the being of the church in actuality.[134] There is, then, "no timeless ahistorical or nongeographical church,"[135] and any account of what the church is must attend to the church as it is particularly and concretely.

Indeed, to fail to attend in ecclesiological description to what the church is in its sociohistorical existence is to deny that it is this concrete and particular

127. Greggs, *Dogmatic Ecclesiology*, 1:xxxiii.

128. Greggs, *Dogmatic Ecclesiology*, 1:xxxvii. The Latin phrase "*pro nobis*" (in the dative) and "*pro nos*" (in the accusative) means "on behalf of us" or "for us."

129. Greggs, *Dogmatic Ecclesiology*, 1:18; see also xxxvi–xl. Greggs is appropriating here Barth's christologically conditioned doctrine of election in relation to the act of the Spirit caus-ing the church to be. See Greggs, *Dogmatic Ecclesiology*, 1:16–18. See also "The Church as the Eventful Act of God," in chap. 5 above.

130. See "Communion Ecclesiology: An Assessment," in chap. 4 above; and "Ideal Ecclesiol-ogy: An Assessment," in chap. 5 above.

131. See Greggs, *Dogmatic Ecclesiology*, 1:18.

132. Greggs, *Dogmatic Ecclesiology*, 1:xxxvii.

133. See Greggs, *Dogmatic Ecclesiology*, 1:xxxviii.

134. See Greggs, *Dogmatic Ecclesiology*, 1:19–21.

135. Greggs, *Dogmatic Ecclesiology*, 1:xlvii.

human community that God has chosen to be in relationship with;[136] but it is also to deny that the church of God exists only as *this* particular and concrete human community. That the church is "an *event* of the *act* of the Holy Spirit" is thus signal in Greggs's ecclesiological thought.[137] As an event of the Holy Spirit's *act*, the agency of divine action is certainly the condition of the possibility of the church's being and the agency of all human action within it.[138] But that the church is an *event* of the Spirit's act means that the church has its being in space and time only as a particular and concrete church—that is, in the context of human fallenness and sin, and among the agency of those who are *simul iustus et peccator*.[139] As Greggs writes, "It is God who fits God's church to meet and to come into being despite the individual and community's sinfulness, creaturely limitations, poverty of worship, and propensity to idolatry. The Holy Spirit speaks through the church as through Balaam's ass—that is, through a divine willing to speak through and create the church in this way."[140] It is imperative, therefore, that in their speech about the church theologians attend to the ways in which the church *does exist* concretely and particularly. True ecclesiological speech *does not exist* apart from description of lived ecclesial life and performed church practice in its particular and concrete sociohistorical existence, which, as Greggs avers, can be variously studied.[141]

For Greggs, then, "There is no way that we can describe the church theologically without speaking of it is as an act of God's grace and a creation of God. But there is *then* the responsibility to speak of *the church* as such as a creation and event of the act of God—that is, as a community in time and space in its empirical and historical reality."[142] It is this fundamental methodological conviction that Greggs seeks to work out, therefore, in his subsequent

---

136. See Greggs, *Dogmatic Ecclesiology*, 1:xliv.

137. Greggs, *Dogmatic Ecclesiology*, 1:8.

138. See Greggs, *Dogmatic Ecclesiology*, 1:9.

139. See Greggs, *Dogmatic Ecclesiology*, 1:10–12.

140. Greggs, *Dogmatic Ecclesiology*, 1:11–12. There is an important point here to be made in relation to the reality of ecclesial sin. Ecclesial sin is not an empirical distortion of the church's true theological identity; neither do all sinful acts of the church remain detached from what the church is truly as the acts of individual Christian believers. See "Ideal Ecclesiology: An Assessment," in chap. 5 above. The point is rather that the church itself is *simul iustus et peccator*; or, as Bonhoeffer puts it, "As a sinful community the church is nevertheless still holy, or rather that in this world it is never holy without also being sinful." Bonhoeffer, *Sanctorum Communio*, 214. Like the individual Christian believer, the corporate community of the church is being sanctified by the Spirit's work of grace.

141. See Greggs, *Dogmatic Ecclesiology*, 1:xxxvi: "Historical, sociological, liturgical, homiletic, psychological, practical, and narrative accounts all have their place (and are used in part as data for the present account)."

142. Greggs, *Dogmatic Ecclesiology*, 1:xxxiv (emphasis original).

speech about how the various modalities of Christ's priesthood take concrete and particular form in the life of the church through the Spirit's work.[143] For example, the modality of oblation takes form in the church's life indicatively, says Greggs, in confession of sin, faithful obedience in word and deed, praise with music and song, monetary giving, and the practice of baptism and Holy Communion.[144] In discussing baptism and Holy Communion, specifically, Greggs stresses that the Christian believer and the church community actively participate in these particular and concrete forms of thanksgiving and praise—that is, they are willed acts of human agency, enacted with the most basic, common, and essential elements of created reality: bread, wine, water, money, and the (fallible and sinful) human voice and body.[145] Significantly, however, all of these concrete and particular forms of thanksgiving and praise are human acts "for which the human is *freed to will*" by the prevenience of the Spirit's redeeming and reordering work of salvation.[146] For Greggs, particular and concrete forms of thanksgiving and praise are human acts of gratitude and grace that are performed *through the Spirit* in response to divine grace, but as such they are also acts that are brought about *by the Spirit* because the grace of God in Christ is itself received *from the Spirit* in the life of the church.[147] When speaking about lived ecclesial life and performed church practice in its sociohistorical existence, there is thus the need for theologians to speak of the agency of human action that takes place *within* the agency of the Spirit's divine action, and of the agency of this divine action that takes place "with a *terminus*" in the human community of the church and the concrete and particular forms and practices that attend to it.[148]

Ecclesiological Ecclesiology: An Assessment

In offering this "thick *theological* description" of the church's human empirical form, Greggs (like Bonhoeffer) gives voice to the concern of ecclesiological ecclesiology to account for the unique nature of what the church is as both creature of God and sociohistorical human community.[149] By recourse to a

---

143. See Greggs, *Dogmatic Ecclesiology*, 1:148–425.

144. See Greggs, *Dogmatic Ecclesiology*, 1:303–30; see also 1:148–201 (on baptism) and 1:202–45 (on Holy Communion).

145. Greggs, *Dogmatic Ecclesiology*, 1:166, 198, 203, 212, 235, 329. While Greggs makes these points in relation to the practice of baptism and Holy Communion, they can equally be applied to the other forms of thanksgiving and praise identified.

146. Greggs, *Dogmatic Ecclesiology*, 1:166 (emphasis added).

147. See Greggs, *Dogmatic Ecclesiology*, 1:303.

148. Greggs, *Dogmatic Ecclesiology*, 1:212 (emphasis added).

149. Greggs, *Dogmatic Ecclesiology*, 1:xxxv (emphasis original).

strict pneumatological determination of ecclesiology, and more specifically to an understanding of the Holy Spirit of God as the divine person in and by whose work the human community of the church exists, ecclesiological ecclesiology works to attend in speech about the church to both the life and work of God as the condition for the possibility of the church's existence and to the church's particular and contingent sociohistorical reality as sinful and fallible. In doing so, ecclesiological ecclesiology might be seen to offer, in light of ecclesiology's most basic task, a reparative theological grammar for ecclesiology per se. This grammar is not one that pries apart in ecclesiological description the asymmetrical relationship of divine and human togetherness in the church's being, and thus, derivatively, it is one that offers an account of divine and human agency. Further, it is a grammar that works to hold together, in accordance with the most basic ecclesiological task, and through reference to the person and work of God the Holy Spirit, the agency of both divine and human action in an appropriately ordered and proportionate way. This grammar is therefore one that the reader might consider to work to mitigate the theological deficiencies that I have suggested exist in relation to each of the first four types of approach to contemporary ecclesiology.

In direct contrast to both empirical and performative ecclesiology, the account of the church that emerges in ecclesiological ecclesiology is strictly dependent upon, and set clearly and methodologically under, a doctrine of God: the church exists in the world as the body of Christ only because of the gracious act and activity of God the Holy Spirit. In ecclesiological ecclesiology, speech about the agency of God's action as the originating and sustaining cause of what the church is as a sociohistorical human community is neither evacuated from ecclesiological description (in contrast to empirical ecclesiology) nor at risk of being obscured within it (in contrast to performative ecclesiology).[150] In ecclesiological ecclesiology, there is, in other words, no sense in which ecclesiology as a doctrine is at risk (as it is in empirical ecclesiology) of being naturalized or de-theologized, or that the human empirical form of the church is absolutely reducible to the category of the empirical or sociological, such that speech about divine action is collapsed into ecclesial human reality, and what the church is might be understood on the basis of human agency alone. But at once, there is also, in ecclesiological ecclesiology, no sense in which the church might be considered (as it is in performative ecclesiology) as one subspecies of created sociality among others, whose distinctiveness as the church is constituted by the agency of Christian believers

150. See chaps. 2 and 3 above.

in lived ecclesial life and performed church practice. Rather, the church is the church *of God*; and it is the church of God only by the work of God the Holy Spirit who creates the church as Christ's body; as a creature of God's grace, the church is, then, sociologically and ontologically distinct from all other human communities in the world.

In this way, the reader might consider ecclesiological ecclesiology to have proper concern for accounting theologically for what the church is in an appropriately *ordered* way: in ecclesiological ecclesiology, theologians first speak about the church as a creature of God and God's gracious acts. In this, the reader might see that ecclesiological ecclesiology affirms the call of ideal ecclesiology to account fully for the church as a creature of God's grace by making methodologically paramount in speech about the church an account of divine agency indexed to a theology of God's aseity.[151] However, the theology of God's aseity on which ecclesiological ecclesiology trades is not one that is focused (as it is in ideal ecclesiology) on the immanent trinitarian life of God. It is instead focused on the being of God *pro nos*—that is, on a theology of God's aseity that is understood and worked out primarily with reference to the being of God who determines Godself to be God "for us" in the person of Jesus Christ, and who makes God's being for us known in this way *in the church* that is brought into being by the act of God the Holy Spirit.[152] Of course, to affirm in this way that an account of theology proper cannot be given in theological inquiry "apart from the life of God as known in the church" might lead the reader to worry about whether ecclesiological ecclesiology—at least from the perspective of ideal ecclesiology—renders too close a connection between God's own being and the being of the church, and thereby risks safeguarding inadequately, in a fashion similar to communion ecclesiology, either the contingent nature of the church or its unqualified difference from the life of God.[153]

The question that the reader may therefore want to register in relation to ecclesiological ecclesiology is whether its specific understanding and working out of a theology of God's aseity in fact results in an account of the church that, proportionately speaking, says too little—or, in the case of

---

151. See chap. 5 above.

152. See Bonhoeffer, *Act and Being*, 91: "Christ is the word of God's freedom. God *is* present, that is not in eternal nonobjectivity but . . . 'haveable,' graspable in the Word within the church" (emphasis original).

153. Greggs, *Dogmatic Ecclesiology*, 1:xxxix. It is on the basis of such an understanding of God's aseity that Bonhoeffer writes, "In order to establish clarity about the inner logic of theological construction, it would be good for once if a presentation of doctrinal theology were to start not with the doctrine of God but with the doctrine of the church." Bonhoeffer, *Sanctorum Communio*, 134. See also chap. 4 above.

Bonhoeffer, specifically, anything at all—about the immanent trinitarian life of God.[154] But, equally, the reader might also want to ask if such an affirmation—that there is no God whose being is independent of the act of God the Holy Spirit who creates the church as a creature of God's saving grace—is not exactly what is needed in ecclesiological description in order to offer a genuinely theological account of the church as a sociohistorical *human* community. For what ecclesiological ecclesiology affirms by speaking in this particular way about the aseity of God is not only the church's contingent nature but also its unqualified difference from God's own life: the church is, after all, the *creature* of God and God's gracious acts; and as the gracious creation of God the Holy Spirit, the church is created external to its sociohistorical existence but as the human community it is in that existence. In ecclesiological ecclesiology, there is, in other words, no sense in which the being of the church is at risk of being overidentified with the being of God, such that the church becomes (as it almost does in communion ecclesiology) "a fourth member of the Trinity," or that the church as Christ's body is seen (as is the tendency in communion ecclesiology) to coinhere with Christ Himself, such that the church is understood to exist in the eschaton.[155]

Further, precisely because the account of divine agency in ecclesiological ecclesiology is indexed to a theology of God's aseity worked out in reference to the being of God as *pro nos* within the church, there is no sense in which the being of the church as a sociohistorical reality is at risk of being either marginalized (in contrast to communion ecclesiology) or dissolved into the eventful act and activity of God (in contrast to ideal ecclesiology), such that what the church is might be understood on the basis of divine agency alone. Put otherwise, when confronted by the actual content of speech about the church in ecclesiological ecclesiology, the proffered account of divine agency and the associated theology of God's aseity works to *relativize* the agency of human action in accounting for the church's human empirical form, but, critically, it does not *minimize* it.

In this way, ecclesiological ecclesiology might be considered by the reader to also have proper concern for accounting theologically for what the church is in an appropriately *proportionate* way: in ecclesiological ecclesiology, although theologians *first* speak about the church as the gracious creation of God the Holy Spirit, they *subsequently* speak about the church as the

154. For further consideration of Bonhoeffer's aversion toward divine metaphysics, see Holmes, "Holy Spirit," 176–77; and Holmes, "Beyond Bonhoeffer," 29–43.

155. Greggs, *Dogmatic Ecclesiology*, 1:8.

sociohistorical human community that the Holy Spirit creates the church
to be. In this, the reader might consider ecclesiological ecclesiology to also
affirm the call of both performative and empirical ecclesiology to account
fully for the church as a lived sociohistorical reality with attendant human
empirical forms and practices.[156] While the church is accounted for in ecclesiological ecclesiology as the church *of God*, it is also spoken about as *the
church* of God, and in such a way that speech about the church is not at
risk (as it is in ideal ecclesiology) of presenting in abstract terms an overly
idealized account of the church that is disconnected from the experience
of lived ecclesial life and neglectful of the church's human empirical form.
In other words, ecclesiological ecclesiology might be said to construe what
the church is (in contrast to both ideal ecclesiology and communion ecclesiology) with full reference to its concrete and particular sociohistorical
existence.

However, in contrast to empirical ecclesiology, ecclesiological ecclesiology
does not attend to the sociohistorical out of a desire to make description of
the church's human empirical form the normative and necessary foundation
of ecclesiology per se. Therefore, it does not consider the fruit of empirical study of the church's phenomenal surface determinative of the church's
being.[157] Rather, ecclesological ecclesiology attends to the sociohistorical
because the act of God the Holy Spirit creates the church in its sociohistorical existence; thus, the church can be understood only by reference to the
Spirit's own act. Of course, this emphasis on the act of the Holy Spirit as
the determinative explanatory power for accounting for the church's human
empirical form might lead the reader to worry about whether ecclesiological
ecclesiology—at least from the perspective of empirical ecclesiology—is in
fact sufficiently oriented away from theological first principles and toward
ecclesial human reality. The question that the reader may want to register
therefore with respect to ecclesiological ecclesiology is whether it results in an
account of the church that is still too disconnected from the church's particular and concrete sociohistorical existence and material descriptions thereof.
The reader might also ask, however, whether a methodological commitment
to the church's intelligibility being strictly dependent on a pneumatological
investigation of the church's being is not exactly what is needed in ecclesiological description in order to offer a genuinely theological account of the
church as the gracious creation of God the Holy Spirit. What is certain is
that ecclesiological ecclesiology serves to remind theologians of the clamant

156. See chaps. 2 and 3.
157. See chap. 2 above.

need to hold together in speech about the church an account of divine and human agency in an ordered and proportionate way to ensure that the church is spoken of as both creature of God and sociohistorical human community, with due concern for the asymmetrical relationship of divine and human togetherness in the church's being.

Conclusion

The motivation behind this book is to encourage those who seek to serve and lead the church to consider what it is they are called to lead and serve, and to engage this question—the question of *what* the church is—before engaging the question of *how* to "be" church or "do" church. To this end, I have sought to present and assess five types of contemporary approach to ecclesiology. Each type has been presented and assessed in relation to a basic theological grammar for accounting for what the church is that was derived from Paul's description of the church in Corinth, focusing on his appropriation in that description of God's covenantal promise to be God as God of a people. That the church is the people *of God* ("I will be their God") and God's *people* ("they will be my people") establishes what I maintain is the most basic ecclesiological task—the task of holding together in speech about the church, in an ordered and proportionate way, an account of both divine and human agency, such that the former relativizes but does not minimize the latter. The church is thereby spoken about as *both* creature of God *and* sociohistorical human community in a way that maintains the asymmetrical relationship of divine and human togetherness in the church's being.

The result, I have attempted to demonstrate, is that the first four types of contemporary approach to ecclesiology, given the most basic ecclesiological task, are to one extent or another theologically deficient. These deficiencies, further, are symptomatic of the problematic tendency in contemporary approaches to ecclesiology to attend either to the church's human empirical form (to "they will be my people") or to the life and work of God (to "I will be their God"), thereby presenting in ecclesiological description theologically disordered and disproportionate speech about the church. Hence I presented and assessed a fifth type of contemporary approach to ecclesiology that corrects, or at least mitigates, the theologically disordered and disproportionate ecclesiological speech of empirical, performative, communion, and ideal ecclesiology. In this consideration, I sought to show the ways in which ecclesiological ecclesiology can be said to hold together in speech about the church what the first four types of approach to contemporary ecclesiology tend to pry apart—that is, the asymmetrical relationship of divine and human togetherness in the church's being. And, derivatively, the way in which ecclesiological ecclesiology proffers an account of divine and human agency. I therefore contend that, given ecclesiology's most basic task, ecclesiological ecclesiology moves toward establishing a reparative theological grammar for ecclesiology per se and offering a genuinely theological account of what the church is.

Of course, whether or not this contention holds good will depend, in part, on the extent to which the reader is convinced by the effectiveness of the analysis I have offered of each type of contemporary approach to ecclesiology; the way in which I have constructed those types; and, indeed, the typology itself. No doubt there will be many who will disagree with the typological construction and analysis presented in this book, not least because of how I have read individual theologians as illustrative of one type of contemporary approach or another. Some of those readings may well be controversial, or at least a matter of dispute. And perhaps some are simply mistaken. It is hoped, however, that what the book presents in relation to each type of contemporary approach to ecclesiology is taken in charity by those who read it, and especially by those whose ecclesiological thought is described in its pages and who are in a position to respond to its reading of their work. Thus if this book, in its attempt to provide a constructive orientation to the field of contemporary ecclesiology, gives rise to fruitful theological discourse by bringing the intricacies of the question of *what* the church is sharply into view among professional theologians or church practitioners, or between teachers and students of ecclesiology, then much of my purpose has been achieved.

I am also hopeful that, in the context of such discourse, questions of ecclesiological method and of what it means to account theologically for what the church is will lead necessarily to questions of how to "be" or "do" church. I am convinced that each type of contemporary approach to ecclesiology presented in this book has any number of practical implications for lived ecclesial life. For example, if the church is just the human social response to the merciful grace of God, why does it matter what form that response takes? If the distinctiveness of the church as a sociohistorical human community is located in Christian belief and practice, why is it important that such practice and belief is more countercultural than culturally relevant? To what extent is the church obliged to examine Christian practice in light of catholic Christian doctrine, with a view to distinguishing in that practice what is proper or foreign to the authentic substance of Christian faith? What is the significance of the celebration of the Eucharist for the church to be the church? How is the church to confront the reality of ecclesial sin as an ever-present aspect of its corporate identity, and what might it mean for the church to confess that sin? If the church exists only as it is turned out toward the world, can a church that pursues its vocation concerned with its own life or institutional survival ever be the church? And if the church is the gracious creation of God the Holy Spirit, with what seriousness can the church pray the age-old prayer of Pentecost, "Come, Holy Spirit," as well as the prayer of the penitent, "Do not take your Holy Spirit from me"? These are just some of the questions that I hope those who read this book might address more substantively than I have been able to do here. In asking and addressing such questions, the reader might join her hope to mine that the reality of how the church is and what the church does will become ever more faithful to the church's own being.

Glossary

ad extra: a Latin term meaning "to the outside." The phrase is (often) contrasted with *ad intra*. *See also* ad intra; opus ad extra.

ad intra: a Latin term meaning "to the inside." The phrase is (often) contrasted with *ad extra*. *See also* ad extra; opus ad intra.

anamnesis: derived from the Greek *ana-*, meaning "back," and *mimnēskesthai*, meaning "to recall" or "cause to remember." *Anamnesis* means "remembrance" or "memorial." Used liturgically, *anamnesis* refers to the eucharistic remembrance (Luke 22:19; 1 Cor. 11:24–25) that recalls and effects, in the present, the past once-for-all event of God's saving work in Christ. The efficaciousness of anamnesis occurs through epiclesis. *See also* epiclesis.

a posteriori: a Latin term used to refer to an assertion that is dependent on, or arises after, experience or empirical verification. *A posteriori* is often contrasted with *a priori*. *See also* a priori.

a priori: a Latin term used to refer to an assertion that is independent of experience or empirical verification. *A priori* is often contrasted with *a posteriori*. *See also* a posteriori.

aseity: derived from the Latin *aseitas*, meaning "self-existence." *Aseitas* is derived from the Latin *a se*, meaning "of itself." Used in relation to God, *aseity* refers to the fact that God is entirely self-sufficient and independent, altogether free from creation in God's own (self-existent) life.

canon: from the Greek *kanōn*, meaning a "straight rod" or "stick" used as a standard of measurement. The word was used figuratively by the early church to refer to the "rule (*kanōn*) of faith" (*regula fidei*), which represented, in summary form, the fixed standard of orthodox Christian understanding in the post-apostolic era.

Cappadocian Fathers: three fourth-century theologians from Cappadocia (a region in what is today Turkey): Basil of Caesarea (ca. 329–79); Gregory of Nyssa (ca. 335–395), who is also Basil's younger brother; and Gregory of Nazianzus (ca. 329–390). Together, the Cappadocians contributed significantly to establishing Christian orthodoxy in christological and trinitarian doctrine in the period between the Council of Nicaea (325) and the Council of Constantinople (381).

Christology: classically, the study of what it means to say that Jesus Christ is fully divine, fully human, and ontologically one person. *See also* hypostatic union.

docetism: the christological heresy that denies the full humanity of Jesus Christ. The word *docetism* comes from the Greek *dokein*, meaning "to seem," and indicates the belief that Jesus only seemed or appeared to be human. Docetism was condemned by Ignatius of Antioch (ca. 35–ca. 107) and ultimately by the Council of Constantinople in 381.

doctrine: from the Latin *docere*, meaning "to teach." Christian doctrine is that which the church (or a particular church) teaches and believes to be a right summary of the teaching of Scripture. *See also* dogma.

dogma: from the Greek *dogma*, meaning "an opinion" or (public) "decree." Christian dogma is the aspect (or aspects) of Christian doctrine that the church (or a particular church) considers authoritative or most essential to the content of Christian truth received by the church from God. Not all doctrines are dogmas, therefore, but all dogmas are doctrines. At its core, Christian dogma is expressed in the conciliar creeds of the fourth century. *See also* doctrine.

doxology: from the Greek *doxologia*, meaning "to speak"—usually by way of liturgical expression—praise and gratitude to God.

Ebionitism: the christological heresy that denies the full divinity of Jesus Christ. Ebionites believed that Jesus was a human being who became the Son of God only through adoption when the Holy Spirit descended upon Him at His baptism. Ebionitism was condemned by Irenaeus of Lyon (ca. 120–202) and Tertullian (ca. 160–240), and ultimately by the Council of Nicaea in 325.

economic Trinity: the term used in Christian theology to designate God as Father, Son, and Holy Spirit in God's salvific and redemptive work in the world, and (often) contrasted with the immanent Trinity. *See also* immanent Trinity.

epiclesis: from the Greek *epiklēsis*, meaning "calling upon" or "invocation," and derived from the Greek, *epikalein*, meaning "to invoke" or "summon." *Epiclesis* refers to the liturgical summoning or invocation of the Holy Spirit, primarily for the purpose of consecrating the elements of bread and wine in the celebration of the Eucharist. In Eastern Orthodox liturgies, the epiclesis is the point at which the bread and wine become the body and blood of Jesus Christ. *See also* anamnesis.

epistemology: from the Greek *epistēmē*, meaning "understanding" or "knowledge," and *logos*, meaning "study." Epistemology is the study of the theory of human knowledge, its nature, sources, and limits.

eschata: a Greek term meaning "last things." See also *eschatology*.

eschatology: from the Greek *eschatos*, meaning "end" or "last," and *logos*, meaning "study." Eschatology is the study of "last things" and in Christian theology is classically concerned with the sequence of four "last things" still to come: death, judgment, heaven, and hell. In twentieth-century systematic theology, however, with the influence of Karl Barth, Dietrich Bonhoeffer, and the so-called "theologians of hope" (Jürgen Moltmann, Johannes B. Metz, Wolfhart Pannenberg, and Gerhard Sauter, for example), the predominant emphasis in presentations of Christian eschatology became an understanding of the *eschaton*—literally, "the last thing"—as yet to come but also already present. That is to say, in Christian theology the *eschaton* is understood to have been inaugurated in the life, death, and resurrection of Jesus Christ and the coming of God the Holy Spirit but also to be awaiting consummation in Christ's future coming in glory. The sovereign reign and rule of God is thus at once a future state and a present reality. *See also* eschata; parousia.

functional Christology: in contrast to classical Christology, the emphasis of study in functional Christology is placed not on *who* Jesus is but on *what* Jesus does in His saving work. *See also* Christology.

hermeneutic: from the Greek *hermēneutikē*, meaning "interpretation." A hermeneutic is an overarching method or theory that one uses in order to interpret and understand a text, broadly conceived.

hypostatic union: a phrase used to refer to the unity of divinity and humanity in Christ. Following the Council of Chalcedon (451), at which the hypostatic union was affirmed, the study of Christology begins (and ends) with an affirmation neither of Christ's two natures, nor His one person, but of both together at once—that is, with an affirmation of the hypostatic union of God and man in the one person of Jesus Christ. This itself affirms that the eternal, divine Word is personally united with the human flesh of Jesus of Nazareth in the incarnation: Christ's humanity has no independent existence apart from the Word, and the full humanity of Christ exists in the Word. In other words, the hypostatic union does not involve any mingling or mixing of divinity and humanity, and after the union the two natures cannot be divided. In the language of Chalcedon, the two natures are "without division or separation," and "without confusion or change." *See also* Christology.

immanent Trinity: the term used in Christian theology to designate God in and with Godself as Father, Son, and Holy Spirit apart from the world, and (often) contrasted with the economic Trinity. *See also* economic Trinity.

Magisterial Reformation: the term used in Christian theology to designate the Protestant Reformation as it was associated most notably with the three major European Reformers Martin Luther (1483–1546), Ulrich Zwingli (1484–1531), and John Calvin (1509–64), and in which the churches of the protest movement established themselves in a relation of interdependence with the authority of civil magistrates. In other words, Magisterial Reformers sought the reform of the church with the support of the state. The term is (often) contrasted with the Radical Reformation. *See also* Radical Reformation.

medieval theology: the theology developed by medieval scholars such as Anselm of Canterbury (1033–1109), Bernard of Clairvaux (1090–1153), Peter Lombard (ca. 1100–60), Bonaventure (ca. 1217–74), Thomas Aquinas (ca. 1225–74), and William of Ockham (ca. 1285–1347).

metaphysics: from the Greek *meta*, meaning "after" or "beyond," and *physikos*, meaning "natural" or "physical." Metaphysics—literally, "beyond the physical"—is the branch of philosophy that studies the ultimate nature of reality and being, and includes ontology in its purview. *See also* ontology.

ontology: from the Greek *ōn*, meaning "being," and *logos*, meaning "study." Ontology is the study of the nature of existence. *See also* metaphysics.

opus ad extra: a Latin phrase used to denote the "outward" (*ad extra*) "work" (*opus*) of God in the world—that is, the work of the economic Trinity. The phrase is contrasted to *opus* (pl. *opera*) *ad intra*. *See also* ad intra; opus ad intra; economic Trinity.

opus ad intra: a Latin phrase used to denote the "inward" (*ad intra*) "work" (*opus*) of God as triune apart from the world—that is, the work of the immanent Trinity. *See also* ad extra; opus ad extra; immanent Trinity.

panentheism: from the Greek *pan*, meaning "all," *en*, meaning "in," and *theos*, meaning "God." Panentheism is the belief that God is *in* all things and all things are *in* God.

pantheism: from the Greek *pan*, meaning "all," and *theos*, meaning "God." Pantheism is the belief that all is God, that God *is* everything and everything *is* God.

parochial church council: the governing body of a parish of the Church of England, consisting of parish clergy, churchwardens, and elected lay representatives.

parousia: a Greek word meaning "presence," used in Christian theology to denote the time when Christ will come again in glory to judge the living and the dead. *See also* eschatology.

patristic: from the Latin *pater*, meaning "father." Patristic theology refers to the theology of the fathers of the early Christian church. The patristic period is commonly understood to end in 749 in the Eastern church with the death of John of Damascus, and in 636 in the Western church with the death of Isidore of Seville.

Pelagianism: the heresy associated with the British monk Pelagius (ca. 354–ca. 420), who developed the idea of salvation unaided—that is, the idea that human beings, by their own willful acting, can bring themselves up out of their fallen, sinful condition and work their way toward salvation, and thereby to the reception of divine grace. Pelagius's views were opposed by Augustine of Hippo and ultimately condemned at the Council of Ephesus in 431.

perichoresis: from the Greek *perichōrēsis*—in Latin, *circumincessio*—meaning "mutual indwelling," "interpenetration," or "coinherence." The term is often invoked in social trinitarianism to indicate that the three distinct persons of Father, Son, and Holy Spirit are one God because each person mutually and perfectly interpenetrates or inheres in the other two; the persons of the Trinity are what they are, in other words, in relation to one another. *See also* social trinitarianism.

phenomenology: from the Greek *phainomenon*, meaning "what appears," and *logos*, meaning "study." Phenomenology is the study of things (phenomena) as they appear to human sense experience from the subjective or first-person perspective, and is typically associated with the work of Edmund Husserl, Martin Heidegger, and Maurice Merleau-Ponty, among others.

pneumatology: from the Greek *pneuma*, meaning "spirit," and *logos*, meaning "study." Pneumatology is the study of the person and work of the Holy Spirit.

predestination: from the Latin *praedestinatio*, meaning "determining beforehand." The term is used in Christian theology to infer the action of God in willing or electing something to a specific destiny before the creation of the world. It is variously understood. John Calvin, for example, uses the term to indicate the eternal divine decree by which God elects or wills some to salvation and others to damnation (see Calvin, *Institutes*, bk. 3, chap. 21). Karl Barth, however, in partial critique of Calvin, uses the term to indicate that the eternal will of God is instead God's decree to be God's own Word, Jesus Christ, such that God's eternal will is to be gracious toward humankind in Christ (see Barth, *CD* II/2, 94–194).

proleptic: from the Greek *prolēpsis*, meaning "an anticipating." The term is used in Christian theology to refer to that which anticipates a future event. For example, the sacrament of baptism can be seen as anticipating the future rising to resurrection life of humans who have died with Christ, and thus as proleptic (see Rom. 6:4–5; Col. 2:12).

Radical Reformation: the term used in Christian theology to designate the Protestant Reformation as it was associated with Andreas Karlstadt (ca. 1486–1541), Conrad Grebel (ca. 1498–1526), and Thomas Müntzer (ca. 1489–1525) among others, and in which the churches of the protest movement established themselves in independence of the authority of civil magistrates. In other words, Radical Reformers sought the reform of the church independent of the state. The term is (often) contrasted with the Magisterial Reformation. *See also* Magisterial Reformation.

regeneration: from the Latin *regeneratio*, meaning "rebirth." Regeneration is the process by which one experiences new life in Christ, being given the gift of faith and the hope of eternal life by God the Holy Spirit (see John 3:3–8; Eph. 2:4–5, 8; and Titus 3:4–8).

simul iustus et peccator: a Latin phrase meaning "at once righteous and a sinner." The phrase was used by Martin Luther to describe the status of the Christian believer who is justified through faith by grace alone but is nevertheless still sinful.

social trinitarianism: a "social" understanding of the Trinity in which the immanent life of God is understood to consist of three interrelated persons united in a communion of mutual love. This loving relatedness of Father, Son, and Holy Spirit—that which is "social" in God's immanent life—is then grounded by (some) social trinitarians in the patristic concept of perichoresis, and seen as a model for created sociality and, in particular, the sociality of the church, which is understood to be "like" the "sociality" of the trinitarian self-relations. *See also* perichoresis.

sociopoiesis: from the Greek *poiēsis*, which is derived from the Greek *poiein*, meaning "to make," "produce," or "bring into existence." *Sociopoiesis* literally means "making the social."

soteriology: from the Greek *sōtēria*, meaning "deliverance" or "salvation," and *logos*, meaning "study." Soteriology is the study of salvation and in Christian theology is classically concerned with the saving work of God effected in the person of Jesus Christ.

spiration: from the Latin *spiratio*, meaning "the act of breathing." The term is used in Christian theology to refer to the act by which the Holy Spirit is said in the Western church to proceed "from the Father and the Son" in a double procession, and in the Eastern church "from the Father" alone in a single procession.

sursum corda: a Latin phrase meaning "lift up your hearts"—literally, "upward hearts." With this bidding in the eucharistic liturgy the presiding priest exhorts the congregation to acknowledge that their existence is entirely dependent on God. As the letter to the Colossians puts it, "Since, then, you have been raised with Christ, set your hearts on things above, where Christ is, seated at the right hand of God. Set your minds on things above, not on earthly things. For you died, and your life is now hidden with Christ in God" (Col. 3:1–3).

synaxis: from the Greek *synaxis*, meaning "gathering" or "assembly." The term is used in the Eastern church to denote an assembly gathered for prayer and worship, generally, as well as an assembly gathered for the celebration of the Eucharist, in what is called the liturgical synaxis. In the Western church the term denotes generally non-eucharistic services of worship and prayer.

theological anthropology: the study of the origin, purpose, and end of humankind as humankind relates to God.

theology proper: the systematic study of the doctrine of God.

Bibliography

Adams, Nicholas, and Charles Elliot. "Ethnography Is Dogmatics: Making Description Central to Systematic Theology." *Scottish Journal of Theology* 53 (2000): 339–64.

Afanasiev, Nicholas. *The Church of the Holy Spirit*. Edited by Michael Plekon. Translated by Vitaly Permiakov. 1971. Reprint, Notre Dame, IN: University of Notre Dame Press, 2007.

———. "Das allegemeine Priestertum in der orthodoxen Kirche." *Eine Heilige Kirche* 12 (1935): 334–40.

Aquinas, Thomas. *Summa Theologica*. Translated by Fathers of the English Dominican Province. 1948. Reprint, Notre Dame, IN: Christian Classics, 1981.

Archbishops' Council, *Common Worship: Services and Prayers for the Church of England*. London: Church House Publishing, 2000.

Aristotle, *Nicomachean Ethics*. Edited by Lesley Brown. Translated by David Ross. New York: Oxford University Press, 2009.

Avis, Paul., ed. *The Oxford Handbook of Ecclesiology*. Oxford: Oxford University Press, 2018.

———. *Reshaping Ecumenical Theology: The Church Made Whole?* London: T&T Clark, 2010.

———. *Theological Foundations of the Christian Church*. Vol. 1, *Jesus and the Church: The Foundation of the Church in the New Testament and Modern Theology*. London: T&T Clark Bloomsbury, 2021.

Badcock, Gary D. *The House Where God Lives: Renewing the Doctrine of the Church Today*. Grand Rapids: Eerdmans, 2009.

Barth, Karl. *Church Dogmatics*. Edited by G. W. Bromiley and T. F. Torrance. Translated by G. W. Bromiley et al. 14 vols. Edinburgh: T&T Clark, 1936–77.

———. *The Epistle to the Romans*. Translated by Edwyn C. Hoskyns. 1933. Reprint, New York: Oxford University Press, 1968.

———. *God Here and Now*. Translated by Paul M. van Buren. London: Routledge & Kegan Paul, 1964.

———. *The Humanity of God*. Translated by Thomas Wieser and John Newton Thomas. Richmond, VA: John Knox, 1960.

———. "The Real Church." *Scottish Journal of Theology* 3 (1950): 337–51.

———. *The Resurrection of the Dead*. Translated by H. J. Stenning. 1933. Reprint, Eugene: Wipf & Stock, 2003.

Basil of Caesarea. *De Spiritu Sancto*. In *St. Basil: Letters and Selected Works*, 1–50. Vol. 8 of *A Select Library of Nicene and Post-Nicene Fathers of the Christian Church*. 2nd series. Edited by Philip Schaff and Henry Wace. 14 vols. New York: Christian Literature, 1890–1900. Reprint, Grand Rapids: Eerdmans, 1983.

———. *Letter XXXVIII*. In *St. Basil: Letters and Selected Works*, 137–41 Vol. 8 of *A Select Library of Nicene and Post-Nicene Fathers of the Christian Church*. 2nd series. Edited by Philip Schaff and Henry Wace. 14 vols. New York: Christian Literature, 1890–1900. Reprint, Grand Rapids: Eerdmans, 1983.

Behr, John. *The Nicene Faith*. Vol. 2 of *Formation of Christian Theology*. Crestwood, NY: St. Vladimir's Seminary Press, 2004.

Bender, Kimlyn J. *Karl Barth's Christological Ecclesiology*. Eugene, OR: Wipf & Stock, 2013.

Boff, Leonardo. *Church: Charism and Power; Liberation Theology and the Institutional Church*. Translated by John W. Diercksmeir. London: SCM, 1985.

———. *Ecclesiogenesis: The Base Communities Reinvent the Church*. Translated by Robert R. Barr. Maryknoll, NY: Orbis, 1986.

Bonhoeffer, Dietrich. *Act and Being: Transcendental Philosophy and Ontology in Systematic Theology*. Edited by Wayne Whitson Floyd Jr. Translated by H. Martin Rumscheidt. Dietrich Bonhoeffer Works 2. Minneapolis: Fortress, 2009.

———. *Discipleship*. Edited by Geffrey B. Kelly and John D. Godsey. Translated by Barbara Green and Reinhard Krauss. Dietrich Bonhoeffer Works 4. Minneapolis: Fortress, 2003.

———. *Ethics*. Edited by Clifford J. Green. Translated by Reinhard Krauss, Charles C. West, and Douglas W. Stott. Dietrich Bonhoeffer Works 6. Minneapolis: Fortress, 2009.

———. *Ethik*. 2nd rev. ed. Edited by Ilse Tödt, Heinz Eduard Tödt, Ernst Feil, and Clifford Green. Dietrich Bonhoeffer Werke 6. Gütersloh: Kaiser, 1998.

———. "Graduation Theses." In *The Young Bonhoeffer: 1918–1927*, edited by Paul Duane Matheny, Clifford J. Green, and Marshall D. Johnson, translated by Mary C. Nebelsick and Douglas W. Stott. 439–41. Dietrich Bonhoeffer Works 9. Minneapolis: Fortress, 2003.

————. "Konkrete Ethik bei Paulus." In *Illegale Theologen-Ausbildung: Finkenwalde 1935–1937*, edited by Otto Dudzus and Jürgen Henkys, et al., 721–38. Dietrich Bonhoeffer Werke 14. Gütersloh: Kaiser, 1986.

————. "Lectures on Christology." In *Berlin: 1932–1933*, edited by Larry Rasmussen, translated by Isabelle Best et al., 299–360. Dietrich Bonhoeffer Works 12. Minneapolis: Fortress, 2009.

————. *Life Together and Prayerbook of the Bible*. Edited by Geffrey B. Kelly. Translated by Daniel W. Bloesch and James H. Burtness. Dietrich Bonhoeffer Works 5. Minneapolis: Fortress, 2005.

————. "The Nature of the Church." In *Ecumenical, Academic, Pastoral Work: 1931–1932*, edited by Victoria J. Barnett, Mark S. Brocker, and Michael B. Lukens, translated by Anne Schmidt-Lange et al., 269–332. Dietrich Bonhoeffer Works 11. Minneapolis: Fortress, 2012.

————. "On Karl Heim's *Glaube und Denken*." In *Berlin: 1932–1933*, edited by Larry Rasmussen, translated by Isabelle Best et al., 243–58. Dietrich Bonhoeffer Works 12. Minneapolis: Fortress, 2009.

————. "Outline for a Book." In *Letters and Papers from Prison*, edited by John W. de Gruchy, translated by Isabel Best et al., 499–504. Dietrich Bonhoeffer Works 8. Minneapolis: Fortress, 2009.

————. *Sanctorum Communio: A Theological Study of the Sociology of the Church*. Edited by Clifford Green. Translated by Reinhard Krauss and Nancy Lukens. Dietrich Bonhoeffer Works 1. Minneapolis: Fortress, 1998.

————. *Schöpfung und Fall: Theologische Auslegung von Genesis 1–3*. 4th ed. Edited by Martin Rüter and Ilse Tödt. Dietrich Bonhoeffer Werke 3. Gütersloh: Gütersloher Verlagshaus, 2015.

————. "Sichtbare Kirche im Neuen Testament." In *Illegale Theologen-Ausbildung: Finkenwalde 1935–1937*, edited by Otto Dudzus and Jürgen Henkys, et al., 422–51. Dietrich Bonhoeffer Werke 14. Gütersloh: Kaiser, 1986.

————. "The Visible Church in the New Testament." In *Theological Education at Finkenwalde: 1935–1937*, edited by H. Gaylon Barker and Mark S. Brocker, translated by Douglas W. Stott, 434–76. Dietrich Bonhoeffer Works 14. Minneapolis: Fortress, 2013.

————. "What Is Church?" In *Berlin: 1932–1933*, edited by Larry Rasmussen, translated by Isabelle Best et al., 262–66. Dietrich Bonhoeffer Works 12. Minneapolis: Fortress, 2009.

Braaten, Carl E. *Mother Church: Ecclesiology and Ecumenicism*. Minneapolis: Fortress, 1998.

Brittain, Christopher C. "Ethnography as Ecclesial Attentiveness and Critical Reflexivity: Fieldwork and the Dispute over Homosexuality in the Episcopal Church." In Scharen, *Explorations*, 114–37.

———. "Why Ecclesiology Cannot Live by Doctrine Alone: A Reply to John Webster's 'In the Society of God.'" *Ecclesial Practices* 1, no. 1 (2014): 5–30.

Browning, Don, ed. *Practical Theology: The Emerging Field in Theology, Church, and World*. New York: Harper & Row, 1983.

Bruce, F. F. *The Acts of the Apostles: The Greek Text with Introduction and Commentary*. 2nd ed. London: Tyndale, 1952.

Brunner, Emil. *The Misunderstanding of the Church*. Translated by Harold Knight. London: Lutterworth, 1952.

Bulgakov, Sergius. *The Bride of the Lamb*. Translated by Boris Jakim. 1945. Reprint, Grand Rapids: Eerdmans, 2002.

Calvin, John. *Institutes of the Christian Religion*. Edited by John T. McNeill. Translated by Ford Lewis Battles. 2 vols. 1960. Reprint, Louisville: Westminster John Knox, 2011.

Cameron, Michael. "The Emergence of *Totus Christus* in Augustine's *Enarrationes in Psalmos*." In *The Harp of Prophecy: Early Christian Interpretation of the Psalms*, edited by Brian E. Daley and Paul R. Kolbet, 205–26. Notre Dame, IN: University of Notre Dame Press, 2015.

Cavanaugh, William T. *Torture and Eucharist: Theology, Politics, and the Body of Christ*. Oxford: Blackwell, 1998.

Church of England. "Statistics for Mission 2011." December 2013. https://www.church ofengland.org/sites/default/files/2017-11/statistics-for-mission-2011.pdf.

———. "Statistics for Mission 2022." December 2023. https://www.churchofengland .org/sites/default/files/2023-11/statisticsformission2022.pdf.

Clough, David L. *On Animals*. Vol.1, *Systematic Theology*. London: Bloomsbury T&T Clark, 2012.

Coakley, Sarah. *God, Sexuality, and the Self: An Essay "On the Trinity."* Cambridge: Cambridge University Press, 2013.

Coleridge, Samuel T. *Opus Maximum*, edited by Thomas McFarland. The Collected Works of Samuel Taylor Coleridge, vol. 15. Princeton: Princeton University Press, 2002.

Cone, James H. *Black Theology and Black Power*. 3rd ed. 1969. Reprint, Maryknoll, NY: Orbis, 2019.

———. *A Black Theology of Liberation*. 3rd ed. 1970. Reprint, Maryknoll, NY: Orbis, 1990.

———. *For My People: Black Theology and the Black Church*. Maryknoll, NY: Orbis, 1984.

———. *God of the Oppressed*. New York: Seabury, 1975.

Congar, Yves. *I Believe in the Holy Spirit*. 3 vols. 1983. Reprint, New York: Crossroad, 2015.

Cottrell, Stephen. "Simpler, Humbler, Bolder: A Church for the Whole Nation which Is Christ Centered and Shaped by the Five Marks of Mission." *General Synod Paper GS2223*. November 2021. https://www.churchofengland.org/sites/default/files/2021-06/gs-2223-vision-and-strategy.pdf.

———. "A Vision for the Church of England in the 2020s." November 2020. https://www.churchofengland.org/sites/default/files/2021-06/a-vision-for-the-church-of-england-in-the-2020s-commentary-by-stephen_cottrell.pdf.

Cross, Terry L. *The People of God's Presence: An Introduction to Ecclesiology*. Grand Rapids: Baker Academic, 2019.

Dalferth, Ingolf U. "Christology and Reconciliation in the Theology of Karl Barth." In *Karl Barth: Centenary Essays*, edited by S. W. Sykes, 14–45. Cambridge: Cambridge University Press, 1989.

Davaney, Sheila Greeve. "Theology and the Turn to Cultural Analysis." In *Converging on Culture: Theologians in Dialogue with Cultural Analysis and Criticism*, edited by Delwin Brown, Sheila Greeve Davaney, and Kathryn Tanner, 3–16. New York: Oxford University Press, 2001.

de Lubac, Henri. *The Church: Paradox and Mystery*. Translated by James R. Dunne. Shannon, Ireland: Ecclesia Press, 1969.

———. *Corpus Mysticum: The Eucharist and the Church in the Middle Ages*. Translated by Gemma Simmons et al. Edited by Laurence Paul Hemming and Susan Frank Parsons. London: SCM, 2006.

———. *The Motherhood of the Church*. Translated by Sergia Englund. San Francisco: Ignatius, 1971.

———. *The Splendour of the Church*. Translated by Michael Mason. London: Sheed and Ward, 1956.

Denzin, Norman K. *Interpretive Interactionism*. 2nd ed. Thousand Oaks, CA: Sage, 2001.

Drane, John. *The McDonaldization of the Church: Spirituality, Creativity, and the Future of the Church*. London: Darton, Longman & Todd, 2000.

Dulles, Avery. *Models of the Church*. Expanded Edition. New York: Image, 1987. First published 1978 by Doubleday (New York).

Dunn, James D. G. *Christianity in the* Making. Vol. 1, *Jesus Remembered*. Grand Rapids: Eerdmans, 2003.

Durham, John I. *Exodus*. Word Biblical Commentary 3. Waco: Thomas Nelson. 1987.

Emerton, David. *God's Church-Community: The Ecclesiology of Dietrich Bonhoeffer*. London: Bloomsbury T&T Clark, 2020.

———. "Jesus Christ: The Centre of the Church." In *Bonhoeffer and Christology: Revisiting Chalcedon*, edited by Matthias Grebe, Nadine Hamilton, and Christian Schlenker, 236–55. London: Bloomsbury T&T Clark, 2023.

Esler, Philip F. "The Adoption and Use of the Word ΕΚΚΛΗΣΙΑ in the Early Christ-Movement." *Ecclesiology* 17, no. 1 (2021): 109–30.

Farrow, Douglas. *Ascension and Ecclesia: On the Significance of the Doctrine of the Ascension for Ecclesiology and Christian Cosmology*. Edinburgh: T&T Clark, 1999.

Fatehi, Mehrdad. *The Spirit's Relation to the Risen Lord in Paul: An Examination of Its Christological Implications*. Tübingen: Mohr Siebeck, 2000.

Feuerbach, Ludwig. *The Essence of Christianity*. Translated by George Eliot. 2nd ed. 1881. Reprint, New York: Dover, 2008.

Ford, David F. "Living Theology in the Face of Death." In Hardy et al., *Wording a Radiance*, 111–36.

Frei, Hans W. *The Identity of Jesus Christ: The Hermeneutical Bases of Dogmatic Theology*. Philadelphia: Fortress, 1975.

———. *Types of Christian Theology*. Edited by George Hunsinger and William Placher. New Haven: Yale University Press, 1992.

Geertz, Clifford. *The Interpretation of Culture*. New York: Basic Books, 1973.

Gibbs, Eddie, and Ryan K. Bolger. *Emerging Churches: Creating Christian Community in Postmodern Cultures*. Grand Rapids: Baker Academic, 2005.

Goldingay, John. *Old Testament Theology*. Vol. 1, *Israel's Faith*. Downers Grove, IL: InterVarsity, 2003.

Greggs, Tom. "*Communio* Ecclesiology: The Spirit's Work of Salvation in the Life of the Church." In *Third Article Theology: A Pneumatological Dogmatics*, edited by Myk Habets, 347–66. Minneapolis: Fortress, 2016.

———. *Dogmatic Ecclesiology*. Vol. 1, *The Priestly Catholicity of the Church*. Grand Rapids: Baker Academic, 2019.

———. "Proportion and Topography in Ecclesiology: A Working Paper on the Dogmatic Location of the Doctrine of the Church." In *Theological Theology: Essays in Honour of John B. Webster*, edited by R. David Nelson, Darren Sarisky, and Justin Stratis, 89–106. London: Bloomsbury T&T Clark, 2015.

Gregory Center for Church Multiplication, The. "Lay-Led Planting." Accessed April 19, 2024. https://ccx.org.uk/myriad-lay-led-planting.

Gunton, Colin E. "Christian Community and Human Society." In *The Christian Faith: An Introduction to Christian Doctrine*, 119–38. Oxford: Blackwell, 2002.

———. "The Church." In *Theology through the Theologians*, 187–205. Edinburgh: T&T Clark, 1996.

———. "The Church on Earth: The Roots of Community." In *On Being the Church: Essays on the Christian Community*, edited by Colin E. Gunton and Daniel W. Hardy, 48–80. Edinburgh: T&T Clark, 1989.

———. "The Community of Reconciliation." In *The Actuality of Atonement: A Study of Metaphor, Rationality and the Christian Tradition*, 173–203. Edinburgh: T&T Clark, 1998.

———. "God the Holy Spirit: Augustine and his Successors." In *Theology through the Theologians*, 105–28. Edinburgh: T&T Clark, 1996.

———. *Intellect and Action: Elucidations on Christian Theology and the Life of Faith*. Edinburgh: T&T Clark, 2000.

———. *The One, the Three and the Many: God, Creation and the Culture of Modernity*. Cambridge: Cambridge University Press, 1993.

———. *The Promise of Trinitarian Theology*. 2nd ed. London; T&T Clark, 1997.

Gustafson, James M. *Treasure in Earthen Vessels: The Church as a Human Community*. New York: Harper & Brothers, 1961.

Gutiérrez, Gustavo. *A Theology of Liberation: History, Politics and Salvation*. Translated and edited by Caridad Inda and John Eagleson. London: SCM, 1974.

Haight, Roger. *Christian Community in History*. 3 vols. New York: Continuum, 2004–8.

Hardy, Daniel W. "Created and Redeemed Sociality." In *On Being the Church: Essays on the Christian Community*, edited by Colin E. Gunton and Daniel W. Hardy, 21–47. Edinburgh: T&T Clark, 1989.

———. *Finding the Church: The Dynamic Truth of Anglicanism*. London: SCM, 2001.

———. "God and the Form of Society." In *The Weight of Glory: A Vision and Practice for Christian Faith; The Future of Liberal Theology; Essays for Peter Baelz*, edited by D. W. Hardy and P. H. Sedgwick, 131–44. Edinburgh: T&T Clark, 1991.

———. *God's Ways with the World: Thinking and Practising Christian Faith*. Edinburgh: T&T Clark, 1996.

———. "A Magnificent Complexity: Letting God be God in Church, Society and Creation." In *The Essentials of Christian Community: Essays for Daniel W. Hardy*, edited by David F. Ford and Dennis L. Stamps, 307–56. Edinburgh: T&T Clark, 1996.

———. "Receptive Ecumenism—Learning by Engagement." In *Receptive Ecumenism and the Call to Catholic Learning: Exploring a Way for Contemporary Ecumenism*, edited by Paul D. Murray, 428–40. Oxford: Oxford University Press, 2008.

Hardy, Daniel W., Deborah Hardy Ford, Peter Ochs, and David F. Ford. *Wording a Radiance: Parting Conversations on God and the Church*. London: SCM, 2010.

Harink, Douglas. *1 & 2 Peter*. SCM Theological Commentary on the Bible. London: SCM, 2009.

Harper, Brad, and Paul Louis Metzger. *Exploring Ecclesiology: An Evangelical and Ecumenical Introduction*. Grand Rapids: Brazos, 2009.

Hauerwas, Stanley. *After Christendom? How the Church Is to Behave If Freedom, Justice, and a Christian Nation are Bad Ideas*. Nashville: Abingdon, 1991.

———. *Christian Existence Today: Essays on Church, World, and Living in Between*. 1988. Reprint, Eugene, OR: Wipf & Stock, 2010.

———. *A Community of Character: Toward a Constructive Christian Social Ethic.* Notre Dame, IN: University of Notre Dame Press, 1981.

———. *Hannah's Child: A Theologian's Memoir.* London: SCM Press, 2010.

———. *In Good Company: The Church as Polis.* Notre Dame, IN: University of Notre Dame Press, 1995.

———. *The Peaceable Kingdom: A Primer in Christian Ethics.* Notre Dame, IN: Notre Dame University Press, 1983.

———. *Sanctify Them in the Truth: Holiness Exemplified.* Edinburgh: T&T Clark, 1998.

———. *With the Grain of the Universe: The Church's Witness and Natural Theology.* Grand Rapids: Brazos, 2001.

———. *The Work of Theology.* Grand Rapids: Eerdmans, 2015.

Healy, Nicholas M. *Church, World and the Christian Life: Practical-Prophetic Ecclesiology.* Cambridge: Cambridge University Press, 2000.

———. "Ecclesiology, Ethnography, and God: An Interplay of Reality of Descriptions." In Ward, *Perspectives on Ecclesiology and Ethnography*, 183–99.

———. *Hauerwas: A (Very) Critical Introduction.* Grand Rapids: Eerdmans, 2014.

———. "Karl Barth's Ecclesiology Reconsidered." *Scottish Journal of Theology* 57 (2004): 287–99.

———. "Practices and the New Ecclesiology: Misplaced Concreteness?" *International Journal of Systematic Theology* 5, no. 3 (2003): 287–308.

———. "What is Systematic Theology?" *International Journal of Systematic Theology* 11, no. 1 (2009): 24–39.

Hector, Kevin W. "The Mediation of Christ's Normative Spirit: A Constructive Reading of Schleiermacher's Pneumatology." *Modern Theology* 24 (2008): 1–22.

Hegel, G. W. F. *Encyclopedia of the Philosophical Sciences in Outline and Critical Writings.* Edited by Ernst Behler. Translated by A. V. Miller, Steven A. Taubeneck, and Diana I. Behler. 1817. Reprint, New York: Continuum, 1990.

Hegstad, Harald. "Ecclesiology and Empirical Research on the Church." In Scharen, *Explorations*, 34–47.

———. *The Real Church: An Ecclesiology of the Visible.* Cambridge: James Clarke, 2013.

Holmes, Christopher R. J. "Beyond Bonhoeffer in Loyalty to Bonhoeffer: Reconsidering Bonhoeffer's Christological Aversion to Theological Metaphysics." In *Christ, Church and World: New Studies in Bonhoeffer's Theology and Ethics*, edited by Phillip G. Ziegler and Michael Mawson, 29–43. London: Bloomsbury T&T Clark, 2016.

———. "The Holy Spirit." In *The Oxford Handbook of Dietrich Bonhoeffer*, edited by Phillip G. Ziegler and Michael Mawson, 168–78. Oxford: Oxford University Press, 2019.

Hooker, Richard. *Of the Lawes of Ecclesiasticall Politie.* Edited by W. Speed Hill. 3 vols. The Folger Library Edition of the Works of Richard Hooker. Cambridge: Belknap, 1977–81.

Hultegren, Arland J. "The Church as the Body of Christ: Engaging an Image in the New Testament." *Word & World* 22, no. 2 (2002): 124–32.

Irving, Alexander. *We Believe: Exploring the Nicene Faith.* London: Apollos, 2021.

Jenson, Matt, and David E. Wilhite. *The Church: A Guide for the Perplexed.* London: T&T Clark, 2010.

Jenson, Robert W. *Canon and Creed.* Louisville: Westminster John Knox, 2010.

———. "The Church and the Sacraments." In *The Cambridge Companion to Christian Doctrine,* edited by Colin E. Gunton, 207–25. New York: Cambridge University Press, 1997.

———. *Systematic Theology.* 2 vols. New York: Oxford University Press, 1997–99.

———. *Unbaptized God: The Basic Flaw in Ecumenical Theology.* Minneapolis: Fortress, 1992.

———. *Visible Words: The Interpretation and Practice of Christian Sacraments.* Minneapolis: Fortress, 1978.

Jinkins, Michael. *The Church Faces Death: Ecclesiology in a Post-modern Context.* New York: Oxford University Press, 1999.

John Chrysostom. *Homilies on the Epistles of Paul to the Corinthians.* Vol. 12 of *A Select Library of Nicene and Post-Nicene Fathers of the Christian Church.* 1st series. Edited by Philip Schaff. 14 vols. New York: Christian Literature, 1886–89. Reprint, Grand Rapids: Eerdmans, 1979.

Jones, Julie Scott, and Sal Watt, eds. *Ethnography in Social Science Practice.* London: Routledge, 2010.

Kärkkäinen, Veli-Matti. *An Introduction to Ecclesiology: Ecumenical, Historical & Global Perspectives.* 2nd. ed. Downers Grove, IL: InterVarsity, 2021.

———. *Pneumatology: The Holy Spirit in Ecumenical, International, and Contextual Perspective.* 2nd ed. Grand Rapids: Baker Academic, 2018.

Kelly, J. N. D. *Early Christian Doctrines.* 5th ed. 1977. Reprint, London: Continuum, 2007.

Kelsey, David H. *Eccentric Existence: A Theological Anthropology.* 2 vols. Louisville: Westminster John Knox, 2009.

Kilby, Karen. "Perichoresis and Projection: Problems with Social Doctrines of the Trinity." *New Blackfriars* 81 (2000): 432–45.

Komonchak, Joseph A. "Ecclesiology and Social Theory: A Methodological Essay." *The Thomist* 45 (1981): 262–83.

———. *Foundations in Ecclesiology.* Supplementary Issue of the *Lonergan Workshop* Journal, vol. 11. Boston: Boston College, 1995.

Korner, Ralph J. *The Origin and Meaning of Ekklēsia in the Early Jesus Movement.* Leiden: Brill, 2017.

Küng, Hans. *The Church.* Translated by Ray and Rosaleen Ockenden. London: Burns & Oates, 1967.

———. *Structures of the Church.* Translated by Salvator Attanasio. London: Burns & Oates, 1965.

Lawrence, James. *Growing Leaders: Reflections on Leadership, Life and Jesus.* Rev. ed. Abingdon, VA: The Bible Reading Fellowship, 2020.

Lindbeck, George A. *The Nature of Doctrine: Religion and Theology in a Postliberal Age.* Louisville: Westminster John Knox, 1984.

Loisy, Alfred. *The Gospel and the Church.* Buffalo: Prometheus, 1988.

Lombard, Peter. *On the Doctrine of Signs.* Book 4 of *The Sentences.* Translated by Giulio Silano. Toronto: Pontifical Institute of Medieval Studies, 2010.

Luther, Martin. *Luther's Works.* Edited by Jaroslav Pelikan, Helmut Lehman, et al. 55 vols. American ed. Minneapolis: Fortress, 1900–86.

Macquarrie, John. *A Guide to the Sacraments.* London: SCM, 1997.

Mawson, Michael. *Christ Existing as Community: Bonhoeffer's Ecclesiology.* Oxford: Oxford University Press, 2018.

McClintock Fulkerson, Mary. *Changing the Subject: Women's Discourses and Feminist Theology.* Minneapolis: Fortress, 1994.

———. "Interpreting a Situation: When Is 'Empirical' Also 'Theological'?" In Ward, *Perspectives on Ecclesiology and Ethnography,* 124–44.

———. *Places of Redemption: Theology for a Worldly Church.* Oxford: Oxford University Press, 2007.

McFarland, Ian A. *From Nothing: A Theology of Creation.* Louisville: Westminster John Knox, 2014.

Mersch, Emile. *The Whole Christ: The Historical Development of the Doctrine of the Mystical Body in Scripture and Tradition.* Translated by John R. Kelly. 1938. Reprint, Eugene, OR: Wipf & Stock, 2011.

Milbank, John. "Ecclesiology: The Last of the Last." In *Being Reconciled: Ontology and Pardon,* 105–37. London: Routledge, 2003.

———. "Enclaves, or Where Is the Church?" *New Blackfriars* 73 (1992): 341–52.

———. "Grace: The Midwinter Sacrifice." In *Being Reconciled,* 138–61.

———. "On Theological Transgression." In *The Future of Love, Essays in Political Theology,* 145–74. London: SCM, 2009.

———. "Stale Expressions: The Management-Shaped Church." In *The Future of Love: Essays in Political Theology,* 264–76. London: SCM, 2009.

———. *Theology and Social Theory: Beyond Secular Reason.* 2nd ed. Malden, MA: Blackwell, 2006.

Moltmann, Jürgen. *The Church in the Power of the Spirit: A Contribution to Messianic Ecclesiology.* Translated by Margaret Kohl. London: SCM, 1977.

———. *The Coming of God: Christian Eschatology.* Translated by Margaret Kohl. Minneapolis: Fortress, 1996.

———. *The Trinity and the Kingdom.* Translated by Margaret Kohl. London: SCM, 1981.

Moran, Dermot. *Introduction to Phenomenology.* New York: Routledge, 2000.

Murray, Douglas. "This Could Have Been a Great Opportunity for the Church." *The Spectator.* June 20, 2020. http://www.spectator.co.uk/article/this-could-have-been-a-great-opportunity-for-the-church.

Newbigin, Lesslie. *The Household of God: Lectures on the Nature of the Church.* London: SCM, 1953.

Niebuhr, H. Richard. *Christ and Culture.* New York: Harper & Brothers, 1951.

Nimmo, Paul T. *Being in Action: The Theological Shape of Barth's Ethical Vision.* London: T&T Clark, 2007.

———. "The Mediation of Redemption in Schleiermacher's *Glaubenslehre.*" *International Journal of Systematic Theology* 5, no. 2 (2003): 187–99.

———. "Schleiermacher on Justification: A Departure from the Reformation?" *Scottish Journal of Theology* 66, no. 1 (2013): 50–73.

Owen, John. *The Church and the Bible.* Vol. 16 of *The Works of John Owen,* edited by William H. Goold. Edinburgh: Banner of Truth, 1968.

Paas, Stefan. *Pilgrims and Priests: Christian Mission in a Post-Christian Society.* London: SCM, 2019.

Pannenberg, Wolfgang. *Systematic Theology.* Translated by G. W. Bromiley. 3 vols. Grand Rapids: Eerdmans, 1991–98.

Pelikan, Jaroslav. *The Christian Tradition: A History of the Development of Doctrine.* Vol. 1, *The Emergence of the Catholic Tradition (100–600).* Chicago: University of Chicago Press, 1971.

Pickard, Stephen. *Seeking the Church: An Introduction to Ecclesiology.* London: SCM, 2012.

Quash, Ben. *Found Theology: History, Imagination and the Holy Spirit.* London: Bloomsbury T&T Clark, 2013.

Radner, Ephraim. *The End of the Church: A Pneumatology of Christian Division in the West.* Grand Rapids: Eerdmans, 1998.

Rasmusson, Arne. *The Church as Polis: From Practical Theology to Theological Politics as Exemplified by Jürgen Moltmann and Stanley Hauerwas.* Notre Dame, IN: University of Notre Dame Press, 1995.

Ratzinger, Joseph Cardinal. *Called to Communion: Understanding the Church Today.* Translated by Adrian Walker. San Francisco: Ignatius, 2008.

———. *Church, Ecumenism, and Politics: New Endeavors in Ecclesiology*. Translated by Michael J. Miller et al. San Francisco: Ignatius, 2008.

Ruether, Rosemary Radford. *Sexism and God-Talk*. London: SCM, 1983.

———. *Women-Church: Theology and Practice of Feminist Liturgical Communities*. San Francisco: Harper & Row, 1985.

Sánchez M., Leopoldo A. *T&T Clark Introduction to Spirit Christology*. London: Bloomsbury T&T Clark, 2022.

Sanders, Fred, and Oliver D. Crisp. *Advancing Trinitarian Theology: Explorations in Constructive Dogmatics*. Grand Rapids: Zondervan, 2014.

Scharen, Christian B., ed. *Explorations in Ecclesiology and Ethnography*. Grand Rapids: Eerdmans, 2012.

———. "'Judicious Narratives', or Ethnography as Ecclesiology." *Scottish Journal of Theology* 58, no. 2 (2005): 125–42.

Schillebeeckx, Edward. *Church: The Human Story of God*. New York: The Crossroad Publishing Company, 1996.

Schleiermacher, Friedrich. *The Christian Faith*. Edited by H. R. Mackintosh and J. S. Stewart. Edinburgh: T&T Clark, 1928.

Schlesinger, Eugene R. "Schleiermacher on the Necessity of the Church." *The Journal of Theological Studies* 66, no. 1 (2015): 235–56.

Schmemann, Alexander. *The Eucharist: Sacrament of the Kingdom*. Translated by Paul Kachur. 1987. Reprint, Crestwood, NY: St. Vladimir's Seminary Press, 2003.

Schüssler Fiorenza, Elizabeth. *In Memory of Her: A Feminist Theological Reconstruction of Christian Origins*. London: SCM, 1983.

Schwöbel, Christoph. "The Creature of the Word: Recovering the Ecclesiology of the Reformers." In *On Being the Church: Essays on the Christian Community*, edited by Colin E. Gunton and Daniel W. Hardy, 110–55. Edinburgh: T&T Clark, 1989.

Sonderegger, Katherine. *Systematic Theology*. 2 vols. Minneapolis: Fortress, 2015–20.

Swinton, John. *Finding Jesus in the Storm: The Spiritual Lives of Christians with Mental Health Challenges*. London: SPCK, 2020.

———. "'Where Is Your Church?' Moving toward a Hospitable and Sanctified Ethnography." In Ward, *Perspectives on Ecclesiology and Ethnography*, 71–92.

Tanner, Kathryn. *The Politics of God: Christian Theologies and Social Justice*. Minneapolis: Fortress, 1992.

———. *Theories of Culture: A New Agenda for Theology*. Minneapolis: Augsburg Fortress, 1997.

Thiselton, Anthony C. *1 Corinthians: A Shorter Exegetical and Pastoral Commentary*. Grand Rapids: Eerdmans, 2006.

Thompson, Marianne Meye. *Colossians and Philemon*. The Two Horizons New Testament Commentary. Grand Rapids: Eerdmans, 2005.

Tomlin, Graham. "It's Far Too Late to Think about Death When You're Dying—Let's Do It Now." *The Times*. February 6, 2021. http://www.thetimes.co.uk/article/its-far-too-late-to-think-about-death-when-youre-dying-lets-do-it-now-3ns35mwfb.

———. *The Widening Circle: Priesthood as God's Way of Blessing the World.* London: SPCK, 2014.

Torrance, Thomas F. *Preaching Christ Today: The Gospel and Scientific Thinking.* Grand Rapids: Eerdmans, 1994.

———. *Reality and Scientific Theology.* 2nd ed. Eugene, OR: Wipf & Stock, 2001.

———. *Royal Priesthood.* Edinburgh: Oliver & Boyd, 1955.

———. *Theology in Reconciliation: Essays towards Evangelical and Catholic Unity in East and West.* 1976. Reprint, Eugene, OR: Wipf & Stock, 1996.

———. *Theology in Reconstruction.* 1965. Reprint, Eugene, OR: Wipf & Stock, 1996.

———. *The Trinitarian Faith: The Evangelical Theology of the Ancient Catholic Church.* 2nd ed. 1991. Reprint, London: Bloomsbury T&T Clark, 2016.

———. "What Is the Church?" *The Ecumenical Review* 11 (1958): 6–21.

Tracy, David. "Foundations of Practical Theology." In Browning, *Practical Theology,* 61–82.

Turner, Philip. *Christian Ethics and the Church: Ecclesial Foundations for Moral Thought and Practice.* Grand Rapids: Baker Academic, 2015.

van der Ven, Johannes A. *Ecclesiology in Context.* Grand Rapids: Eerdmans, 1996.

van Nieuwenhove, Rik. *An Introduction to Medieval Theology.* 2nd ed. Cambridge: Cambridge University Press, 2022.

Volf, Miroslav. *After Our Likeness: The Church as the Image of the Trinity.* Grand Rapids: Eerdmans, 1996.

von Rad, Gerhard. *Old Testament Theology.* Vol. 1. Translated by D. M. G. Stalker. Edinburgh: Oliver & Boyd, 1962.

Ward, Graham. *Cultural Transformation and Religious Practice.* Cambridge: Cambridge University Press, 2005.

Ward, Pete. *Liquid Church.* Peabody, MA: Hendrickson, 2002.

———. *Liquid Ecclesiology: The Gospel and the Church.* Leiden: Brill, 2017.

———. *Participation and Mediation: A Practical Theology for the Liquid Church.* London: SCM, 2008.

———, ed. *Perspectives on Ecclesiology and Ethnography.* Grand Rapids: Eerdmans, 2012.

———. *Selling Worship: How What We Sing Has Changed the Church.* Milton Keynes, UK: Authentic Media, 2005.

Webster, John. *God without Measure: Working Papers in Christian Theology.* 2 vols. London: T&T Clark Bloomsbury 2016.

———. *Holiness.* London: SCM, 2003.

———. *Holy Scripture: A Dogmatic Sketch*. Cambridge: Cambridge University Press, 2003.

———. "'In the Society of God': Some Principles of Ecclesiology." In Ward, *Perspectives on Ecclesiology and Ethnography*, 200–222.

———. Introduction to *The Oxford Handbook of Systematic Theology*. Edited by John Webster, Kathryn Tanner, and Iain Torrance, 1–15. New York: Oxford University Press, 2007.

———. "On Evangelical Ecclesiology." *Ecclesiology* 1.1 (2004): 9–35.

———. "Theological Theology." In *Confessing God: Essays in Christian Dogmatics II*, 11–31. 2nd ed. London: Bloomsbury T&T Clark, 2016.

———. *Word and Church: Essays in Christian Dogmatics*. Edinburgh: T&T Clark, 2001.

Welch, Claude. *The Reality of the Church*. New York: Scribner's Sons, 1958.

Williams, A. N. *The Architecture of Theology: Structure, System, and Ratio*. Oxford: Oxford University Press, 2011.

Williams, Rowan. "Not Being Serious: Thomas Merton and Karl Barth." *Dr Rowan Williams 104th Archbishop of Canterbury*. 10 December 2008. http://rowanwilliams .archbishopofcanterbury.org/articles.php/1205/not-being-serious-thomas-merton -and-karl-barth.html.

Wittgenstein, Ludwig. *Philosophical Investigations*. Translated by G. E. M. Anscombe et al. Rev. 4th ed. Oxford: Wiley-Blackwell, 2009.

Wood, Susan K. "Robert Jenson's Ecclesiology from a Roman Catholic Perspective." In *Trinity, Time, and Church: A Response to the Theology of Robert W. Jenson*, edited by Colin E. Gunton, 178–87. Grand Rapids, Eerdmans, 2000.

Wooden, Anastacia K. "Eucharistic Ecclesiology of Nicolas Afanasiev and Its Ecumenical Significance: A New Perspective." *Journal of Ecumenical Studies* 45 (2010): 543–60.

———. "The Limits of the Church: Ecclesiological Project of Nicolas Afanasiev." PhD diss., Catholic University of America, 2019.

Wright, N. T. *The Climax of the Covenant: Christ and the Law in Pauline Theology*. London: T&T Clark, 1991.

Wyatt, Tim. "Explained: Why Tensions Are Running High in the CofE's Church Planting Row." *Premier Christianity*. August 24, 2021. http://www.premierchristianity .com/news-analysis/explained-why-tensions-are-running-high-in-the-cofes-church -planting-row/5439.article.

Yeago, David S. "The Church as Polity? The Lutheran Context of Robert W. Jenson's Ecclesiology." In *Trinity, Time, and Church: A Response to the Theology of Robert W. Jenson*, edited by Colin E. Gunton, 201–37. Grand Rapids: Eerdmans, 2000.

Zizioulas, John D. *Being as Communion: Studies in Personhood and the Church*. 2nd ed. London: Darton, Longman & Todd, 2004.

———. "The Church as Communion." *St. Vladimir's Theological Quarterly* 38 (1994): 3–16.

———. *Communion and Otherness: Further Studies in Personhood and the Church.* Edited by Paul McPartlan. London: T&T Clark, 2006.

———. "Ecclesiological Presuppositions of the Holy Eucharist." In *The One and the Many: Studies on God, Man, the Church, and the World Today*, edited by Gregory Edwards, 61–74. Alhambra, CA: Sebastian Press, 2010.

———. "L'eucharistie: quelques aspects bibliques." In *L'eucharistie*, by J. Zizioulas, J. M. R. Tillard, and J. J. von Allmen, 11–74. Églises en Dialogue 12. Paris: Mame, 1970.

———. "Le mystère de l'église dans la tradition orthodoxe." *Irénikon* 60 (1987): 325–35.

———. "The Mystery of the Church in Orthodox Tradition." *One in Christ* 24 (1988): 294–303.

———. "The Pneumatological Dimension of the Church." In *The One and the Many: Studies on God, Man, the Church, and the World Today*, edited by Gregory Edwards, 75–90. Alhambra, CA: Sebastian Press, 2010.

Author Index

Subject Index

anamnesis, 90, 93

anthropology, theological, 13

aseity, of God, 8–9, 13, 15

  and ecclesiological ecclesiology, 128–29, 152–53

  and ideal ecclesiology, 101, 107, 119, 122–23, 125

blueprint ecclesiology, 61–66

Cappadocian Fathers, 79, 91

The Christian Faith (Schleiermacher), 54–56

Christology

  and ecclesiology, 78, 94, 98–99, 130n2

  and empirical ecclesiology, 37–39

  functional, 52

  and pneumatology, 81n26, 116n108

church

  actualization of, 133–36, 138–41, 142–44, 148–50

  as already completed in Christ, 133

  as anticipation of communion, 78–84

  as body of Christ, 115–16, 133, 135, 139, 146–47

  as Christ's risen body, 84–90, 98–100

  as communion, 84–91

  as community of salvation, 144

  confusion of with the Realm of God, 131

  as created sociality, 66–71

  as creature of God's grace, 102, 128, 153

  decline, xiii, xiv

  dependence on God for existence, 7–10

  as divine and human reality, 7, 11

  doctrine of as extension of doctrine of God, 102–6, 119–22

  and the economic acts of God, 113–16

  Eucharist as source of, 111–13

  as an event of the Holy Spirit's act, 142–50

  as eventful act of God, 119–22

  as an ever-new event, 121

  existence of by God's own act, 132–33

  focus of on how to be or do, xv–xvi

  founding of at Pentecost, 100, 116n108, 136, 140, 142–43, 147, 159

  fullness of in the Eucharist, 91–96

  and God's covenant, 6–10

  God's election as ground of, 120–21

  as God's people, 9–10, 130, 157

  as graced community, 60

  grounding of in triunity of God, 79–84, 94–95, 113–16

  historical givenness of, 94

  historicizing approach to understanding of, 131–32

  as the human community of God the Holy Spirit, 131–42

  inseparability of divine essence and human empirical form of, 131–32

  as *koinōnia*, 81–84, 91, 94–98, 114–15, 128

  as loving community of and in the Spirit, 137

  as mediator of Gospel for the world, 146–47

  as mother, 5n12

  as movement moved by God, 102–8

  and narratives of the endless genesis of, 111–12